TERRORISM AND GLOBAL DISORDER
POLITICAL VIOLENCE IN THE CONTEMPORARY WORLD

ADRIAN GUELKE

I.B. TAURIS
LONDON · NEW YORK

Published in 2006 by I.B.Tauris & Co Ltd

6 Salem Road, London W2 4BU
175 Fifth Avenue, New York NY 10010
www.ibtauris.com

In the United States of America and Canada distributed by
Palgrave Macmillan a division of St. Martin's Press
175 Fifth Avenue, New York NY 10010

A full CIP record for this book is available from the British Library
A full CIP record is available from the Library of Congress

Library of Congress Catalog Card Number: available

ISBN10: 1 85043 803 X (Hb)
ISBN13: 978 1 85043 803 8 (Hb)
ISBN10: 1 85043 804 8 (Pb)
ISBN13: 978 1 85043 804 5 (Pb)

International Library of War Studies 8

Typeset in Janson by Keystroke, 28 High Street, Tettenhall, Wolverhampton
Printed and bound in India by Replika Press Pvt. Ltd.

For innocent victims of terrorism and of the war against terrorism

Contents

Preface

While human beings tend quickly to forget the ravages caused by epidemics or the death toll from natural disasters, even when they occur on a vast scale, memories of the carnage caused by war, terrorism or other forms of political violence rarely fade. This is in part because the purposeful nature of such violence demonstrates what human beings are capable of doing to each other. Our knowledge of past atrocities thus stimulates our fear of becoming victims of similar or worse outrages in the future. Such fear is buttressed by the fact that it is quite impossible to predict the future course of human violence, since both intentions and capabilities are constantly in flux. And this is particularly true of the small sub-state groups that engage in terrorism. Consequently, there are limits to the reassurance that any analyst of political violence can offer to the fearful reader. Indeed, to offer any reassurance at all may create a hostage to fortune, since the possibility of another tragedy on the scale of 9/11 can never be ruled out. However, what the reader is entitled to expect is that the analysis of what has already happened should aim to be objective and this is what I have striven to achieve in this book.

This is the third book I have written for I.B. Tauris. My first was also on the subject of terrorism. It focused on the onset of an age of terrorism that could be dated from the late 1960s. Terrorism then was related to the emerging post-colonial era. This book focuses on the phenomenon as it has developed in the context of the global disorder and uncertainty that followed the end of the cold war. I am most grateful to Dr Lester Crook for suggesting to me that I should write this book. I was able to find a wealth of material that helped me to get to grips with what has sometimes been dubbed the new terrorism. A realization that has been brought home to me by my work on the manuscript is how crucial a difference there is between violent groups seeking to operate at a global level and groups confining their actions to a region in which conflict is already taking place. This is a distinction that political leaders in many countries have tended to gloss over. In the process they have tended to magnify the actual threat that the rare groups with global ambitions pose to most people's security.

Conducting the research for this book has also increased my concern that the political exploitation of the issue of terrorism has become a major threat to the civil liberties that form an essential basis for constitutional government. Much is written these days about the promotion of democracy, as if the mere holding of multi-party elections was a panacea for all political ills. Yet democracy itself is a hollow concept in the absence of a constitutional order and without guarantees for basic civil rights. These are being eroded in many countries, not least the United States and Britain, in the name of the war against terrorism. The appalling deeds that have been justified by neo-conservatives and others under the rubric of the war against terrorism provide one reason why I have chosen to dedicate this book both to innocent victims of terrorism and to those of the war against terrorism. The capacity of terrorism to bring out the very worst in any society may be seen in the fact that the latter vastly outnumber the former.

I owe a large debt of gratitude to colleagues at many universities round the world who have influenced my ideas during discussions on this and related topics over the years. Students at Queen's in the course of many classes, particularly at post-graduate level, have provided me with a vital sounding board for my ideas and I am grateful for their contribution to my thinking. I am also grateful to my family. My wife, Brigid, helped to compile the index and read the proofs. John and Kate contributed ideas. I would also like to thank a number of people who assisted in the production of the book, including Dr Lester Crook, Dr Richard Willis, Liz Friend-Smith, Kate Sherratt, Stewart Fields and Ellie Rivers. The usual disclaimer applies. None of the people I have thanked bear any responsibility for any shortcomings in what follows.

Adrian Guelke, Belfast, May 2006

CHAPTER I

Introduction

A day of infamy

The question this book seeks to answer is this: did the world change fundamentally on 11 September 2001 as a result of al-Qaeda's assault on America? The proposition that the world changed on that day, which has been advanced by a number of the leading political figures in the West, including the British Prime Minister, Tony Blair, is controversial for a number of reasons. One is that the simultaneous attacks on the World Trade Centre and the Pentagon followed an undoubted watershed in world affairs, the collapse of communism in Eastern Europe and the demise of the Soviet Union. This raises the issue of whether it is credible to contend that the world changed fundamentally twice in little more than a decade. One line of argument suggested by the proximity of the two sets of events is that the second was in fact the product of the first, in other words, that the end of the cold war paved the way to the terrorism of al-Qaeda. Afghanistan provides the most obvious link between the two sets of events, since the country was the birthplace of al-Qaeda, while the cost of the occupation of Afghanistan was a contributing factor to the shift in Soviet foreign policy that made possible the peaceful transformation of Eastern Europe.

A second reason why the proposition of the fundamental significance of 9/11 is contentious has been its employment by a number of governments to justify extraordinary security measures that impinge on basic civil liberties in the wake of 9/11. Indeed, it might also be argued with considerable force that what made 9/11 a turning point in world affairs was not the intrinsic significance of the day's events themselves, but the use made of them to launch a new phase of Western foreign policy by the governments of the United States and the United Kingdom. Further, it might be contended that these governments' reactions to the events of 9/11, including the invasion of Iraq, have engendered the very conflict with the Muslim world that the perpetrators of the assault on America were seeking. Consequently, both those fearful of further attacks on the scale of 9/11 and critics of Western policy, groups that are by no means mutually exclusive, are to be found among supporters of the proposition that 9/11 deserves to be treated as a major turning point in world affairs. For reasons that will be explained through the course of this book, it is utterly impossible to predict whether or not terrorist attacks on the same or even larger scale than 9/11 will take place in the course of the next 20 years and as long as such a possibility exists, this argument is difficult to refute altogether. However, it remains a central contention of this book that the significance of 9/11 has fundamentally been misunderstood, in part because of a failure to distinguish between terrorism at a local or regional level, which is commonplace, and the relatively rare phenomenon of terrorism that is global in its scope.

While argument over the meaning of the events of 11 September 2001 continues to be intense, the bare bones of what happened that day are not in dispute. In quick succession teams of hijackers seized and took control over four American airliners on domestic routes within the United States of America. One jet (American Airlines flight no. 11) was deliberately crashed into the North Tower of the World Trade Centre in New York; another (United Airlines flight no. 175) into the South Tower. A third plane (American Airlines flight no. 77) was crashed into the Pentagon in Washington DC. The fourth (United Airlines flight no. 93) came down in a field in Pennsylvania following a struggle between the hijackers and the passengers. Slightly fewer than three thousand people died in these attacks, the overwhelming majority in New York, though in the immediate aftermath of the attacks there were fears that the death toll would be much higher. In the words of the title of Fred Halliday's book they were 'two hours that shook the world'.[1]

Inevitably, the issue of who was responsible for the atrocities has been the occasion of a greater measure of argument, especially as they were not accompanied either by any claim of responsibility or by the publication of political demands linked to the attacks. Nevertheless, within the mainstream of international opinion, there was relatively little dispute, almost from the outset, that the perpetrators of these attacks were followers of Osama bin Laden, the leading figure in a violent, Islamic fundamentalist network known as al-Qaeda ('the Base', in English). The initial impression of bin Laden's responsibility hardened further after a taped conversation, in which he discussed the attacks and more specifically the collapse of the World Trade Centre's towers, was released by the Bush Administration. But despite the weight of evidence implicating al-Qaeda, some sections of world opinion remained stubbornly resistant to the notion of bin Laden and al-Qaeda's guilt and provided a market for conspiracy theories that implicated others in the perpetration of the attacks. A far more serious contention, which is discussed further below, was that the attacks could have been prevented. The most radical version of this contention was that the Bush Administration (or in some accounts the government of another state) chose to allow the attacks to take place for its own purposes. More common was the more reasonable contention that incompetence on the part of the authorities contributed to their failure to prevent the attacks.

Al-Qaeda had previously attacked American targets outside the United States. In particular, the network had simultaneously attacked the American embassies in the capitals of Kenya and Tanzania on 7 August 1998. In November of that year a New York federal court returned indictments against Osama bin Laden and other members of al-Qaeda in connection with the embassy bombings. In October 2000, a suicide bomb attack killed 17 American sailors on the USS Cole when it was refuelling at the port of Aden in Yemen, an attack attributed to followers of bin Laden. Perhaps more pertinently, members of an organization, Egypt's Islamic Group, which was to develop strong links with al-Qaeda, had attacked the World Trade Centre in February 1993. However, both the scale and the nature of the atrocities of 11 September were of a different order of magnitude to previous attacks linked to al-Qaeda. Admittedly, hundreds of people had been killed in the attacks on the African embassies. In particular, in the attack on the American embassy in Nairobi 201 Kenyans and 12 Americans were killed, while 11 Tanzanians died in the attack on the embassy in Dar es Salaam. But the fact that the overwhelming majority of the victims were citizens of poverty-stricken states in the Third World of relatively little interest to the Western media in normal times inevitably dampened the impact of the lethal scale of the attacks. It was only in retrospect that the significance of the readiness of al-Qaeda to inflict indiscriminate carnage in foreign countries far outside any arena of conflict in Muslim lands was appreciated.

Discussion of the meaning of these events typically took two forms in the immediate aftermath of 11 September: emphasis on the unprecedented nature of the attacks and comparison of these events with a previous, traumatic episode in America's history, Japan's attack on Pearl Harbour on 7 December 1941. Writers who took the first approach noted that there had been instances in which hundreds of people had been killed in a single act of terrorism or a closely related series of such acts. However, there had been no previous case in which the actions of a sub-state entity had resulted in the deaths of thousands in a matter of hours. Indeed, it was a common assumption in much of the literature on terrorism in the 1970s that sub-state groups engaged in clandestine violence sought, as the saying went, 'few dead, but many watching'. But some writers, most notably Brian Jenkins, had drawn attention to a trend towards increasingly lethal acts of terrorism. The issue is addressed further in Chapter 8.

The scale of the attacks prompted some writers to question the adequacy of labelling them as acts of terrorism and to coin such terms as super-terrorism[2] and hyper-terrorism to convey the unprecedented nature of what had happened. However, for a variety of reasons, neither of these terms secured wide acceptance or became accepted in common usage. One reason was that the addition of the prefix super- or hyper- to a concept as absolutist as terrorism tended to diminish rather than enhance the term's force. Another was that the attacks of 11 September quickly became part of a longer-standing concern of those writing in the field of terrorism and this was that some day terrorists might acquire and use weapons of mass destruction, whether nuclear, biological or chemical. A factor in the growth of concern over this issue was a lethal attack on the Tokyo subway system by a Japanese religious cult, Aum Shinrikyo, which used Sarin nerve gas. This concern was given additional weight by the distribution of small quantities of anthrax through the US postal system in October 2001. The motivation of the perpetrator or perpetrators remained obscure, but these cases did, however, underline the vulnerability of society to such attacks.[3]

Concern over weapons of mass destruction fitted neatly into the wish of the Bush Administration to link its response to the attacks of 11 September to the issue of state sponsorship of terrorism. The two issues were connected in so far as it was generally considered to be beyond the capacity of sub-state groups on their own to manufacture weapons of mass destruction. This tied in neatly with a concern over the behaviour of rogue states within the international political system, especially as one of the criteria for the use of the rogue state label was state sponsorship of terrorism. Admittedly, in his initial response to the attacks of 11 September, President Bush showed that he was aware of the danger of being drawn into consideration of these much wider issues and carefully limited himself to tackling terrorism with a global reach. This committed the United States only to dealing with the al-Qaeda network or others who sought to follow its example. In particular, President Bush attempted to divorce the problems in the Middle East peace process from the attacks of 11 September. The attempt prompted a response from the Israeli Prime Minister, Ariel

Sharon, that 'Israel will not be Czechoslovakia'.[4] Czechoslovakia had been sacrificed in a vain effort to appease Hitler and Sharon wanted to alert American opinion to the possibility that the Bush Administration might wish to detach its war against terrorism after 11 September from the ongoing conflict between Israel and the Palestinians. The moment of tension between Israel and the United States passed quickly as Bush himself opted for a broader definition of the problem of terrorism that included Palestinian suicide bombers operating in Israel within its compass.

The broad approach paid handsome electoral dividends for the Republican Party in the mid-term elections of 2002. It also fitted in with the pre-existing political agenda of the Administration's neo-conservatives. However, a strong case can be made that the narrower approach that Bush adopted at the outset had in fact been the more sensible response to the attacks of 11 September. The danger that rogue states might supply sub-state groups with weapons of mass destruction was not any greater after 11 September than it had been before the attacks. While the nightmare scenario of deaths on a scale larger than in any previous series of terrorist attacks had come to pass, it had not occurred in any of the ways that writers on the use of weapons of mass destruction by terrorists had ever imagined. The possibility that terrorists might crash aircraft into buildings or into crowds had received attention, but it did not number among the worst fears of either analysts or governments and it was not one of the possibilities considered in the context of the use of weapons of mass destruction. It was only after the event that full cognisance was taken of how large civilian airliners might be deployed as flying bombs capable of causing deaths on a very large scale.

It is worth underlining just how far the attacks of 11 September 2001 confounded expectations of what might happen next in the realm of terrorism. Fear of an escalation of terrorist violence centred for the most part on the use of chemical, biological or nuclear weapons. In so far as there was recognition that terrorists might find a way of turning the operation of technology against the most technically advanced societies, it concerned the latest technological developments, such as the internet.[5] Cyberterrorism, as it was dubbed, was a major preoccupation among analysts of new terrorist possibilities. What virtually nobody foresaw was the use of a longstanding vulnerability in a new way. The hijacking of civilian airliners was not a new phenomenon. Indeed, it was nearly as old as civil aviation. The first hijacking occurred in the 1930s. However, hijacking only became associated with the concept of terrorism in the late 1960s. This was a reflection of the intentions of the hijackers.

The purpose of the early hijackers had been to persuade the pilot by the threat of force to take them to a different destination. In the late 1940s the perpetrators were often fleeing Communist regimes in Eastern Europe, which made for lenient treatment of the crime in the West. In the early 1960s there was a rash of hijackings to Havana in Cuba, as well as in the opposite direction of refugees from Castro's regime. The tactic of hijacking for the purpose of taking hostages was a novelty introduced by Palestinian groups in the late 1960s. The first hijacking of this new type took place in July 1968. Three members of the Popular Front for the Liberation of Palestine (PFLP) diverted an El Al jet to Algiers where they held the passengers and crew hostage. The threat to passengers increased media interest and coverage of hijackings. It also prompted strong counter-measures by the authorities and a hardening of attitudes towards the crime of hijacking for any purpose. Hijacking was henceforth included among the tactics employed by terrorists.

The world discovered on 11 September 2001 that the hijacking of airliners could be put to a much more lethal use than just the taking of hostages, serious though such a crime was. Hijacking for the purpose of hostage-taking clearly presented a threat to the lives of the passengers and crew of any airliner the hijackers seized, as well as to the members of the units of special forces deployed by governments to end hijackings without concessions to the hijackers' political demands. However, it did not present a threat to the general public at large on the scale that was to be demonstrated by the attacks of 11 September. The incidence of the hijacking of civilian airliners reached a peak in the period 1969 to 1972, with more than 50 hijacks in each of the four years. At the same time, incidence of hijacking simply for the purpose of diverting the plane to another destination declined.

That was not because the motive to use this means to flee uncongenial regimes disappeared but because of much greater hostility by the authorities towards hijacking, regardless of its purpose. It is striking that the United States, which had been one of the countries most affected by hijacking for this purpose, was scarcely touched by the more lethal form of hijacking practised by Palestinian groups such as the PFLP. There were only four cases in which a US carrier was caught up in a hijacking that resulted in any fatalities between 1970 and the attacks of September 2001. By far the most serious of the episodes – and also the only one hijack to originate within the United States – was the result of the actions of a disgruntled former employee of the airline affected. The low level of security on domestic routes within the United States prior to September 2001 was a consequence of the perception that the threat of hijacking lay elsewhere, primarily on international routes and on other continents. Paradoxically it was because no significant political group sought to exploit this vulnerability in the last three decades of the twentieth century that the counter-measures common elsewhere had not been introduced on domestic routes within the United States.

The attacks of 11 September 2001 forced governments round the world to consider what the consequences of hijacking for the purpose of using a seized airliner as a flying bomb might be on their territory (and, in some cases, further afield). Reflecting the earlier preoccupation with terrorist use of weapons of mass destruction, the nightmare scenario was that a team of suicide hijackers might seize a civilian airliner for the purpose of crashing it into a nuclear power plant. There were also considerable fears that the country's political leadership or sites of historic or symbolic importance might be targeted. Security was tightened up at airports across the world, with the objective not merely of preventing any such possibilities, but also to reassure the travelling public. This took the form of stopping passengers boarding commercial airliners with items such as metal spoons and nail scissors. Searches before passengers were allowed to board their plane became more thorough and in some cases passengers were required to remove their shoes and take off belts during this process.

In the aftermath of 11 September there was a sharp decline in the incidence of hijackings across the world. According to the ASN Aviation Safety Database, there were no further hijackings of civilian airliners in the world in 2001 after 11 September. There were five hijackings involving a total of two fatalities in 2002 and seven hijackings involving no deaths in 2003. By contrast, there had been 23 hijackings in 2000. Even at their peak, hijackings represented a far smaller threat to the safety of aviation than did accidents. However, because of the risk that hijackers may turn an airliner into flying bomb, it is likely that the authorities will try to ensure that the incidence of hijacking round the world remains as close to zero as they can possibly achieve. Thus, in so far as 11 September was a watershed in the use of violence, it was a self-negating one. The cancelling of transatlantic flights in the course of 2003 and 2004 underlined how seriously the threat is taken and the lengths to which the authorities are prepared to go to avoid any possibility of the seizure of an airliner by an al-Qaeda cell.

Of course, it is possible to argue that with the passage of years, those responsible for airline safety, including the governments, airports and carriers may become more complacent about the possibility of a repeat of 11 September and that preventing a further 11 September depends on continuing vigilance. Further, civil aviation remains vulnerable to other forms of attack, as was underlined by the case of the shoe bomber, Richard Reid. This was a failed attempt in December 2001 by a follower of bin Laden to destroy an airliner during a transatlantic flight with explosives he had smuggled on board in his footwear. Given the number of passengers on the largest jumbo jets in commercial service, bringing down an airliner might by itself cause hundreds of deaths. What is more, as was underlined by the case of the Pan Am flight brought down over Lockerbie in Scotland in December 1988, an airliner brought down by a bomb may cause additional deaths on the ground. Two planes on domestic flights from Moscow were downed by bombs in August 2004.

On top of these considerations, account also needs to be taken of the power of imitation. This should not be exaggerated, however. Thus, it is easier to list reasons why sub-state groups engaged in political violence (in conventional terms, terrorists) would be unwilling to follow al-Qaeda's example. First, very few groups would seek to justify such totally indiscriminate carnage. Second, as was entirely predictable, the scale of the attacks of 11 September resulted in extensive international cooperation to root out the al-Qaeda network. Despite the unpopularity of the Bush Administration in very many countries as a consequence of its unilateralism and extremism on issues such as the threat posed to the planet by global warming, the condemnation of the attacks on America was practically universal. So too was the readiness to cooperate in measures against al-Qaeda. While this did not prevent fresh outrages by groups loosely linked to the al-Qaeda network in 2002 and 2003, none of these attacks took place in the industrialized world or in countries without a large Muslim population. The first major attack by jihadists on a member of the European Union took place in Spain in March 2004. A second major such attack took place in London in July 2005. Third, the strategic calculation behind al-Qaeda's assault on America remained obscure, even though bin Laden's ultimate objective of restoring the power of the Muslim world in global affairs was evident.

However, none of these considerations means others might not copy the methods of al-Qaeda. Already there have been a number of reports of small aircraft being deliberately crashed into buildings. It was to be expected that embittered individuals seeking to end their own lives might choose this spectacular method of conveying their anger with the world. Further, as the pair who carried out the shootings at the Columbine High School in Colorado in 1999 underline, such behaviour may not be confined to the actions of lone individuals. It is certainly not beyond the bounds of possibility that members of an apocalyptic religious cult might attempt to emulate al-Qaeda's attacks on the twin towers of the World Trade Centre. It is less likely but by no means impossible that a politically motivated group might follow al-Qaeda's example, particularly an organization espousing a nihilist ideology or arising from a community in a brutalizing conflict that considered itself abandoned by world opinion and with nothing to lose. The Palestinians' feeling of abandonment by the international community was certainly a factor in the resort to hijacking for the purpose of taking hostages by Palestinian groups in the late 1960s.

While the taking of hostages is undoubtedly an outrageous crime, however, it hardly compares with killing people by the thousand. So the readiness of a group to take hostages to attract publicity to a cause neglected by the international community cannot be read as indicating a preparedness to kill on a much larger scale. Behind the fear that 11 September 2001 has set the scene for still further and worse horrors to come lies the belief that the mentality of the perpetrators of the assault on America was such that, as the British Prime Minister, Tony Blair put it, 'if they could have killed 30,000 or 300,000 they would have rejoiced in it'.[6] From this perspective, the reason that sub-state groups engaged in covert violence have not killed by the thousand in the past has not been moral or political, but technical constraints. They have simply lacked the technical means. Consequently, so the argument goes, if terrorists were to acquire the means for mass destruction, there would be virtually no limit to the havoc they might wreak.

What this argument fails to get to grips with is that the relationship between the scale of the violence a sub-state group might seek to inflict and the nature of its political objectives. Thus, the scale of al-Qaeda's attacks and the global character of its objectives were and are connected. By contrast, the groups associated with the onset of the age of terrorism in the late 1960s and examined in a previous work by this author[7] generally pursued national objectives, even when these were couched in terms of fighting imperialism. Notwithstanding the much exaggerated influence of globalization, human beings continue to live in societies relatively independent of each other politically. Consequently, most political organizations, including sub-state groups using political violence, seek primarily to influence events at this level. That begs a rather obvious question. What accounts for the emergence of a network of Islamists seeking to bring about change at a global level? One possible answer is their perception that the ending of bipolarity has created the opportunity for the world to be shaped on the basis of new principles. This explains the appeal of Huntington's thesis that the ideological conflicts of the past are being replaced by a clash of civilizations to advocates of a global jihad against the West, a topic analysed further in Chapter 2. Another way of making the same point is the proposition that the global disorder spawned by the end of the cold war created the conditions for the rise of al-Qaeda.

It is worth underlining the difference between the international conditions in the late 1960s and those obtaining in the 1990s and beyond. In the late 1960s violent groups seeking to extend the concept of self-determination to justify its application beyond the colonies of the European empires encountered strong opposition from the international community. Among other elements, this took the form of United Nations declarations upholding the territorial integrity of the existing states. These also emphasized the norm of non-intervention in the internal affairs of states, except in blatant cases of continuing minority or colonial rule. By contrast, the 1990s were characterized by diminishing respect for the norm of non-intervention, as well as by international acquiescence in the break-up of states. This paved the way to a substantial increase in membership of the United Nations, as well as the emergence of political entities in effective control of territory but lacking formal international recognition. This backdrop of global disorder has been reflected in resort to military force by leading states in the world without legal authorization. It has also provided encouragement to a very small number of radical Islamists to develop a strategy that is global both in its ambitions and in its theatre of conflict.

As well as exploiting the known vulnerability of commercial aviation to hijacking at the point where security was at its weakest, al-Qaeda adopted an approach to the breaching of society's defences against covert violence that had been used since the early 1980s in the Middle East and South Asia. The al-Qaeda cells that attacked America were on a suicide mission. The willingness of perpetrators to die themselves as part of an attack is by no means a new phenomenon. It was a feature of the activities of an eleventh-century Persian religious sect to which we owe the term, assassin. The assassins stabbed their victims to death in public places, with no expectation that they would be able to escape the scene of the crime. Their reign of terror was brought to an end when the Mongols stormed the sect's mountain fortress. Towards the end of the Second World War, Japan trained a number of its pilots for suicide missions. These kamikaze attacks typically involved the deliberate crashing of a plane into a warship. Use of the suicide tactic by contemporary sub-state groups dates back to the early 1980s. The tactic was first used in Lebanon, Kuwait and Sri Lanka. The most significant of the attacks that used this tactic took place in Lebanon in 1983. The American embassy in Beirut was attacked in a suicide truck bombing which killed 49 people on 18 April. Then on 23 October 1983, a suicide truck bomb was driven into the barracks of the US marines in Beirut and moments later another such attack took place on the barracks of the French army in Beirut. The first attack killed 241 people; the second 58. Claims of responsibility for these attacks were made by Islamic Jihad, which was used as a *nom de guerre* by Hezbollah (The Party of God), a radical Shi'ite Muslim organization established in Lebanon in 1978.

Strikingly, the attacks of 23 October employed a tactic that was later to be associated with al-Qaeda: that of attacking a number of targets at the same time. This maximized the impact of their actions, as well as ensuring that the authorities were not forewarned as to likely targets or methods of attack. Even more significantly, the attacks of 23 October achieved their objective of driving American and French forces out of Lebanon. One implication of these events seemed to be that killing a lot of people at the same time could change the policy of governments. Another was the effectiveness of suicide attacks in achieving this result. Not surprisingly, other sub-state groups sought to emulate Hezbollah's example, so that the incidence of suicide attacks spread to other countries. The result was that in the course of the 1990s suicide attacks took place in countries as diverse as Algeria, Argentina, Croatia, India, Israel, Kenya, Sri Lanka, Tanzania and Turkey. The success of the attacks of October 1983 in persuading the Americans and the French to withdraw also encouraged the further use by Hezbollah of the tactic in Lebanon against the presence of Israeli forces. Hezbollah's campaign of violence was also ultimately successful in achieving its objective of a complete Israeli withdrawal from Lebanon in 2000.

In an article in the August 2003 issue of the *American Political Science Review*, Robert Pape argues that the impetus behind suicide terrorism is largely instrumental and that the perception that the tactic has proved successful has encouraged its spread.[8] Nevertheless, the view persists that the use or non-use of the tactic of suicide attacks cannot be explained in purely instrumental terms and that has continued to be the case even after the events of 11 September 2001. For example, after an attack in Karachi in May 2002, in which 11 French engineers and three others were killed, in the speculation as to what group might be responsible for the attack, much was made of the fact that Pakistani extremist groups had no history of suicide attacks. A report in the *Christian Science Monitor* quoted a political analyst as saying that 'Arabs have a history of suicide attacks, but Pakistanis have never been known to indulge in such acts'.[9] In a similar vein, when a military base was attacked in the Philippines killing three soldiers, an army spokesman declared 'We do not have a history of suicide bombings among Filipinos'.[10] The same disposition to blame outsiders was evident when the UN Headquarters in Baghdad was attacked in August 2003. In a report on 21 August 2003 Radio Free Europe quoted Philip Mitchell of the International Institute of Strategic Studies to the effect that Iraqis did not have a history of such attacks.

The attribution of responsibility for acts of violence to outsiders is to be found throughout the history of violence. In fact, it always has been the case that particularly outrageous acts of violence tend to be attributed to outsiders as long as there is any uncertainty over the identity of the perpetrators. While outsiders may play a role in importing new forms of violence into a previously unaffected society, imitation is a significant source of spill-over, a topic examined further in Chapter 7. Another common assumption in the reporting of suicide attacks is that religious belief of some kind underpins the readiness of the perpetrators to sacrifice their own lives. Yet the group that carried out the largest number of suicide attacks in the last decades of the twentieth century was the Liberation Tigers of Tamil Eelam (LTTE or Tamil Tigers) and it was motivated not by religion but by nationalism. However, understandably when Americans were faced with the terrible events of 11 September 2001, they did not seek an explanation for it in the evolution of the use of political violence by sub-state groups in either Lebanon or Sri Lanka. Rather they looked to events in their own history that bore comparison with the attacks that day.

The event that most closely resembled 11 September 2001 was the attack on Pearl Harbour by the Japanese on 7 December 1941. There were some obvious similarities between the two. There was the surprise nature of the attacks, as well as their unprovoked character. The manner in which the attacks shattered the peace the country was enjoying also seemed eerily similar. The traumatic nature of the events provided a further basis of comparison, as did the sense of outrage the two events provoked. The words of President Franklin Roosevelt after Pearl Harbour that 7 December 1941 was a date that would live in infamy seemed tailor-made for the attacks of 11 September 2001. While the analogy of Pearl Harbour suggested that a large challenge faced the country, the comparison was also ultimately reassuring in suggesting that this latest challenge to the security of the United States could and would be overcome. The abstract concept of war against terrorism gained meaning from the implicit analogy with the war that followed Pearl Harbour. It even suggested a tolerable timeframe for the completion of the task. A further similarity was the roughly comparable figure for the numbers killed in the two attacks.

There were of course important differences between the two events. Al-Qaeda was not a state but a transnational network. Admittedly, it did not exist entirely without reference to state authority and the safe haven provided for al-Qaeda by the Taliban regime gave the first phase of President Bush's war against terrorism a concrete objective attainable by the deployment of conventional, military forces. However, after the overthrow of the Taliban regime, the next objective for a 'war against terrorism' was much less clear-cut. In this context, an early mistake in the strategy of the United States was not completing the job of the pacification of Afghanistan. That permitted some of the rural areas of the country as well as those of neighbouring Pakistan to continue to provide cover for at least part of the al-Qaeda network. Another large difference between the two events lay in the relationship between means and ends. At Pearl Harbour the Japanese navy attacked America's Pacific fleet with the intention of striking at America's capacity to intervene to prevent Japanese conquests in Asia. The link between ends and means is obvious. It is far more difficult to discern what al-Qaeda hoped to achieve through the killing of a large number of civilians of various nationalities in the United States.

Comparison of 11 September and Pearl Harbour was a theme of many editorials that appeared in the American press in the immediate aftermath of the attacks in 2001. The popular press used the analogy to set the terms for America's response. For example, the *New York Post* proclaimed: 'Nothing less than unconditional victory was acceptable six decades ago. Nor is it today.'[11] How America had responded to Pearl Harbour was seen as presaging the country's reaction to 11 September. The *Washington Times* declared: 'The "sleeping giant" feared by Adm. Yamamoto, architect of the surprise attack on the American fleet at Pearl Harbor, has been reawakened.'[12] In its editorial, the *Washington Post* recalled with approval Roosevelt's words after Pearl Harbour that 'we will not only defend ourselves, but will make certain that this form of treachery shall never endanger us again'.[13] Given its comparison of the two events, the *Post*'s editorial carried the implication that the country had failed to uphold Roosevelt's commitment that such an event should never be allowed to happen again. The blame, according to the editorial, was that 'in the past the United States has shied away from squarely confronting regimes that were linked to terrorist attacks against Americans'.[14] It advocated the identification and elimination of 'all sources of support for terrorist networks that would wage war on the United States' and that if necessary America 'must act alone'.[15]

It should be noted that in normal circumstances, government and media are reluctant to use the term, 'war', in connection with the covert violence or terrorism of sub-state groups because of the implication that those who carry out such acts are combatants. They usually prefer to describe terrorism as a crime and the perpetrators of such actions as criminals. It can be argued that there is no necessary conflict between the two characterizations, as is suggested by the term, 'war crime'. Indeed, in the aftermath of 11 September, it was argued that the scale of the attacks on America meant that a case could be made against the perpetrators under the rubric of a war crime or a crime against humanity before the International Criminal Court. This was despite the fact that terrorism *per se* did not fall within the remit of the court. However, that was hardly a consideration as far as the United States government was concerned, given America's rejection of the court. What made the language of war attractive was the implication that a single set of enemies could be identified and vanquished. The uncomfortable implication of treating the events of 11 September 2001 as a crime was that there was no guarantee that other groups would not copy their methods. From this perspective, bringing the perpetrators of 11 September to justice and even uprooting the whole of the al-Qaeda network offered no assurance that there could never be a repeat of the carnage that occurred on that day.

However, it would be wrong to give the impression that the analogy with Pearl Harbour was one that was reassuring in all its aspects to the American public. The comparison has some distinctly darker dimensions. These include the failure to anticipate the attacks, the political exploitation of the attacks and the racial backlash to which the two events gave rise. The unexpected nature of Pearl Harbour and 11 September raised obvious questions about American intelligence-gathering efforts. In the case of 11 September the initial impression was that the attacks had come out of a clear blue sky, as it were, with nothing to alert the authorities in advance about the dangers that the country faced. The chapter heading on the tragedy in Peter Bergen's book, *Holy War, Inc.*, conveys this well. It is 'While America Slept'.[16] It underscores Bergen's analysis that neglect of appropriately focused intelligence-gathering was largely to blame for America's lack of preparedness. Bergen describes what happened on 11 September as 'the most significant failure in the history of American intelligence-gathering' and he comments scathingly:

> 'American Taliban' John Walker Lindh, a hapless twenty-year-old Californian, had ended up fighting with the Taliban and meeting bin Laden in Afghanistan. Meanwhile, American intelligence agencies – funded to the tune of thirty billion dollars a year – were somehow unable to replicate Lindh's feat and found themselves utterly surprised by al-Qaeda's assaults on the 'homeland'.[17]

Subsequently, in much the same way as happened in the case of Pearl Harbour, a much more complex picture emerged that the authorities had in their possession all manner of pieces of information that might have alerted them to the attacks. Some writers took the next step of arguing that these should have alerted the authorities. And going even further than that there was a small minority who discounted mere incompetence and placed a sinister construction on the failure of the authorities to act on the information that was available. Lending verisimilitude to this proposition was a document produced in 2000 by *The Project for the New American Century*, a neo-conservative ginger group. It called for radical change in American foreign policy but accepted that this shift might take place slowly unless there was 'some catastrophic and catalyzing event, like a new Pearl Harbor'.[18]

When what the United States authorities knew before 11 September is put together, it does indeed seem odd or even worse that nobody put the pieces together and realized the danger facing the country. However, this view from hindsight is very simplistic. It takes no account of the mountain of information that pointed in other directions and the difficulty before the event of extracting the relevant clues from all the other information in the possession of a number of different agencies of government. The point is well made in Desmond Ball's chapter on intelligence in the edited volume, *Worlds in Collision*.

> In retrospect, there is much which could and should have been detected before September 11 (especially concerning the activities of the hijackers in the US in the preceding months). But the warning signs were never explicit, and they were drowned in a mass of confusing and contradictory information, including a series of reports of possible terrorist attacks in May–June 2001 – which, when proven false, may have contributed to a relaxation of diligence by the relevant agencies. In Roberta Wohlstetter's terms, 'relevant signals, so clearly audible after the event, [were] partially obscured before the event by the surrounding noise'.[19]

In short, what America lacked before 9/11 was not information but the capacity to separate the chaff from the wheat. However since 9/11, far from learning this lesson, the Bush Administration has sought to increase the quantities of information at its disposal by every possible means, including the authorization of torture and other abusive treatment of prisoners. But sustaining the belief that there was more to the failure to anticipate the attacks than the competence or foresight of the authorities was suspicion of the intentions of the occupant of the White House in both 1941 and 2001. The accusation on the right against President Roosevelt was that he used Pearl Harbour as an opportunity to bring about a much more radical change in American foreign policy than responding to this act of Japanese aggression demanded. Similarly, in the case of 11 September President Bush has been accused of exploiting al-Qaeda's assault to justify a pre-existing foreign policy agenda, which included intervention in Iraq. In both cases, a few analysts on the extreme fringes of opinion have argued on the basis of their exploitation of the attacks on America that Roosevelt and/or Bush in one way or another connived at the attacks taking place in the first place.

In the wake of Pearl Harbour, 110,000 people of Japanese ancestry living in the United States, many of them American citizens, were interned in camps in the interior of the country, far from the homes many of them had made on the West Coast of the United States. In the immediate aftermath of 11 September, there were fears that the government might be tempted to subject the country's three million Arab-Americans to similar treatment. Following 11 September there were some attacks on Arab-Americans as well as on Muslims in general. However, these attacks were strongly condemned by the Bush Administration. The consensus that the treatment of Japanese-Americans during the Second World War had been a shameful episode in the country's history counted against any direct repetition of that mistake. At the same time, the Bush Administration's conduct of its war against terrorism has entailed serious violations of fundamental human rights and the rule of law. This issue is discussed further in Chapter 9.

Statements by the Bush Administration after 11 September, as well as by other governments, stressed that the actions of al-Qaeda should not be seen as representative either of the Arab world or of Muslims. In particular, Western political leaders emphasized the many statements made by Muslim religious leaders condemning the attacks as contrary to Islam and the teachings embodied in the Koran. Nevertheless, a widespread fear in the West was that the attacks were symptomatic of a fault-line between Western liberal-democracies and the Islamic world. This issue is addressed next. Through the course of the book, different dimensions of the relationship between terrorism and the structure of the international political system since the end of the cold war are addressed. This is a much wider agenda than simply consideration of the events of 11 September 2001 and reaction to them. Even if President Bush had chosen to confine the war against terrorism to uprooting al-Qaeda, there would be a justification for pursuing this broader agenda. At the very least, it is necessary to get to grips with the possibility that al-Qaeda's techniques might be imitated by other violent transnational networks, as well as with possible sources for the growth of such networks.

This is not intended as a counsel of despair. Rather, the argument of this book is that there is nothing inevitable about the future of terrorism. Though the past cannot be changed, it is also possible in this field, as it is in others, to consider how things might have been different. In particular, had more capable and visionary leaders with higher standards of political integrity been in charge of the principal powers since the end of the cold war, a number of the horrors this book analyses might never have come to pass. And the threat of future violence might also have been less. However, that does not mean that the price paid for the mistakes made by the leaders in power at the time of 9/11 will primarily take the form of further terrorism. Indeed, the damage may well be much wider than anything that could possibly be encapsulated in the concept of terrorism.

Notes

1 It is from the title of his book on the attacks on America: Fred Halliday, *Two Hours that Shook the World: September 11, 2001 – Causes and Consequences*, Saqi Books, London 2002.
2 See, for example, Lawrence Freedman (ed.), *Superterrorism: Policy Responses*, Blackwell, Oxford 2002.
3 The two cases are discussed in detail in Chapter 8.
4 Quoted in Suzanne Goldenberg and Virginia Quirke, 'Israel attacks US campaign', *Guardian*, 5 October 2001.

5 Use of the internet by terrorists has continued to be a major concern. See, for example, Joseph Nye, 'How to counter terrorism's online generation', *Financial Times*, 13 October 2005.

6 The words are those used by Blair, in a speech given on 5 March 2004, which was published in full online by BBC News.

7 Adrian Guelke, *The Age of Terrorism and the International Political System*, I.B. Tauris, London 1995.

8 Robert A. Pape, 'The Strategic Logic of Suicide Terrorism' in *American Political Science Review*, Vol. 97, No. 3, August 2003, pp. 343–61.

9 Mohammad Afzal Niazi quoted in Jawad Naeem, 'Suicide attacks hit Pakistan', *Christian Science Monitor* (Boston), 9 May 2002.

10 'Abu Sayyaf suspected in Philippine blast', CNN.com, 3 October 2002.

11 *New York Post* (New York), 12 September 2001.

12 *Washington Times* (Washington DC), 12 September 2001.

13 Quoted in the *Washington Post* (Washington DC), 12 September 2001.

14 Ibid.

15 Ibid.

16 Peter L. Bergen, *Holy War, Inc.: Inside the Secret World of Osama bin Laden*, Phoenix, London 2002, p.24.

17 Ibid., p. 226.

18 Quoted in 'The Plan: Were Neo-Conservatives' 1998 Memos a Blueprint for Iraq War?', abc.NEWS.com, 10 March 2003.

19 Desmond Ball, 'Desperately Seeking Bin Laden: The Intelligence Dimension of the War against Terrorism' in Ken Booth and Tim Dunne (eds), *Worlds in Collision: Terror and the Future of Global Order*, Palgrave Macmillan, Basingstoke 2002, p. 60.

CHAPTER 2

A clash of civilizations?

In 1993 America's leading international relations journal, *Foreign Affairs*, published a controversial article by a distinguished American political scientist, Samuel Huntington. It was entitled 'The Clash of Civilizations?'.[1] The piece was commonly interpreted as predicting that conflict between the West and Islam was inevitable. In truth, some of Huntington's own pronouncements contributed to this view of what he was saying. In the aftermath of 11 September Huntington was widely credited with having anticipated such a development, compounding the original overstatement of his arguments. For example, shortly after 11 September the British *Sunday Times* described his piece as 'uncannily prescient' and reproduced the entire article for the benefit of the paper's readers.[2] The obvious implication was that it had predicted the attacks on America. However, in fact, the question mark in the title mattered. Further, the article ranged much more widely than simply the future of relations between the West and Islam after the end of the cold war. Before considering the content of the article, it is worth putting the piece in the context of the author's earlier writings. Huntington's first major work was published in 1957. His book, *The Soldier and the State*, was a controversial study of civil–military relations.[3] Huntington achieved further fame in the 1960s and 1970s for his analysis of the reasons for political instability in the Third World.[4] One implication of his analysis appeared to be that rural insurgencies could be countered by rapid urbanization. He was accused in this context of influencing the conduct of American counter-insurgency policies in Vietnam and elsewhere.

Huntington next became associated with the analysis of the successive waves of democratization that have occurred since the end of the Second World War. In his studies of democratization he formed the view that Islam as a belief system was inimical to the spread of liberal-democracy. He was by no means alone in holding such a negative view of the influence of Islam. His 1993 article drew heavily on the writings of Bernard Lewis. Lewis argued that the failure of Islamic societies to adapt to modernization accounted for their antagonism to the West and in fact the title of Huntington's article came from a piece Lewis had published in 1990. Lewis had been propounding this thesis for a very considerable time, going back to the early 1970s. Lewis's thesis had started out as a way of explaining the hostility of Arab states towards Israel that implied that it existed totally independently of Israeli policies or actions. It had considerable appeal to those who advocated unconditional support for the state of Israel in its conflicts with the Arab world.

The scope of Lewis's case widened considerably with the growth of Islamic fundamentalism linked to the Iranian revolution of 1979. Thereafter books such as John Laffin's *The Dagger of Islam*, published in 1979, popularized the notion of an Islamic threat to the West.[5] So the idea of conflict between the West and Islam was well established before the end of the cold war. Huntington's 1993 article, by relating the potential for conflict between the West and Islam to a new phase in international relations, put the problem in a far more serious light than that of a conflict made more visible by the waning of bipolarity. Indeed, a common criticism of Huntington's thesis was precisely that during the cold war, antagonism between America and the Soviet Union had tended to overshadow all other conflicts and it was inevitable that the end of the cold war would lead to greater attention being paid to other conflicts.

The point of departure of Huntington's article was the identification of different phases in the history of international relations since the formation of the modern international political system as a result of the Peace Treaty of Westphalia of 1648. Huntington identified three past phases in the history of the international political system; an era of conflict among princes, kings and emperors; an era of conflict among nations; and the era of conflict between ideologies. A characteristic of each of these phases was that they were primarily conflicts within Western civilization itself. This was even true of the last phase, misleadingly labelled a conflict between East and West. This was not the case in a cultural sense, Huntington argued. In fact, Marxism was a Western ideology and its appeal in the Third World was as a modernizing ideology that would enable backward societies to catch up with industrially developed capitalist states.

After making the case that the end of the cold war did represent a definitive end to the conflict of ideologies, Huntington went on to argue that the next phase of world history could be characterized by a clash of civilizations. He asserted: 'The next world war, if there is one, will be a war between civilizations.'[6] Huntington claimed that seven or possibly eight civilizations covered the globe: Western, Confucian, Japanese, Islamic, Hindu, Slavic-Orthodox, Latin American and African. He argued that 'the most important conflicts of the future will occur along the cultural fault lines separating these civilizations from one another'.[7] He provided six different reasons for this expectation. First, he asserted that the differences between civilizations were basic and that while not totally immutable they were unlikely to disappear soon. Second, the shrinking of the world as a result of the information revolution had increased the interactions among peoples of different civilizations, intensifying civilization-consciousness. Third, global economic change was tending to separate people from longstanding local identities, as well as weakening the nation-state as a source of identity. Fourth, '[a] West at the peak of its power confronts non-Wests that increasingly have the desire, the will and the resources to shape the world in non-Westernways'.[8]

The importance of this factor was enhanced by the passing of a generation of Third World leaders who had been educated in the West and absorbed its culture. Fifth, he argued that the relatively immutable character of cultural characteristics and differences made them less amenable to compromise than economic or political ones. Finally, Huntington argued that the trend towards regional economic blocs that broadly coincided with the boundaries of particular civilizations was enhancing civilization-consciousness.

The increased importance of the role of civilizations in global politics made the fault lines between civilizations potential flash points for conflict. Thus, Huntington argued that with the disappearance of cold war divisions in Europe, 'the cultural division of Europe between Western Christianity, on the one hand, and Orthodox Christianity and Islam, on the other, has re-emerged'.[9] He accepted that relations between different civilizations have varied widely, but contended that relations between Islam and other civilizations have tended to be violent. As he put it, 'Islam has bloody borders'.[10] He placed special emphasis on a history of conflict between Islam and the West going back 1,300 years. He was pessimistic about the future.

> This centuries-old military interaction between the West and Islam is unlikely to decline. It could become more virulent. The Gulf War left some Arabs feeling proud that Saddam Hussein had attacked Israel and stood up to the West. It also left many feeling humiliated and resentful of the West's military presence in the Persian Gulf, the West's overwhelming military dominance, and their apparent inability to shape their own destiny. Many Arab countries, in addition to the oil exporters, are reaching levels of economic and social development where autocratic forms of government become inappropriate and efforts to introduce democracy become stronger. Some openings in Arab political systems have already occurred. The principal beneficiaries of these openings have been Islamic movements. In the Arab world, in short, Western

democracy strengthens anti-Western political forces. This may be a passing phenomenon, but it surely complicates relations between Islamic countries and the West.[11]

Huntington concluded the article by accepting some qualifications to his arguments while restating his central hypothesis. This was that 'conflict between civilizations will supplant ideological and other forms of conflict as the dominant global form of conflict'.[12] At the same time, Huntington acknowledged that civilization identities would not replace all other identities, that nation-states would survive and that conflict would take place within civilizations as well as between them.

As Huntington anticipated it would, his article provoked a firestorm of criticism. He produced a fuller version of his argument in a book published in 1996, in which he expanded on the significance of what he described as the Islamic Resurgence which he saw as being fuelled by demographic factors.[13] The book proved just as controversial as the article had been. Fred Halliday referred to Huntington's book-length formulation of his thesis as 'particularly clear, polemical and utterly irresponsible'.[14] John Esposito criticized Huntington for playing into 'old stereotypes by characterizing Islam and the West as age-old enemies'.[15] Five main themes can be identified in the criticisms Huntington's thesis encountered prior to 11 September.

First, it was argued that he did not take sufficient cognizance of the huge power imbalances in his world of civilizations. No other civilization was a match for the West. Islam, even less than some of the other rivals to Western civilization, simply did not have the capacity to mount a significant challenge to the reality of Western dominance. From this perspective the world was entering a period of domination by the West and, within that grouping, of American hegemony. Second, it was argued that he overestimated the clarity of divisions among civilizations. While many accepted the case he made that modernization was not equivalent to Westernization, borrowing between civilizations was commonplace and promoted by the intensity of interactions that was the product of globalization. The very processes of interaction themselves played their part in undermining the basis for separate or separable civilizations. Third, the organization of the international political system into sovereign states gave an importance to the interests of states that tended to undercut solidarity on the basis of the membership of a common civilization. Fourth, many of the critics argued that conflict within the Muslim world especially was of much greater importance than conflict between Islam and any other civilization.

In fact, especially after the events of 11 September 2001, Huntington himself has put considerable stress on conflict within the Muslim world by referring to the post-cold war era as 'an age of Muslim wars',[16] involving both conflict with other civilizations and between Muslims. Some writers regard his acknowledgement of the extent of conflict among Muslims as an indication that he has retreated from his original thesis. For example, Tariq Ali argues that the notion of an age of Muslim wars undercuts his original thesis. 'This simplistic notion leaves his whole conception of "wars of civilisation" hopelessly mired in a fundamental contradiction. Either we are seeing an "age of Muslim wars" or a "a clash of civilisations". It can't be both. In fact, it is neither.'[17]

However, this circle is easier to square than Ali supposes, in so far as it is possible to argue that conflict within the Muslim world is connected to relations with other civilizations. It is a common-place of inter-communal violence that it also generates conflict within the groups affected. To falsify Huntington's thesis on this score, it would be necessary to establish that the conflicts within the Muslim world were unconnected to its relations with other civilizations. This is far from being an easy task.

Huntington's general response to criticisms has been to deny that they invalidate the basic thrust of his argument. Disarmingly he has accepted that the picture he had painted of the world was an oversimplification. In a piece published the same year as his original article, Huntington responded to his critics by comparing his division of the world in cultural terms with the cold war paradigm that prevailed before the coming down of the Berlin

Wall and the collapse of the Soviet Union. The cold war paradigm divided the world into three groupings, mainly affluent liberal-democratic states led by the United States, Communist states dominated by the Soviet Union and non-aligned states in the Third World outside the first two camps. This framework could not account for everything in world politics, including major developments such as the Sino-Soviet split.

> Yet as a simple model of global politics, it accounted for more important phenomena than any of its rivals: it was an indispensable starting point for thinking about international affairs; it came to be universally accepted; and it shaped thinking about world politics for two generations.[18]

Huntington made similar claims for his framework, the heart of which was potential, if not actual, conflict between the West and Islam.

> The debates the civilization paradigm has generated around the world show, that in some measure, it strikes home; it either accords with reality as people see it or it comes close enough so that people who do not accept it have to attack it.[19]

These passages also underscore the extent of Huntington's ambition. It was to establish out of the flux and chaos of the post-cold war world a framework that nobody could easily gainsay. In particular, one implication of the case he made was that once such a framework was adopted by the policymakers, especially in the United States, the overwhelmingly dominant force in world politics, academics would have little choice but to accept its force, as had happened during the cold war.

The fifth common theme of critics of Huntington is that the most dangerous aspect of his analysis was that it had the potential to create the very clash of civilizations that it forecast as likely to occur. That such a criticism could be made was in itself a remarkable tribute to Huntington's influence on the world as an academic. While Huntington has followed the American practice of moving between university and government and briefly served in both the Johnson and Carter Administrations, his influence has been entirely independent of his short-lived forays into politics, but reflects simply the force of his ideas. The overwhelming majority of academics write with the freedom that comes from knowing that nothing they publish is ever likely to affect the course of world events, whether for good or ill. While many writers reacted to the events of 11 September as a vindication of Huntington's analysis and as a striking demonstration of his prescience, Huntington himself tended to be rather more circumspect in his comments on 11 September. He was wise to do so. It was said unkindly of another great American thinker, the naval historian, Alfred Thayer Mahan, because his ideas contributed to a naval arms race in the first decades of the twentieth century that he was one of the causes of the First World War. It might similarly have been said that the author of 'The Clash of Civilizations?' was one of the causes of 11 September.

Jihadists, that is to say, Muslims advocating an Islamic resurgence through violent means, understandably were fully in accord with Huntington's assumption of the incompatibility of the West and Islam.[20] The point has been underlined by a number of Huntington's critics writing both before and after 11 September. For example, in his book on 11 September, Fred Halliday notes:

> All over the Middle East, especially in Saudi Arabia and reportedly in Japan as well, Huntington finds favour among the anti-modernists, particularists, nationalists and fundamentalists. Why? Because Huntington says that East and West are separate, we are all distinct and there will inevitably be conflict.[21]

Halliday argues passionately that neither Islam nor the West can sensibly be treated as monolithic entities. In this context, he is even critical of well-meaning efforts to promote dialogue between Christians and Muslims on the grounds that they reinforce simplistic conceptions of a single other. He highlights the variations to be found in the interpretation of Islam and the conflicting interests of states in which Muslims form a majority of the population. He also dismisses the notion of a single West.

> There *is* no one West – not in international relations terms, not in political terms and, most important of all, there is no one West in terms of political values. People often say that human rights or sovereignty are 'Western' concepts, yet they are concepts that did not arise out of some undifferentiated West. They emerged out of conflicts between individual countries involving movements for the rights of people to vote, for the rights of women or for the rights of trade unions or other groups.[22]

While the events of 11 September were interpreted by some as proof of the correctness of Huntington's thesis on the clash of civilizations, what Halliday labelled 'faultline babble'[23] formed only an undercurrent in the reactions to the attacks on the American mainland. In part, that was because Huntington's contention that the reaction to the attacks had been on civilizational lines was hard to sustain in the light of the near universal condemnation of al-Qaeda's assault. As Amitav Acharya pointed out, 'Governments, including those presiding over Islamic nations, not only condemned the terrorist attacks on the US, many also recognized its right to retaliate against the Taliban.'[24] In part, paradoxically, this was because Huntington's thesis was actually interpreted by many policymakers as a warning of the danger of conflict along civilizational lines, if they permitted an Islamophobic reaction to 11 September. Political leaders in the United States, Britain, France and Germany, among others, emphasized that al-Qaeda did not speak for Islam and that the actions of the suicide hijackers had been entirely contrary to the precepts of Islam as a religion.

However, there was a third more important reason why Huntington's framework did not take hold in the manner that might have been anticipated prior to 11 September. That was because there was another frame of reference in which the assault on America could be placed and which more importantly also provided the basis for the government's response to the attacks. This frame of reference characterized the events themselves as acts of terrorism of such a scale that they demanded the response of a war against terrorism. As noted in Chapter 1, President Bush's initial public statements on 11 September referred to terrorism or terrorists with a global reach. For example, in his address to both houses of Congress on 20 September 2001, President Bush devoted a large part of his speech to al-Qaeda, which he described as 'a collection of loosely affiliated terrorist organizations'. He also spoke of al-Qaeda's close relationship to the Taliban regime in Afghanistan, but at the same time he drew a very clear distinction between al-Qaeda and Muslim countries in general. He went on:

> The enemy of America is not our many Muslim friends; it is not our many Arab friends. Our enemy is a radical network of terrorists, and every government that supports them. Our war on terror begins with al-Qaeda, but it does not end there. It will not end until every terrorist group of global reach has been found, stopped, and defeated.[25]

Few people doubted that what Bush meant by terrorists with a global reach was any group minded to attack the territory of the United States. In particular, he was not announcing an open-ended war against every organization in the world engaged in political violence, particularly if the organization's campaign of violence was primarily confined to the territory of its governmental adversary. The reassurance of a limited war dampened the impact of some of the more strident parts of the speech, including his declaration that 'either you are with us or you are with the terrorists'.[26] If President Bush had stuck to the terms of this speech, America's response to 11 September might have been limited to a campaign primarily directed at uprooting al-Qaeda's network. Admittedly, even a campaign wholly confined to al-Qaeda would have been complicated by the network's links through affiliates to places such as Kashmir, Chechnya and the Philippines suffering deep-rooted conflicts. But aside from such pitfalls such an approach would have been uncontentious and might well have proved successful considering the extent of al-Qaeda's international isolation after 11 September, as well as the unpopularity of the Taliban regime in Afghanistan.

However, it is now evident, in a way which was not publicly apparent at the time, that the generally prudent approach Bush outlined in his speech to Congress did not represent his real attitude. In fact, it seems that he was intending from the outset to use 11 September as justification for taking action against Iraq. This became evident in 2002 when Bush opted for a much broader interpretation of the war against terrorism. The advantage of this approach to the Administration was that it chimed in well with the public mood in the United States. There were uglier elements to this mood that included the wish to see a large number of Arabs killed in retaliation for 11 September. Targeting Iraq tapped into a longstanding hostility towards the Arab world that pre-dated concerns over the growth of Islamic fundamentalism and the perception of it as a threat to Americans. The much broader notion of the war against terrorism established a flexible framework within which the Bush Administration could pursue a pre-existing foreign policy agenda. Whether or not this was originally the Bush Administration's intention, this approach was politically divisive both within the United States and internationally. It also prolonged the crisis over 11 September. It thereby ensured that there would be no danger that the war might have seemed over by the time of the 2004 Presidential election. That might have meant that the electorate would have primarily judged his Administration on the issue of the economy rather than the conduct of foreign policy. The nightmare for Bush was that in these circumstances he might have suffered the same fate as his father. His correct assumption was that a political context in which security loomed larger than any other issue would favour the incumbent.

While Bush's conduct in the year following 11 September mainly won praise, there were a few critics of the framing of America's response in terms of a war against terrorism. One criticism was that the concept of terrorism represented an abstraction and that it made no sense to wage a war against an abstraction. A similar criticism was that terrorism was a methodology, in other words, a particular if unpleasant and reprehensible way of pursuing political ends through violence, and it made little sense to fight a methodology without any regard to context or objectives. William Pfaff combines both criticisms in complaining at the Bush Administration's 'intellectually incoherent elevation ... of terrorism, a tactic or method of combat employed throughout the ages, to metaphysical standing as Terror, a phenomenon which American arms were expected to conquer'.[27]

A further criticism of the use of the rubric of terrorism to frame America's response to the events of 11 September was that without the qualification of global reach the scope of a war against terrorism was potentially limitless. This was because the concept might be applied to almost any act of lethal violence with a social or political objective. Consequently, an extensive interpretation of the concept could theoretically commit America to endless entanglement in conflicts across the world. However, the consensus among commentators was that there was little danger that this would occur as the Bush Administration had no intention of allowing itself to be drawn into conflicts in which it had no stake. The Irish and Basque cases were given as examples. A different sort of criticism was that the notion of a war against terrorism was inappropriate because it treated the perpetrators of terrorist acts as warriors rather than criminals. From this perspective, what was required was the identification of the perpetrators by the usual methods of criminal investigation, so that they could be charged with the appropriate offences and brought to justice. Of course, such a course of action depended on the willingness of other countries to cooperate in the investigation of the crimes committed and to hand over suspects against whom a prima facie case could be made.

In the first phase of the war against terrorism, criticism of the Bush Administration tended to be relatively muted. This was because most people were ready to judge the Bush Administration by its actions and in the months immediately after 11 September these were regarded by most of world public opinion as compatible with the legitimate defence of its citizens. In particular, there was little criticism of the stringent nature of the Bush Administration's ultimatum to the Taliban regime or of its unwillingness to allow more time for diplomacy before launching military attacks on Afghanistan. The refusal of the Taliban regime to surrender Osama bin Laden after his indictment by an American court in connection with the attacks on the American embassies in East Africa in 1998 suggested that the diplomatic route was unlikely to yield significant results. Of course, it could be argued that after 11 September there was much greater pressure on the Taliban regime to comply with the demands of the outside world to cease its assistance to al-Qaeda. In fact, the belief that the Taliban regime could be persuaded to expel al-Qaeda from Afghanistan formed the basis for diplomatic initiatives by the government of Pakistan in the weeks immediately following 11 September. The failure of these initiatives reinforced the assumption by Western analysts of a relationship of interdependence between the Taliban and al-Qaeda.

This assumption is central to Lawrence Freedman's analysis of the conflict between America and al-Qaeda in Booth and Dunne's edited volume on the aftermath of 11 September published in 2002. He describes the rapid evolution of American thinking on this issue in the weeks after 11 September.

By the end of September, as the US began to understand the symbiotic relationship between the two, the focus shifted to take in the Taliban as well as al-Qaeda. The idea that the relationship was one of guest and host had been shattered: the two were clearly intertwined, so that the defeat of one would create a crisis for the other.[28]

Freedman argued forcefully that al-Qaeda's roots in Afghanistan made it highly vulnerable to the counter-attack that America launched in the closing months of 2001.

> It suited al-Qaeda to give the appearance of being shadowy and ubiquitous, a network of groups spread around the world, harboured unwittingly in Western countries as much as in countries blatantly hostile to the West. The enemy appeared to lack military capabilities, a capital city or even, despite the focus on Osama bin Laden himself, a supreme leader and hierarchical chain of command. Yet this impression was wrong. Evidence gleaned after the fall of the Taliban regime demonstrated that Osama bin Laden was fully *au fait* with the operation [i.e. 11 September]. The description of al-Qaeda as being non-state was not accurate in that it had gained its base and sanctuary in Afghanistan by effectively sponsoring and then taking over the Taliban regime, and through the gradual integration of its fighters with those of the Taliban.[29]

The relationship with the Taliban gave al-Qaeda a secure base for training and planning its international operations, but it also made the organization vulnerable to the deployment of conventional military forces. The presence within Afghanistan of forces opposed to the Taliban regime meant that it was even possible to achieve the objective of overthrowing the Taliban regime without deployment of American ground forces. The combination of American air power and the Northern Alliance proved remarkably effective in routing the Taliban. Its stronghold in the North of the country, Mazar-e-Sharif, fell on 8 November 2001. That was followed less than a week later by the fall of the capital city, Kabul. There was stronger resistance to the progress of the Northern Alliance in the South, reflecting the Taliban's Pashtun ethnic base. But by the end of 2001, no major city remained under the control of the Taliban and American efforts were focused on driving al-Qaeda out of the Tora Bora caves, which provided the organization, as it appeared, with its last hiding place within Afghanistan.

The speed of the Northern Alliance's victory and the low cost to the United States of the victory in terms of lives of American servicemen were widely seen as an impressive demonstration of America's great power in the post-cold war world. Two concerns surfaced at the time of these events. The first concern arose from the very large number of civilian casualties caused by American aerial bombardment, particularly carpet-bombing with daisy-cutters. The claim that American action had caused a larger number of civilian deaths in Afghanistan than the total number of people killed in the attacks of 11 September attracted considerable comment.[30] As in the war in Kosovo in 1999, American tactics appeared designed to minimize casualties among the American military at the expense of the local civilian population. In the case of Kosovo these tactics perversely bore a relationship to the humanitarian justification advanced for the military action. This was because the humanitarian nature of the action was assumed to mean there would be a very low level of tolerance for American military casualties among the American public. However, the American public's willingness to accept a higher level of casualties in Afghanistan in pursuit of the objective of eliminating the threat from al-Qaeda did not change the attitude of the forces themselves to taking casualties.

The other concern to surface was fear that the publicity given to civilian casualties in Afghanistan would cause hostility towards the United States among Muslims in other parts of the world. Indirect evidence that this was indeed the case was provided by a Gallup poll conducted in December 2001 and January 2002. Respondents in seven countries (Indonesia, Iran, Kuwait, Lebanon, Morocco, Pakistan and Turkey) were asked if they considered American military intervention in Afghanistan to be justified. A large majority (77 per cent) considered that it was not justified. However, in the same survey over two-thirds of the respondents (including for this question people in Jordan and Saudi Arabia as well as the other seven countries) also considered the attacks on America to be morally unjustifiable.[31] Yet while the concept of terrorism provided the basis on which the Bush Administration might have both cultivated and drawn on a global consensus condemning the attacks of 11 September, it made little effort to do so. On the contrary, the instinct of the Administration, especially its neo-conservatives, was to seek to polarize opinion over its response to the attacks. There was an electoral pay-off within the United States for the adoption of an aggressive, unilateralist approach, while internationally it served the purpose of furthering the agenda the neo-conservatives had been pushing for prior to 11 September.

A third concern over American military operations in Afghanistan arose much later in the course of 2003, 2004 and 2005. This was that the task of rooting out al-Qaeda from Afghanistan had not been completed. In particular, the focus of American and other international forces on the control of the cities meant that developments in the country's rural areas were neglected, permitting a partial revival of the Taliban in ethnically Pashtun areas of the countryside. Further, the combination of a partial Taliban revival and the weak hold of the Pakistani authorities on the tribal (largely Pashtun) areas bordering Afghanistan created space for the establishment of relatively safe havens for the remnants of al-Qaeda. This was most clearly reflected in the failure to capture some of the leading figures in al-Qaeda in the course of 2001 and 2002, including Osama bin Laden himself.

The failure can partly be attributed to the obsession of President Bush and neo-conservatives in his Administration with regime change in Iraq. But it also stemmed from the Administration's wish to limit the involvement of other external forces in military operations in Afghanistan, except for a narrowly defined role in peacekeeping. In this context, even the British government's offer to provide ground forces for the initial assaults on the Taliban and al-Qaeda was turned down by the Bush Administration. It was also in part a consequence of the alliances the Administration entered into with local forces in Afghanistan. Rivalries among different local factions, as well as their own separate agendas, ensured that their cooperation with the Americans was never total. One area in which there was obvious conflict between the interests of the international community and the forces that overthrew the Taliban regime was the production of heroin. In fact, discouragement of the cultivation of the opium poppy had been a factor in the Taliban regime's loss of support in the course of 2000 and 2001. One consequence of its overthrow was a large expansion in Afghanistan's production and trading of narcotics. This might be seen as the temporary price to be paid for addressing the more immediate threat that terrorism with a global reach emanating from Afghanistan posed to the international community. But at the same time the lawlessness inevitably associated with the trade in narcotics itself poses a formidable obstacle to the objective to which the international community has paid frequent lip service, the establishment of stable, constitutional government in Afghanistan. Further, even the argument that such an outcome provides the only guarantee against Afghanistan's once again becoming a base for groups like al-Qaeda has failed to secure for the government of Afghanistan the assistance it needs to tackle the country's economic dependence on drugs.

It is open to argument as to whether a larger multilateral campaign to rid Afghanistan of al-Qaeda in the final months of 2001 and the first half of 2002 could have prevented subsequent al-Qaeda-related atrocities, including the attacks in Bali, Madrid and London. It would seem to be an implication of Freedman's emphasis on al-Qaeda's dependence on the Taliban regime that a more thorough purging of Afghanistan might well have reduced the network's capacity to carry out attacks in other parts of the world. Against this view it can be argued that Freedman overstates the extent of central control by al-Qaeda from Afghanistan. The contrary position is that al-Qaeda has always been a very loose, transnational network of like-minded jihadists and that consequently the complete uprooting of those based in Afghanistan would have made relatively little difference to its capacity. From this perspective, the subsequent attacks in Bali and elsewhere simply underline the point that Afghanistan was not crucial to the operation of the network. However, this position would seem to take too little account of the place of Afghanistan in the overall history and development of al-Qaeda, as is discussed in the next chapter.

A more reasonable proposition would be that the overthrow of the Taliban regime did substantial damage to al-Qaeda. That atrocities have continued to be committed by groups related to al-Qaeda can be attributed to six main factors. First, the new rulers' hold on Afghanistan was not sufficient to rid the country completely of al-Qaeda. That was compounded by the balance of political forces in Pakistan that gave al-Qaeda a further haven in areas of Pakistan bordering Afghanistan. Second, the al-Qaeda network had established roots in other parts of the world far beyond Afghanistan or Pakistan even before 11 September 2001. Third, the nature of al-Qaeda changed as a result of the measures taken to suppress it. It underwent a process of mutation, with some analysts positing that this will spawn the creation of new generations of al-Qaeda. Fourth, just as al-Qaeda itself had copied methods that had been used by Hezbollah in Lebanon, including near-simultaneous attacks on more than one target and the sacrifice of the lives of the militants in the attacks, so other jihadists have imitated al-Qaeda. Consequently, suicide terrorism or martyrdom operations, as well as the synchronization of multiple attacks, have become part of the methodology of a variety of groups.

Fifth, al-Qaeda has become a label that is almost automatically attached to attacks on Westerners. In particular, tourists have been targeted in a considerable number of attacks attributed to al-Qaeda since 9/11. Examples are a suicide car bomb attack in Mombasa, Kenya, that killed 15 people in November 2002, a simultaneous attack on a number of targets in Casablanca, Morocco, that killed 43 people in May 2003, a truck bomb attack on the Hilton hotel in Taba, Egypt, that killed 30 people in October 2004, and the bomb attacks on Sharm el Sheikh, Egypt, that killed 88 people in July 2005. However, it is far from clear whether all these cases are in fact connected to al-Qaeda's global strategy, since groups with purely national objectives have attacked tourists in the past.[32] Sixth, the policies of the West, but most particularly those of the government of the United States, have continued to alienate large parts of both the Muslim and Arab worlds. This has aided jihadists everywhere in their recruitment of new supporters.

In the context of consideration of Huntington's thesis of a clash of civilizations, by far the most important of the six factors is the last. One interpretation of President Bush's response to the events of 11 September was that he was intent on avoiding confrontation with the Muslim world. The use of the concept of terrorism for framing America's response to the atrocities, speeches denying any connection between most followers of the Muslim religion and bin Laden and the avoidance of language that lent any credibility to Huntington's thesis seemed to point in that direction. The initiation of military operations in Afghanistan did not contradict this picture since they could be interpreted as necessary for American self-defence. The assumption was that after the uprooting of al-Qaeda had removed any implication of appeasing terrorism, it would be possible for the United States government to take steps to address the grievances of the Muslim and Arab worlds. Thereby it would defuse the issues that had generated any support for bin Laden or that had created fertile ground for recruitment by jihadist organizations.

There were even hopes that after the military campaign in Afghanistan the United States government might seek to promote a resolution of the impasse in the Israeli–Palestinian peace process. These hopes and assumptions proved to be very wide of the mark. After Afghanistan President Bush turned to the issue not of addressing alienation in the Muslim world but of regime change in Iraq. Even then the British Prime Minister, Tony Blair, tried to sustain the illusion that this objective was compatible with the pursuit of a balanced settlement to the Israeli–Palestinian conflict. In fact, the war in Iraq proved to be the prelude to the abandonment of the United States of America's longstanding commitment to United Nations resolution 242 of 1967. This resolution called on Israel to withdraw from the territories it had occupied as a result of the six-day war. The Bush Administration declared that it was ready to support the Sharon government in Israel in its intention to hold on to major settlements on the West Bank on a permanent basis, as well as to support its rejection of any right of return by Palestinian refugees to an enlarged Israel.

While this dramatic shift in America's position announced in April 2004 meant that the radical and confrontational nature of the Bush Administration's foreign policy could no longer be denied, the interpretation of its motives still remained open to question. Consequently, there was still room for debate over the future direction of policy. Thus, in so far as it seemed possible during the course of 2004 to attribute both the conduct of the war in Iraq and support for Sharon to domestic electoral considerations, it remained possible to suggest that in due course some moderation in the character of American foreign policy might occur once Bush was safely re-elected. Of this, there has been little sign. On the contrary, appointments during his second term have emphasized Bush's commitment to the neo-conservative agenda for the aggressive maintenance of America's global hegemony. At the same time, there has been some moderation of the Israeli–Palestinian conflict itself but primarily as a result of the actions of the parties themselves rather than any change in the approach of the United States to the issue. However, the sheer cost of American military interventions, especially in Iraq, may ultimately impose some constraint on the Bush Administration's actions.

In any event, it is evident that the Bush Administration did not adopt the rubric of terrorism to frame its response to the events of 11 September so as to avoid confrontation with either the Arab or the Muslim worlds. Thus, far from it being the case that Huntington's thesis of a clash of civilizations has been rendered redundant by the way in which the Bush Administration reacted to 11 September, it has taken an even more malign form than the way in which Huntington formulated it. The use of the concept of terrorism, not merely to apply to the atrocities carried out by al-Qaeda, but to all manner of hypothetical threats, has permitted the Bush Administration to frame its foreign policy objectives in highly moralistic terms, as a conflict between good and evil. The result has been the propagation of the view of America's being engaged, less in a conflict between civilizations as in a conflict between civilization and barbarism.

It may be objected that this paints far too bleak a picture of American foreign policy. In particular, Bush does not conceive of most Muslims as America's enemies. Further, it is also the case that most Muslims do not see America as their enemy, despite the efforts of bin Laden and others sharing his views to persuade them otherwise. Indeed, it is questionable whether most Muslims in any event attach primary political importance to their identity as Muslims. National, linguistic and ethnic identities are frequently more important than religious identity in the political sphere, while commitment to secular political ideologies also tends to mute the influence of religion on political life. What is evident is that the Bush Administration has not considered it necessary to avoid actions that seem likely to increase hostility towards the United States. Further, in considering its response to 11 September, the Administration has not dwelt on why there might be hostility towards the United States in some parts of the world or considered it worthwhile to seek to address these. Admittedly, the question of why 'they hate us' has been much debated in the United States. However, posing the issue in this way is hardly conducive to analysing the impact of American foreign policy on attitudes towards the United States. It is also not conducive to differentiating between opposition to particular aspects of American foreign policy and the very much rarer occurrence of a generalized dislike of the American way of life. Thus, there has been little effort made by the Bush Administration to understand why there might be disgruntlement in parts of the Muslim world with American actions since the end of the cold war.

Rather the emphasis has been on the failure of modernization in the Muslim world, with this being seen as the primary source of hostility towards the United States as the exemplar of successful modernization. This argument, which has formed a leitmotiv of the writings of Bernard Lewis, conveniently portrays Americans as the unwitting and wholly innocent victims of other people's entirely unjustified antagonism. Just as importantly, it also undercuts the notion that any benefit would accrue to the United States from any efforts it made to accommodate specific political grievances of people in the Muslim world. Such assumptions perhaps explain the Bush Administration's failure to recognise what might seem not only obvious but also to require appropriate action. This is that the growth of jihadist organizations has been fuelled by violent political conflicts across the Muslim world. Regardless of their origins, it might seem almost self-evident that America would have an interest in their resolution because of their spill-over effects and their capacity to pose a threat to the maintenance of order in the international political system. Yet members of the Bush Administration have for the most part been contemptuous of the efforts of its predecessor to act as a mediator in the resolution of regional conflicts. The inclination of the Administration has been to reject the view that this role should form a part of America's post-cold war mission in the world.

The crude assumption that the sole purposes of American foreign policy should be the furtherance of American interests and values and the advancement of American power has reinforced the view that there is little reason for the United States to promote political accommodation in societies embroiled in conflict. From this perspective, America's interest lies in supporting those advancing free markets and democracy, while it is also generally in the country's interest to eschew alliances with governments that do not represent these values. Further, in so far as conflicts in the Muslim world can be attributed to 'civilizational failure', promoting political accommodation might be viewed as ineffectively addressing the symptoms of a much deeper malaise. By implication, since America is identified with free markets and democracy, concentration on the aggressive pursuit of American interests, according to this view, is to everyone's benefit in the long run. Where the thesis of a clash of civilizations fits into such a perspective is that it provides a readymade explanation of resistance to American interventions, without according such resistance any legitimacy. While Huntington's thesis has not formed the basis of the Bush Administration's response to 11 September, at a sub-terranean level, its influence has remained profound in providing its adherents with a simple key for understanding the world's woes.

Notes

1 Samuel P. Huntington, 'The Clash of Civilizations?', *Foreign Affairs*, Vol. 72, No. 3, Summer 1993, pp. 22–49.
2 The *Sunday Times* (London), 14 October 2001.
3 Samuel P. Huntington, *The Soldier and the State: The Theory and Practice of Civil-Military Relations*, Vintage Books, New York 1957.
4 Samuel P. Huntington, *Political Order in Changing Societies*, Yale University Press, New Haven 1968.
5 John Laffin, *The Dagger of Islam*, Sphere, London 1979.
6 Huntington, 'The Clash of Civilizations', p. 39.
7 Ibid., p. 25.
8 Ibid., p. 26.
9 Ibid., pp. 29–30.
10 Ibid., p. 35.
11 Ibid., pp. 31–2.
12 Ibid., p. 48.
13 Samuel P. Huntington, *The Clash of Civilizations and the Remaking of World Order*, Simon & Schuster, New York 1996, pp. 109–20.
14 Fred Halliday, *Two Hours that Shook the World: September 11, 2001 – Causes and Consequences*, Saqi Books, London 2002, p. 194.
15 John L. Esposito, *Unholy War: Terror in the Name of Islam*, Oxford University Press, New York 2002, p. 127.
16 In 'Special Davos Edition' of Newsweek, December 2001–January 2002.
17 Tariq Ali, *The Clash of Fundamentalisms: Crusades, Jihads and Modernity*, Verso, London 2003, p. 308.
18 Samuel P. Huntington, 'If Not Civilizations, What?', *Foreign Affairs*, Vol. 72, No. 5, November/December 1993, p. 187.
19 Ibid.
20 The term, jihadist, is used in this sense throughout this book, generally in preference to Islamic fundamentalist or Islamist. One reason for this usage is the importance of recognizing the existence

of Islamist political parties competing for votes in many countries
that do not condone the use of violence to further political objectives
wherever there are opportunities for peaceful political competition.
The same is true of groups that might reasonably be labelled Islamic
fundamentalists. It may be fairly pointed out that neither liberal nor
orthodox Muslim scholars interpret the concept of jihad as providing
a licence for political violence, but by the same token they would
certainly not call themselves jihadists.

21 Halliday, *Two Hours that Shook the World*, p. 194.
22 Ibid., p. 197.
23 Ibid., p. 194.
24 Amitav Acharya, 'State–Society Relations: Asians and World Order
    after September 11' in Ken Booth and Time Dunne (eds), *Worlds in
    Collision: Terror and the Future of Global Order*, Palgrave Macmillan,
    Basingstoke 2002, p. 195.
25 'Text: Bush address to Congress', *BBC News Online*, 21 September
    2001.
26 Ibid.
27 William Pfaff, 'The American Mission?', *New York Review of Books*
    (New York), Vol. LI, No. 6, 8 April 2004, p. 24.
28 Lawrence Freedman, 'A New Type of War' in Booth and Dunne,
    Worlds in Collision, p. 39.
29 Ibid., p. 38.
30 A study by an American academic, Professor Marc Herold, that the
    number of Afghan civilians killed by US bombs had surpassed the
    death toll from the attacks on 9/11 received wide coverage. See, for
    example, 'Afghanistan's civilian deaths mount', report on http://news.
    bbc.co.uk for 3 January 2002.
31 *Financial Times*, 28 February 2002.
32 The targeting of tourists is examined further in Chapter 7.

CHAPTER 3

Blowback

In his book on the attacks on America on 11 September 2001, *Two Hours that Shook the World*, Fred Halliday defines blowback as follows:

> Somewhat evasive term, said to be a CIA slang, for activities carried out by former Western clients, such as the Afghan guerrillas who later turn against the West. Examples of exculpatory passive: 'the pen *was* lost', '*it* slipped' rather than '*I* lost it', '*I* knocked it over'.[1]

Peter Bergen also refers to the concept in his book, *Holy War, Inc.* In fact, he devotes a whole chapter entitled 'Blowback: The CIA and the Afghan War' to this issue. However, he is critical of accounts that portray the CIA as directly responsible for sponsoring the activities of Osama bin Laden and his band of Arab Afghans during the war against the Soviet occupation of Afghanistan. He puts the main blame for this development on Pakistan's Inter-Services Intelligence Directorate (ISI) and concludes:

> They [the Pakistanis] funneled millions of dollars to anti-Western Afghan factions, which in turn trained militants who later exported jihad and terrorism around the world – including to the United States. Such an unintended consequence of covert operations is known in spook parlance as 'blowback'.[2]

How and why Western support for the Afghan resistance to Soviet occupation should have ended up in helping to create al-Qaeda forms the subject of this chapter. To explain the context, a brief history of the development of Afghanistan as a modern state is necessary, though perhaps it might be more accurate to characterize the country's political evolution as a quest for modernization that has yet to be fulfilled.

The origins of Afghanistan as a state, as opposed to its being merely a component in the building of empires by the region's many conquerors, can be traced to 1747. In that year, a meeting of tribal chiefs in what was known as a *Loya Jirga*, a concept that still has resonance in present-day Afghanistan, chose Ahmad Shah Abdali as their king. He changed the name Abdali to Durrani, inaugurating a long-lived monarchy that survived to the 1970s. He also built an impressive empire that encompassed part of present-day Pakistan and India, including Kashmir. It was the contraction of Ahmad Shah's empire under subsequent rulers that ultimately determined the boundaries of the state. The country's past glories explain the disposition within Afghanistan towards irredentism rather than partition, as well as the suspicious attitude of neighbouring states towards the promotion of Afghan nationalism.

During the nineteenth century, two expanding empires, the Russian and the British, threatened the independence and even the very existence of Afghanistan. The determination of the British to prevent the Russians from securing a pathway to the warm waters of the Indian Ocean lay at the root of two wars between Britain and Afghanistan. The history of Afghanistan during the nineteenth century was dominated by the twin themes of internal disorder and external intervention. It was the era of the Great Game in which Britain as the stronger of the two imperialisms took preventive action to prevent the Russians from gaining a foothold in Afghanistan from which they might threaten British India. The Afghan wars had a considerable impact on popular culture in Britain. It was reflected in the stereotype of Afghans as fearsome bearded warriors and in the frequency with which Afghan cities featured in street names in estates from the Victorian era.

The First Afghan War between 1839 and 1842 arose out of a British desire to replace a rather competent Afghan ruler and one by no means unfriendly to the British. It was not a successful venture. The last year of the war was marked by a catastrophic retreat of British forces from Kabul to Jalalabad in January 1842. According to legend, an assistant surgeon, Dr William Brydon, was the sole survivor out of a force of 16,500. In fact, this was an exaggeration. He was the only European to make it to Jalalabad. But by no means all of those who were taken prisoner were killed and a number were ultimately rescued when British retribution for these events followed. That was followed by withdrawal. The Second Afghan War between 1878 and 1880 was scarcely any more sensible in its conception. It arose out of a Russian diplomatic mission to Kabul, a mission not sought by the Afghan government of the time. The outcome of the conflict was the Afghan government's agreement to British supervision of its foreign affairs, a position that lasted to 1919.

For three-quarters of the twentieth century, half a dozen monarchs ruled over Afghanistan, but without the stability that such continuity might seem to imply. Resistance to modernization and a propensity towards warlordism retarded the country's development through much of the century. Habibullah Khan, whose main achievement was to keep Afghanistan out of the First World War, reigned from 1901 to 1919 when he was assassinated. His successor, Amanullah Khan launched the Third Afghan War to free the country from British supervision. After Afghan victories on the ground the British resorted to an air war. Negotiations followed the inconclusive outcome of the war. They led to the Treaty of Rawalpindi under which Afghanistan at last achieved effective independence. Amanullah introduced reforms aimed at the modernization and secularization of Afghan society. The reforms encountered resistance and proved to be Amanullah's undoing. He was forced to abdicate in January 1929. A period of instability followed during which a Tajik brigand, Bacha-i-Saqqa, briefly seized Kabul. In October 1929 Nadir Shah Ghazi became king. His assassination in 1933 led to the accession to the monarchy of his nineteen year-old son, Mohammed Zahir Shah. He ruled the country from 1933 to 1973. He remained an important figure in exile during the years of Soviet occupation, the civil wars that followed and the period of Taliban rule. It even seemed possible at the close of 2001 that he would figure in the plans for the post-Taliban era, though by then he was in his late 80s.

An important figure during Zahir Shah's reign was his cousin, Mohammed Daud. He was Prime Minister between 1953 and 1963. In this capacity, he 'introduced a major programme of social and economic modernization, drawing economic aid from the Soviet Union'.[3] In fact, Daud sought support for his programmes from both superpowers, but the higher priority Washington gave to relations with Pakistan was an obstacle to the development of close relations between the United States and Afghanistan. This was because Daud's championing of Pashtun ethnic interests was a source of friction between Afghanistan and Pakistan. It was one of the factors that contributed to Daud's dismissal by Zahir Shah. A new constitution was adopted in 1964 and Zahir Shah, while retaining considerable power, took steps in the direction of transforming the monarchy into a constitutional one. In 1971 and 1972 Afghanistan suffered a severe drought. The economic consequences of the drought and anger over corruption in government undermined the popularity of the regime, paving the way for Daud to seize power in a military coup d'état in July 1973. Daud turned Afghanistan into a republic with himself as President. He introduced a new constitution in 1977.

A year later in April 1978 Daud was himself overthrown and killed in a coup led by Mohammed Taraki. Taraki was the Secretary-General of the People's Democratic Party of Afghanistan (PDPA). This was the country's Communist Party. Taraki headed the Khalq (or masses) faction of the party. Taraki was ousted and killed by his deputy, Hafizullah Amin, in September 1979. By this time, the reforms promulgated by the regime had given rise to a full-scale revolt against the PDPA's rule. The insurgency had attracted the interest and support of the United States. The aid to the insurgents was channelled through Pakistan so that the United

States could deny Afghan and Soviet charges of intervention. Alarmed by the prospect of the violent overthrow of an ideological ally, the government of the Soviet Union intervened militarily in the conflict in December 1979. Moscow regarded Amin as a liability and its forces captured and executed him, implausibly claiming that he had been a traitor and agent of American imperialism. The Soviet Union installed in power the exiled leader of the Parcham (or flag) faction of the PDPA, Babrak Kamal.

Despite the support of Soviet forces numbering 120,000 at their peak, Kamal was never able to establish effective control over the country as a whole, in the face of the revolt of the Mujahidin. This was the collective name the media applied to the insurgents against the Soviet occupation of Afghanistan between 1979 and 1989. How the Mujahidin were and to some degree continue to be seen in the West is captured by the US State Department's translation of the term as 'freedom fighters'. A more literal translation of both Mujahid and Mujahidin is provided by Fred Halliday in the section on keywords in his book on the impact of 11 September upon world politics:

> **Mujahid, pl. Mujahidin** One who wages *jihad*, used in modern political discourse to denote nationalist and Islamist fighters, e.g. during the Algerian war of independence (1954–62), the anti-monarchical resistance to the Shah (1971–79) and the Afghan anti-communist war (1978–92).[4]

In fact, the religious dimension of the Mujahidin was of immense importance. It attracted relatively little attention during the years of the Soviet occupation. The media interpreted the conflict simply as a nationalist struggle by the Afghan people against a puppet regime supported by an oppressive foreign presence. Few saw the supporters of the regime as beleaguered modernizers overwhelmed by the forces of rural conservatism. Just as importantly little attention was paid to the fact that the collective term, Mujahidin, covered a wide range of different organizations. These represented a variety of both ethnic groups and attitudes towards

religion and were only very loosely held together by their commitment to the common objective of ending the Soviet occupation.
Further, while there was some coverage of the extent to which
the organizations that made up the Mujahidin received outside
material help in their fight against the Soviet Union, external
involvement in the struggle for power among different elements
of the Mujahidin was largely disregarded in the Western media.

Under Gorbachev, the Soviet Union ended its disastrous
intervention in Afghanistan in line with the general direction of
the country's foreign policy away from ideological confrontation
with the non-Communist world. In May 1986 Moscow replaced
Babrak Kamal with Muhammed Najibullah. In 1988 the Soviet
Union agreed to withdraw its forces from Afghanistan, a process
which was completed in terms of an agreed timetable by 15
February 1989. In retrospect, it is tempting to interpret Soviet
withdrawal from Afghanistan as the prelude to the collapse of
Communism in Eastern Europe and to the eventual disintegration
of the Soviet Union itself. However, it was far from being the only
factor in the demise of the Soviet system. The system's economic
failings and its incapacity to adjust to the oil shocks of the 1970s
and to technological innovations such as the microchip were more
significant. This was notwithstanding the high cost of the Afghan
intervention in terms both of money and lives, as well as its
demoralizing impact on Soviet society. Yet inevitably for groups
that had fought in Afghanistan, the notion that their actions had
brought about the destruction of a superpower had potent appeal.

Jihadists were not alone in drawing this conclusion from the
events of the late 1980s. A particularly striking statement of this
thesis was put forward by President Carter's former National
Security Advisor, Zbigniew Brzezinski, in an interview he gave in
1998. Brzezinski had been responsible for the policy of channelling aid to insurgents after the 1978 coup and before the
intervention of Soviet forces. Indeed, the intention behind this
policy had precisely been to bring about Soviet intervention, on
the calculation that it would prove as debilitating for the Soviet
Union as American intervention in Vietnam had been for the

United States. Brzezinski was challenged as to the consequences of America's promotion of the jihadists and made this reply: 'Which was more important in world history? The Taliban or the fall of the Soviet empire? A few over-excited Islamists or the liberation of Central Europe and the end of the cold war?'[5]

To the surprise of much of the world, the puppet regime of Mohammed Najibullah did not collapse immediately on the withdrawal of Soviet forces. Indeed, it outlasted the Soviet Union itself. Admittedly, its survival was as much a reflection of the divisions within the Mujahidin as its own political strength. At the time of the completion of the Soviet withdrawal, an interim government had been established in Peshawar, Pakistan, by seven of the groups that made up the Mujahidin. However, the alliance was by no comprehensive or representative of all the elements that had opposed the Soviet occupation. Consequently, both the United States and (less surprisingly) the Soviet Union took the view that Najibullah should stay in power until internationally recognized elections could be held. This did not in the end turn out to be a viable option as the regime lost ground to the forces supporting the Peshawar alliance. In April 1992 Najibullah's position finally became untenable and he took refuge in the United Nations compound in Kabul where he remained until his capture and execution by the Taliban in September 1996.

In accordance with an agreement among Mujahidin leaders, Burhanaddin Rabbani became the first President of the Islamic State of Afghanistan, as the country was renamed in 1992. Rabbani had founded Jamiat-i-Islami in 1973. He was a moderate Islamist who came from Afghanistan's second largest ethnic group, the Tajiks, who comprised approximately a quarter of the country's population. Pashtuns formed the largest ethnic group comprising approximately 40 per cent of the population. From the outset there was a violent struggle for power among the different factions of the Mujahidin. Ethnic and sectarian differences played an important role in the factionalism that beset the country. These tended to coincide with and reinforce regional divisions facilitating the emergence of local strong men. In short, they created the conditions for warlordism. Compounding the country's problems was the involvement of neighbouring states in its conflicts. Amalendu Misra describes the situation after the fall of Najibullah as follows:

> Far from helping to ease the civil war in the country, regional powers such as India, Iran and Pakistan actively encouraged factional fighting, and vied with each other for power and dominance in this chaotic atmosphere. By the year 1994 Afghanistan had become really and truly an anarchical place. The idea of Afghanistan as a coherent polity had dissipated completely. Its definition as a country was held together by images of lawlessness, the destitution of people living within it, and the extreme violence that everyone experienced there. Afghanistan, at this juncture, truly manifested the classic symptoms of a failing or failed state.[6]

The anarchic conditions in much of the country and the absence of Pashtun representation at the highest levels of government prompted a movement among Pashtuns to replace the government in Kabul. It was called the Taliban, the Persian plural for *talib*, meaning a student from a religious institution. The name reflected the fact that the core of its support came from recruits from religious schools called madrassas that were to be found in both Afghanistan and Pakistan. The Taliban first emerged in the province of Kandahar in January 1994, when Mullah Omar and students from his madrassa in the village of Singesar in the Argestan district of Kandahar attacked and defeated a local warlord who had been responsible for the rape of local women and other atrocities. From these small beginnings a much larger movement developed as the fame of its exploits against the worst manifestations of warlordism spread. By the end of 1994 governments outside of Afghanistan, most particularly that of Pakistan, had taken note of the movement's emergence.

Among the factors that helped to propel the Taliban into becoming a national movement were the support of the government of

Pakistan, its student army recruited from both Afghanistan and Pakistan, and its base in the country's largest ethnic group, the Pashtuns. In September 1996 the Taliban captured Kabul. Najibullah was executed and Rabbani fled, while the Taliban leader, Mullah Mohammed Omar, declared that the state would be run wholly in accordance with Islamic principles and to this end renamed the country the Islamic Emirate of Afghanistan. There was a generally hostile international reaction to the extreme policies promulgated by the Taliban. These included the abolition of education for women, draconian punishments for a very wide range of offences and prohibitions on the most basic forms of entertainment such as popular music and kite-flying. In May 1997 Pakistan recognized the Taliban as the lawful government of Afghanistan. Saudi Arabia and the United Arab Emirates followed suit. However, continued fighting and the opposition to the Taliban in the north of Afghanistan provided grounds for other governments to withhold recognition.

One cause of the international hostility towards the Taliban was its relationship with Osama bin Laden and al-Qaeda, as discussed in greater depth below. This increased in 1998 as a result of the bombing of American embassies in East Africa by al-Qaeda, atrocities that prompted the Clinton Administration to launch cruise missile attacks on al-Qaeda bases in Afghanistan. Another reason for international hostility towards the regime was the manner in which it extended its control of the country, including the massacre of thousands of Hazara, Uzbek and Tajik civilians in the city of Mazar-i-Sharif in the same month as the embassy bombings, August 1998. In the perspective of the Taliban this was retaliation for the killing of large numbers of its supporters in the city in the previous year. By the end of 1998, the Taliban regime was in control of approximately 90 per cent of Afghanistan, but as a consequence of outrage at its actions, it continued to be denied recognition as the lawful government of Afghanistan. The main exceptions to Taliban control were the Panjshir valley and a corner in the north-east of the country. Together these provided a base for opponents of the regime who had joined forces in what became known as the Northern Alliance. This grouping drew its support from minority ethnic and sectarian groups that had been increasingly alienated by the policies pursued by the Taliban.

The regime's lack of international legitimacy gave its opponents the incentive to continue fighting, while also increasing the regime's dependence on its few allies such as al-Qaeda. In 1999 and 2000 the Taliban launched offensives against the remaining areas of the country not under the movement's control, but there were also successful counter-offensives by the Northern Alliance, led by the Tajik leader, Ahmad Shah Massoud. In February 2001 the regime attracted further international attention and condemnation when Mullah Omar ordered the destruction of gigantic statues of the Buddha that dated back to the second century. By this time the international community had imposed sanctions against Afghanistan over the regime's failure to cooperate in the combating of international terrorism, most clearly through the safe haven it afforded Osama bin Laden and other leading figures in al-Qaeda. Two days before the attacks on America, on 9 September 2001, suicide bombers posing as journalists killed Massoud.

The events of 11 September prompted an ultimatum from the United States to the Taliban regime both to surrender bin Laden and to take other action to prevent its territory from being used as a safe haven by al-Qaeda. The United States government made it clear that it was unwilling to haggle over the terms of the regime's cooperation. In the light of both the public mood in the United States and the Taliban's previous resistance to American demands over the issue, there was little expectation of a response from the regime that would avert military action against it. Indeed, American retribution against the Taliban regime was swift. Less than a month after the attacks on America, US forces started the air war against the Taliban, with the firing of cruise missiles against military targets on 7 October 2001. In a gesture of international solidarity, British forces also took part in these attacks. The principal aim of the aerial bombardment was to lend support to a ground offensive launched by the Northern Alliance. There was a relatively brief period of stalemate before the defences of the Taliban were cracked, leading to the fall of Kabul on 13 November.

In a meeting in Bonn, Germany, in December Afghan opponents of the Taliban agreed to establish an interim government headed by a supporter of King Zahir Shah, Harmid Karzai. Karzai was confirmed as the ruler of Afghanistan by the holding of a traditional Loya Jirga or Grand Council in June 2002. Karzai was given the task of presiding over the drawing up of a new constitution and the holding of general elections in 2004. From an international perspective, the urbane and modest Karzai was hailed as an attractive leader ideally suited to rehabilitate Afghanistan's reputation after the extremism of the Taliban. Initially the rapid collapse of the Taliban regime had seemed an extraordinarily impressive demonstration of American power, considering the difficulties that the British empire had encountered in the country in the nineteenth century and the Soviet Union in the twentieth century. The fact that it had been achieved without having to invade the country with a massive army made it appear even more impressive.

However, the situation in Afghanistan had been far from normalized. The old problems of local resistance to the central government quickly re-emerged. The various components of the Northern Alliance were at one with the international community in wanting to overthrow the Taliban regime. But once that objective had been achieved, they had an agenda of their own that diverged markedly from that of the international community in significant respects. In addition, the ethnic base of the Northern Alliance meant that securing the allegiance of the Pashtuns to the new dispensation was always likely to prove difficult, despite all the efforts made by the Americans and others to ensure the representation of Pashtuns in the interim government.

These circumstances in combination with the diversion of American troops and attention to the war in Iraq created the conditions for a revival of the Taliban in rural areas of Afghanistan, particularly in the Pashtun heartland of Kandahar province. The failure of the Bush Administration to establish the conditions for the eradication of al-Qaeda in Afghanistan provides the basis for scathing criticism of the Administration by the former head of counter-terrorism in the Clinton and Bush Administrations, Richard Clarke.[7] He argues that an obvious objective of the United States after 11 September was 'that al-Qaeda's sanctuary in Taliban-run Afghanistan had to be occupied by U.S. forces and the al Qaeda leaders killed'.[8] He continues:

> Unfortunately, Bush's efforts were slow and small. He began by again offering the Taliban a chance to avoid U.S. occupation of their country and, when that failed, he initially sent in only a handful of Special Forces. When the Taliban and al Qaeda leaders escaped, he dispatched additional forces but less than one full division equivalent, fewer U.S. troops for all of Afghanistan than the number of NYPD [New York Police Department] assigned to Manhattan.[9]

He elaborates on this criticism in the final chapter in the book in which he addresses the question, what should the Administration have done in Afghanistan after 11 September.

> The United States should have inserted forces into Afghanistan to cut off bin Laden's escape routes and to find and arrest or kill him and his deputies. After the U.S. finally introduced ground forces into Afghanistan and began sweep operations looking for al Qaeda and the Taliban, America and its coalition partners (including France and Germany) should have established a security presence throughout the country. They did not. As a result, the new Afghan government of President Hamid Kharzi was given little authority outside the capital city of Kabul. There was an opportunity to end the factional fighting and impose an integrated national government. Yet after initial efforts to unite the country, American interest waned and the warlords returned to their old ways. Afghanistan was a nation raped by war and factional fighting for twenty years. It needed everything rebuilt, but in contrast to funds

sought for Iraq, U.S. economic and development aid to Afghanistan was inadequate and slowly delivered.[10]

To assess Clarke's case against the Bush Administration, a fuller account is needed of the links between al-Qaeda and Afghanistan. Osama bin Laden established strong links with Afghanistan during the Soviet occupation in the 1980s. He was a key figure in Saudi Arabia and Pakistan's support for the jihad against the Soviet occupation of Afghanistan in the 1980s. And insofar as the United States provided Pakistan with much of the wherewithal to back the jihad, bin Laden may be regarded as indirectly a beneficiary of American as well as Saudi largesse, hence the basis for the argument that the subsequent emergence of al-Qaeda was a case of blowback. As it turned out, America's material support for the Mujahidin played a vital role in their ultimate victory. In particular, at a critical juncture in the war, the supply of Stinger missiles (shoulder-launched surface-to-air missiles) to the Mujahidin provided them with an effective counter to armoured Soviet helicopters that had threatened the rebels' control of the rural areas of Afghanistan.

But in spite of the scale of America's assistance to the Mujahidin, American political influence over the different factions that made up the Mujahidin was limited. This was a product in part of when America had begun supporting the opposition to Communist rule in Afghanistan. This had predated direct Soviet military intervention in December 1979. Under a presidential directive of 3 July 1979, Jimmy Carter authorized covert support for the resistance to the government in Kabul. The channelling of American aid indirectly through other parties was designed to counter claims by the Soviet Union both before and at the time of direct Soviet military intervention of American intervention in the conflict. The argument that its actions constituted counter-intervention to the illegitimate interference in the domestic affairs of Afghanistan of other states, most particularly the United States, was an important element in the Soviet government's justification of its actions. The Carter Administration strongly denied Soviet claims and sought to sustain the fiction of its non-involvement by using Pakistan as a conduit for its aid to the rebels. This practice continued even after the entrenchment of Soviet occupation had removed the need for the United States to be able to deny its connection to the Mujahidin. This was also despite the fact that the scale of American aid in the 1980s had made its involvement in the conflict obvious across the world.

The important political consequence was that successive American governments exercised little influence over the factional politics of the Mujahadin. The common interest of the United States, Pakistan and Saudi Arabia in securing the withdrawal of the Soviet Union from Afghanistan and the ending of Communist rule in the country overlaid large differences in their longer-term political objectives. Pakistan had a strong interest in preventing Afghan nationalists with potentially irredentist ambitions from gaining power in Kabul, while Saudi Arabia had a stake in using the conflict to advance its conservative version of the Muslim religion, Wahhabi Islam. Pakistani and Saudi interests dictated the terms on which the war against the Soviet occupation should be fought. This was more as a religious crusade against infidels than as a struggle for self-determination by the Afghan people. That paved the way for the creation of a Muslim international brigade to fight the Soviet occupation. The most important person in this crusade was Osama bin Laden.

Osama bin Laden was born in Riyadh, Saudi Arabia, on 10 March 1957. His family came from al-Rubat, a village in Yemen. His father, Mohammed bin Laden emigrated from Yemen to Saudi Arabia where he made a fortune in construction. His efforts laid the basis for what ultimately became a multi-billion dollar business. Osama's father had several wives and Osama was the seventeenth son, among a total of 52 children. Mohammed bin Laden died in 1967 in a plane crash. Osama bin Laden graduated with a degree in public administration from the King Abdulaziz University in Jeddah in 1981. At university he came under the influence of Islamists (in other words adherents of the view that the religion ought to form the basis of one's actions in the political realm). Among these influences, the most significant, as well as the most radical, was that of Abdullah Azzam, a member of the Muslim Brotherhood, a long established Islamist movement in the Arab world. Esposito describes Azzam as 'an advocate of a militant global jihad ideology and culture'.[11]

Early in 1980 Osama bin Laden travelled to Pakistan to meet up with leaders of the resistance to the Soviet occupation of Afghanistan and on his return to Saudi Arabia he lobbied for support for the Mujahidin. He became fully engaged in the jihad in 1982 when he entered Afghanistan, contributing both equipment and funds to the resistance. In 1984 with increasing numbers of Arabs joining the struggle in Afghanistan, bin Laden established the House of the Supporters (Beit al-Ansar), a guesthouse in Peshawar, Pakistan, for Arabs on their way to join the jihad, the first of many such facilities. At about the same time Abdullah Azzam set up the Afghan Services Office (Mekhtab al-Khadamat). With money raised by bin Laden largely from the Saudi government, the scope of these activities expanded, channelling many thousands of Muslim volunteers into the jihad against the Soviet occupation. These volunteers became known not entirely appositely as the Arab Afghans. None were Afghans and by no means all of them were Arab. However, most did come from three Arab countries: Saudi Arabia, Yemen and Algeria. Estimates of the number of Arab Afghans who participated in the jihad in Afghanistan vary considerably. Bergen estimates that during the entire course of the war they numbered in the low tens of thousands.[12] He argues that they were vastly outnumbered by the number of Afghan participants in the resistance to Soviet occupation and concludes that their contribution was 'insignificant from a military point of view'.[13] On this basis, even on the contestable assumption that the Afghan war played a critical role in the eventual demise of the Soviet Union, their involvement was unnecessary to secure the Soviet Union's defeat in Afghanistan. What followed from the Arab Afghan involvement in Afghanistan therefore could not be interpreted as a price worth paying for the much larger objective of the liberation of Eastern Europe, as Brzezinski wished to have it.

In contrast to Bergen's assessment of their military contribution, the political consequences of the involvement of the Arab Afghans in the conflict were to prove huge. From the outset, Azzam and bin Laden put the war in Afghanistan in a much wider context. Thus, Azzam, in explaining that the duty of Muslims to defend Muslim territory placed an obligation on Muslims to participate in the jihad in Afghanistan, declared:

> This duty will not end with victory in Afghanistan; jihad will remain an individual obligation until all other lands that were Muslim are returned to us so that Islam will reign again: before us lie Palestine, Bokhara, Lebanon, Chad, Eritrea, Somalia, the Philippines, Burma, Southern Yemen, Tashkent and Andalusia.[14]

These words have been widely quoted since 11 September but attracted little interest at the time they were made. In general, the ideology of the jihadists during the course of the war against the Soviet occupation of Afghanistan received scant attention in the West. Even after the Soviet withdrawal, there was initially little recognition of the extent to which jihadist violence in other parts of the world had its origins in the extremely brutal war against the Soviet occupation. Similarly, little attention was paid outside the region to the factional politics within Afghanistan after the Soviet withdrawal.

It took a number of years for connections to be made between the growth of terrorism linked to Islamic fundamentalism in the 1990s and the war in Afghanistan in the 1980s. The role of the Arab Afghans in the spreading of political violence to other lands was slow to be recognized. And even after the events of 11 September there remains a reluctance to trace the origins of present-day jihadist terrorism to the ideological form that opposition to the Soviet intervention in Afghanistan took. A partial justification for this reluctance is that events after the Soviet withdrawal from Afghanistan did not follow a straightforward path. In the aftermath of the Soviet withdrawal from Afghanistan in February 1989, bin Laden founded al-Qaeda (the Base). Bergen suggests that it initially had two purposes.[15] One was to provide documentation on the fate of those who had joined the jihad under the auspices of the Afghan Service Office to assist families in tracing relatives. The second and more significant purpose was to recruit an inner group from the Arab Afghans to continue the jihad after Afghanistan. This inner group was carefully vetted in the recognition that a number of Middle Eastern governments had been monitoring who had volunteered to fight in Afghanistan. However, at this point it was far from clear in what direction the jihad would be pursued.

Abdullah Azzam, the ideologist of a global jihad, was assassinated in Pakistan in November 1989. By this time Osama bin Laden had returned to Saudi Arabia where he was hailed as a hero of the anti-Soviet jihad in Afghanistan. Initially, with the encouragement from inside the Saudi government he turned his attention to politics in Yemen. However, the complex politics of Yemen was soon overshadowed by events elsewhere in the region. In August 1990 Iraq invaded Kuwait. The invasion was a direct threat to Saudi Arabia itself. To the disgust of bin Laden the Saudi government sought military help from the United States. Bin Laden's offer to enlist Arab Afghans to defend the Kingdom failed to move the Saudi government. Bergen argues that bin Laden viewed the dispatch of American troops to the Kingdom of Saudi Arabia in August 1990 as an event scarcely less significant than the Soviet intervention in Afghanistan in December 1979. Bin Laden now found himself ostracized. In 1991 he returned to Afghanistan, but the shifting alignments of the Mujahidin factions struggling for power in post-Soviet Afghanistan made him seek a more secure haven. This he found for a time in Sudan. A radical Islamist government had come to power in Sudan in 1989 as a result of a military coup d'état. As a country riven by regional, racial, religious and ethnic conflicts, Sudan provided a favourable environment for the flourishing of ideologies that justified the use of violence for political ends. Bin Laden forged a close relationship with Hassan al-Turabi, the leader of Sudan's National Islamic Front and an influential supporter of the military regime.

This relationship made it possible for bin Laden to establish a haven in Sudan. It was cemented further by the investments that bin Laden made in what was and remains a very poor country. Bin Laden's business activities also provided a convenient cover for the development during this period of al-Qaeda as a global jihadist network. An early indication of the intentions of the global jihadists was the bombing of the World Trade Centre in New York in February 1993. Six people died in this attack and hundreds were injured. At the time, the name al-Qaeda meant little to the investigators and contemporary accounts focused on the role played by a close affiliate of al-Qaeda, an Egyptian organization, Islamic Jihad. Similarly, the part played by jihadists in assisting militias in Somalia in their attacks on American forces and even their involvement in a bomb attack in Riyadh in November 1995 that killed five Americans had not yet alerted the American authorities or the international community at large to the significance of bin Laden's network. Bin Laden's Sudanese haven facilitated meetings between his group and other violent Islamist movements, most significantly, the Lebanese Shia group, Hezbollah. Hezbollah had pioneered two significant developments in the realm of clandestine violence: suicide missions and the launching of simultaneous attacks on a number of targets. These techniques were to be imitated by al-Qaeda. They had been used by Hezbollah with devastating effect against American and French forces in Beirut in 1983 and achieved their purpose in causing a rapid withdrawal of Western forces from Lebanon.

In 1996, in part as a result of American pressure on the Sudanese government, bin Laden was forced to leave Sudan. He returned to Afghanistan in May that year. Fortuitously, his return coincided with the rise to power of the Taliban. Bin Laden quickly forged a close relationship with the new movement and its leader, Mullah Mohammed Omar. The haven in Afghanistan, permitting the establishment of secure training camps and facilitating recruitment, emboldened bin Laden to expand the activities of the al-Qaeda network and to launch larger and larger attacks. The most devastating of these attacks prior to the events of 11 September was the simultaneous bombing of the American embassies in Kenya and Tanzania on 7 August 1998. Over two hundred people, mainly locals, were killed in the two attacks. The Clinton Administration responded by launching cruise missile attacks on al-Qaeda bases in Afghanistan, as well as on a pharmaceutical plant in Sudan where it alleged production of agents for chemical warfare had been taking place. Among those killed in the attacks on Afghanistan were members of a Kashmiri jihadist organization. This underlined the fact that al-Qaeda was connected through affiliated organizations and groups to conflicts in many parts of the world that involved Muslims. A number of these conflicts, such as the Kashmiri, Kosovan and Chechen conflicts were not viewed by the West in these terms, but rather conceived as primarily nationalist conflicts in which people were engaged in a struggle for self-determination. Different views existed as to the legitimacy of these struggles, but none was seen in the same light as the use of violence to further a fundamentalist interpretation of Islam.

Bin Laden had made his own intentions plain in two declarations issued well before the attacks on America's African embassies. The first of these declarations was entitled 'The Declaration of Jihad on the Americans Occupying the Country of the Two Sacred Places' and was issued in August 1996. Its title underlined the priority bin Laden placed on the removal of American troops from Saudi Arabia, which he regarded both as a religious affront to Muslims and as signifying the political weakness of the Islamic world. The second declaration of 23 February 1998 announced the formation of the World Islamic Front against the Jews and the Crusaders. It is reproduced as an appendix in Halliday's book on the events of 11 September 2001. Halliday calls it al-Qaeda's founding statement. He bases that in part on the range of co-signatories of the declaration. These are clearly intended to signal how global al-Qaeda had become and the extent of its reach. The most widely quoted section of the declaration was its self-described *fatwa* to attack Americans and their allies.

> The ruling to kill the Americans and their allies – civilians and military – is an individual duty for every Muslim who can do

it in any country in which it is possible to do it, in order to liberate the al-Aqsa Mosque and the Holy Mosque from their grip, and in order for their armies to move out of all the lands of Islam, defeated and unable to threaten any Muslim.[16]

Unsurprisingly, in the wake of these declarations and the attacks on America's African embassies, dealing with the threat posed by al-Qaeda became the major preoccupation of the Clinton Administration's Counter-terrorism Security Group under Richard Clarke. Yet until the events of 11 September 2001, neither the issue of the threat from al-Qaeda nor that of international terrorism more widely had a high political profile in the United States. In particular, how to meet such threats was not a matter of partisan debate, further limiting the political salience of these issues. Clarke's book recounts his efforts to raise the profile of the threat from al-Qaeda at the policymaking level. False alarms in the past, such as the initial speculation that jihadists had been responsible for the Oklahoma City bomb in 1995 and the downing of a TWA jet in 1996, may have contributed to a tendency to discount the significance of bin Laden's rhetoric. Even those who did not discount his rhetoric may have doubted the capacity of the global jihadists to launch a large-scale attack on the United States or within the West more widely.

Clarke made some headway during the Clinton Administration in persuading senior members of the Administration to take the threat from al-Qaeda seriously. Admittedly, the focus was on immediate issues such as thwarting any attempt by al-Qaeda to use the coming of the millennium to stage a spectacular attack. There was much less of a focus on the sources of alienation within the Muslim world fuelling recruitment to al-Qaeda, though Clarke does argue that preventing al-Qaeda from exploiting ethnonational conflicts in the former Yugoslavia was a factor in American intervention in the Balkans. When President Bush took office, Clarke found to his dismay that the senior members of the Administration were both ill-informed on the subject of al-Qaeda and strongly disinclined to believe that a network without state backing could pose a serious threat to the security of the United States. Even the events of 11 September 2001, while having a profound impact on American political discourse did not change opinion within the Bush Administration fundamentally. The neo-conservatives remained committed to their project of American hegemony during the twenty-first century and used the events of 11 September to justify a pre-existing foreign policy agenda. The disdain for the Clinton Administration's approach to foreign policy, especially its efforts to mediate in regional conflicts, also remained unchanged.

These attitudes were reflected in the Bush Administration's response to the events of 11 September, particularly its emphasis on the efficient use of American military power to strike back at America's enemies. In this context, there is a strong element of benefit of hindsight in Clarke's criticism that the Bush Administration did not launch its assault on Afghanistan even earlier. Much more justified is his criticism that the Administration's policy towards Afghanistan after the fall of the Taliban regime created the conditions for the revival of the Taliban movement, as well as the continuing use of both Afghanistan and Pakistan by al-Qaeda. The Bush Administration's contemptuous attitude towards nation-building and its unwillingness to assume such a role in Afghanistan back up Clarke's criticism. Yet it might be argued that creating a stable, democratic government in Afghanistan lies beyond the capacity of the international community, whatever resources are put into the country. This is because of the prevalence in Afghanistan of regionally based warlordism in undermining the creation of an effective central government.[17] There is also the closely related problem of the huge contribution made to the economy of a desperately poor society by opium. By 2004, there had been a twenty-fold increase in the production of opium since the fall of the Taliban regime, indicating the scale of the difficulty the international community faces.[18] It might also be argued that the fall of the Taliban regime struck a very large blow against al-Qaeda and that the remnants of the organization do not pose a threat comparable to that of before 11 September.

It might also be argued that cynical political calculation lay behind the failure of the Bush Administration to complete the task of uprooting al-Qaeda in Afghanistan in the early months of 2002. With the 'war' over, it would have been much more difficult to enlist support for other parts of the Administration's foreign policy agenda. It would also have been difficult to have made the 'war on terrorism' into a wedge issue in partisan American politics, enabling Republican candidates in the mid-term elections of 2002 to 'run on the war' in the revealing phrase of Bush's adviser on elections, Karl Rove.[19] By this Rove meant not just the military action that the government had undertaken in Afghanistan but the clear prospect that there would be military intervention in Iraq. The next chapter examines how and why the Bush Administration waged war on the regime of Saddam Hussein in Iraq, though plainly there was no connection between the regime and the events of 11 September or more generally any alliance or practical cooperation between the Iraqi regime and al-Qaeda. In fact, from time to time spokespersons of the Administration admitted as much. However, that did not in the least deter the senior members of the Administration from the President downwards from making speeches clearly intended to convey to their audiences that there was a close relationship between Saddam Hussein and bin Laden. Nor did it in the least deter neo-conservatives in the media from propagating the same untruths.

Notes

1 Halliday, *Two Hours that Shook the World: September 11, 2001 – Courses and Consequences*, Saqi Books, London 2002, p. 11.

2 Peter L. Bergen, *Holy War, Inc.: Inside the Secret Worlds of Osama bin Laden*, Phoenix, London 2002, p. 70.

3 J. Denis Derbyshire and Ian Derbyshire, *Political Systems of the World*, Chambers, Edinburgh 1989, p. 583.

4 Halliday *Two Hours that Shook the World* p. 17.

5 Quoted in John K. Cooley, *Unholy Wars: Afghanistan, America and International Terrorism* (Second Edition), Pluto Press, London 2000, p. 20.

6 Amalendu Misra, *Afghanistan: The Labyrinth of Violence*, Polity, Cambridge 2004, pp. 61–2.
7 Clarke chaired the Counter-terrorism Security Group (CSG) from 1992 to 2001.
8 Richard A. Clarke, *Against All Enemies: Inside America's War on Terror*, Free Press, New York 2004, p. 245.
9 Ibid.
10 Ibid., pp. 277–8.
11 John L. Esposito, *Unholy War: Terror in the Name of Islam*, Oxford University Press, New York 2002, p. 9.
12 Bergen, *Holy War, Inc.*, p. 58.
13 Ibid.
14 Quoted in Bergen, *Holy War, Inc.*, p. 56.
15 See Bergen, *Holy War, Inc.*, pp. 62–3.
16 Quoted in Halliday, *Two Hours that Shook the World*, p. 219.
17 Afghanistan's continuing problems were extensively examined in *Independent*, 15 November 2005, under the heading, 'Afghanistan: The war with no end'.
18 See, for example, 'The new challenge of fighting druglords', *Financial Times*, 19 August 1994.
19 See, for example, James Carney, 'General Karl Rove, Reporting for Duty', 29 September 2002 at http://www.time.com.

CHAPTER 4

Diversion

Iraq was a high priority for George W. Bush from the day of his inauguration as President of the United States in January 2001. Numerous accounts of the inner workings of the Bush Administration have emphasized that long before the events of 11 September 2001 Bush was preoccupied with bringing about regime change in Iraq. Despite the absence of evidence of any involvement by Iraq in the events of 11 September 2001, there was a determination within the Administration in the aftermath of the assault on America to use it to justify direct American military action against Iraq. Saddam Hussein had long been a figure of hate in the United States and the Bush Administration could count on that in arguing the case for military action. The ideological gulf between Saddam Hussein and Osama bin Laden and the fact that there was mutual hostility between jihadist groups and Saddam Hussein's regime were disregarded in the context of a much cruder and crasser equation. This was that the assault on America had stemmed from the country's support for Israel. That generated a strong desire for revenge against the Arab world as the primary source of antagonism to the Jewish state. That desire was not assuaged by the overthrow of the Taliban regime in Afghanistan. This was more especially because of the failure to capture bin Laden at the time of its fall, but also because of the absence of strong antipathy towards Afghanistan as such.

By contrast, American hostility towards Iraq dated back to 1958 when a leftist military regime came to power in Baghdad overthrowing a pro-Western monarchy. Ironically, there was a slight improvement in relations between the two countries after Saddam Hussein became President in 1979. The main reason for the change was the Iranian revolution of the same year. Iraq attacked Iran in 1980 leading to a long and costly war. Though America remained basically neutral with an interest, as Henry Kissinger put it, that both sides should lose, it tilted increasingly towards Baghdad in the later stages of the war. One sign of that was the removal of Iraq from America's list of terrorist states. Iraq had been labelled a terrorist state for giving support to the Kurdish Workers Party (PKK) in Turkey. However, the thawing of relations between Iraq and the West proved short-lived. On 2 August 1990 Iraq invaded and occupied Kuwait. Saddam Hussein miscalculated the response of the international community to what was a clear violation of one of the most basic principles of the world since the end of the Second World War and the setting up of the United Nations.

Relations between Iraq and Kuwait had deteriorated following the end of the war between Iraq and Iran – commonly referred to as the First Gulf War – in 1988. Disputes over the payment of debts incurred by Iraq during the eight-year war, the rights to oilfields straddling the two countries' border and oil pricing contributed to the antagonism between the two Arab states. The American government made its neutrality in relation to these disputes clear to the parties. Saddam Hussein wrongly interpreted this stance as an indication that the United States would not oppose an Iraqi military take-over of Kuwait. Much of international reaction to the invasion of Kuwait centred on Iraq's violation of the basic international norms of respect for the sovereignty, territorial integrity and independence of a member state of the United Nations. The outrage at the violation was compounded by Iraq's announcement on 28 August 1990 that it was annexing Kuwait as the country's nineteenth province. The desire of most member states of the United Nations for the restitution of Kuwaiti sovereignty assisted George H.W. Bush in putting together a very broad international coalition committed to use whatever means were needed to secure an Iraqi withdrawal. This included military action, but strictly confined to the removal of Iraq from Kuwait.

From the outset, American concerns went beyond simply the question of the violation of international norms. An immediate fear following the invasion was that Iraq might invade Saudi Arabia and thereby gain control of a large proportion of the world's supply of oil. Thus, the objective of Operation Desert Shield entailing the dispatch of a large force of American troops to Saudi Arabia was to protect the Kingdom against invasion in the first instance. Operation Desert Storm, the use of force by America and other countries to expel Iraq from Kuwait, followed in 1991 after the failure of attempts to secure Iraq's withdrawal through negotiations and the imposition of economic sanctions. The ground war against Iraqi positions in Kuwait took place after prolonged aerial bombardment of Iraqi forces both in Kuwait and in Iraq itself. The international forces ranged against Iraq quickly overwhelmed the Iraqi forces occupying Kuwait. An indication of Saddam Hussein's priorities was that he did not commit the Republican Guards, his elite forces, to the defence of Kuwait.

The ease of victory presented the Americans whose forces had dominated the coalition against Iraq with a dilemma. To proceed to Baghdad would run counter to the basis on which they had mobilized the international community, including many Arab states, against Iraq. But to stop fighting after Iraq's withdrawal from Kuwait might mean leaving Saddam Hussein in power and still in possession of weapons of mass destruction, another of America's major concerns. Revolts against Saddam Hussein's rule by both Kurds and Shi'ites appeared to offer America a way out of this dilemma and President George H.W. Bush eagerly supported their rebellions in both the hope and the expectation that they would bring about the fall of the regime. In fact, the Kurdish and Shi'ite revolts helped to consolidate Saddam Hussein's position because they roused the worst fears of the Sunni minority which dominated Iraq as to the consequences of the fall of the regime. Saddam Hussein used the Republican Guards to suppress the rebellions. The brutality with which the revolts were suppressed led to a humanitarian emergency in Iraq. Its most visible manifestation was a flood of Kurdish refugees into Turkey.

With the attention of the media still on Iraq, Western governments came under pressure from public opinion to intervene. At a meeting of the European Community on 8 April 1991 a plan to establish a safe haven for the Kurds in Northern Iraq was approved and two days later the Bush Administration warned Iraq to end all military activity in the area. These measures to protect the Kurds were followed in August 1992 by the establishment of a no-fly zone over southern Iraq, under which the Iraqi air force was not permitted to operate south of 32 degrees north. These steps were justified in terms of a concept that was by no means entirely new but which achieved altogether greater importance in world affairs than ever before. This was the concept of humanitarian intervention, an oxymoron in so far as it came to be used to justify the use of force on a massive scale to achieve its objectives.[1]

On the face of it the concept is ambiguous since it is not evident from the words themselves that the term, 'humanitarian', does not apply to the means employed but rather to the ends being used to justify the intervention. Further, the fact that a state advances humanitarianism as its justification for intervention, does not necessarily mean that this was its actual or sole motivation. But so quickly has the concept become absorbed into the bloodstream of Western societies that in practice there is virtually no ambiguity in its current usage. In particular, it is now universally understood that humanitarian intervention by states involves the use of massive military force, the (ostensible) purpose of which is to achieve humanitarian ends. The similarity with justification of terrorism is striking, namely that the nobility of the cause is regarded as excusing any means employed. In both cases, too, transferring moral responsibility for the consequences of one's actions to one's adversary remains a favourite ploy as in the statement: 'Look what he – they – made me do'.

It is worth reflecting at some length on this major and sudden change in world affairs. Up to the end of the cold war, the attitude of the international community towards intervention had been expressed in a series of declarations by the United Nations General Assembly that condemned intervention for any reason whatsoever in the strongest terms. This outlook was upheld by the General Assembly in resolutions that condemned Soviet intervention in Afghanistan and American intervention in Grenada by large majorities. It is not surprising that vulnerable, newly independent states in Asia and Africa that had emerged as a result of decolonization should have strongly supported the notion that intervention in the affairs of other states had no place in a post-colonial world. But even the former imperial powers themselves were willing to endorse the norm of non-intervention as a safeguard against Communist subversion. A further factor that made the most powerful states in the world ready to forswear intervention in principle was the belief that the gains of intervention were likely to be outweighed by the costs. This was especially the case in a bipolar world where action by one side could be expected to prompt counter-intervention from the other bloc.

The end of the cold war and the revolution in military technology as a result of the advent of the microchip changed these calculations radically. The demise of Communism in Eastern Europe freed Western policymakers from a paradigm in which the world was viewed through the prism of bipolarity. In particular, fear of Soviet subversion no longer dominated the foreign policy agenda of Western states. But it also meant that conflict in other parts of the world could no longer be explained in terms of the machinations of the Kremlin. It necessitated other interpretations of conflicts that had previously been seen in East–West terms. Two interpretations proved popular in the years that followed the coming down of the Berlin Wall. The first was that conflict was caused by 'ancient hatreds'. This provided a plausible explanation for the ethnic conflict that erupted in countries previously behind the Iron Curtain. The second was that the political ambitions and greed of 'evil men' were the cause of conflict.

Neither explanation placed any responsibility at the door of the foreign policy of Western states for any of the conflicts. Conveniently, too, neither explanation treated poverty, inequality or a struggle over scarce resources as a source of conflict. That might have suggested that the international community had some responsibility to address such sources of conflict through measures to reduce global economic inequality and not just to treat their symptoms intermittently. Consequently, both explanations might be regarded as self-serving from a Western perspective and that, no doubt, contributed to their appeal and widespread acceptance in the Western media. However, the 'ancient hatreds' interpretation of events and the 'evil men' interpretation did have rather different implications for the conduct of foreign policy. Thus, the 'ancient hatreds' view suggested that external intervention was unlikely to achieve a permanent end to the conflict, while by contrast the 'evil men' view suggested that their removal from power was all that stood in the way of a country's normalization and re-integration into the community of nations.

In practice, the 'ancient hatreds' view tended to prevail in the early stages of conflict, while the 'evil men' view tended to emerge when the effects of the conflict spilled across international frontiers and began to threaten international peace. At the same time, the revolution in military technology meant that the costs of military intervention in other countries' internal conflicts no longer appeared prohibitively high. Indeed, in so far as the 'evil men' theory appeared credible, it seemed a relatively simple matter to use military force to secure their removal from power. To those who swallowed this theory of conflict, Western leaders after the end of the cold war were to be faulted not for the adoption of aggressive policies that set aside the norm of non-intervention but for lacking the will to bring about an end to evil.

The Second Gulf War had started out as a collective effort by the international community under the leadership of the United States to restore the sovereignty and independence of a member state of the United Nations. It was successful in this purpose. Yet, ironically, it quickly led to action at odds with a fundamental principle of the post-colonial world order, the norm of non-intervention. The expulsion of Iraq from Kuwait reinforced the authority of the United Nations, but the subsequent limits placed on Iraqi sovereignty ran counter to its basic principles. The unified response of the international community to the invasion of Kuwait gave way to disagreement among the major powers as to how to treat Iraq after the war. While the objective of ensuring that Iraq did not possess weapons of mass destruction that might pose a threat to neighbouring countries enjoyed wide support, there were frequent disagreements as to the best means of addressing the issue. There were also differences in the assessment of Iraq's capabilities. The absence of agreement prompted the United States to take military action without the authority of the Security Council against the regime of Saddam Hussein. It was supported in doing so by Britain and indeed British forces participated in Operation Desert Fox in December 1998 and in attacks on Iraq's air defence network in February 2001.

With the passage of time, differences in approach towards the Iraqi regime hardened rather than diminished. Thus, American politicians increasingly took the view that nothing less than the removal of Saddam Hussein and the Baath party from power was required. However, most member states of the United Nations were in favour of an easing of the economic sanctions that had been imposed on Iraq, especially as it became evident that they had caused a humanitarian catastrophe by depriving Iraqis of essential medical supplies. The United Nations estimated that as many as half a million Iraqi children had died as a result of the interruption of medical supplies to the country. Even this failed to persuade American and British leaders that the policies they had adopted for the containment of Saddam Hussein had been misconceived. They also appeared blind to the impact of their policies on opinion in the Arab world. In this context, there was a connection between Iraq and al-Qaeda, though hardly the one conceived by Bush Administration and propagandists in the United States to justify the war against Iraq. Thus, the suffering of the people of Iraq featured prominently in al-Qaeda's statement of 23 February 1998 that purported to issue a *fatwa* which asserted that it was the duty of Muslims to kill Americans and their allies.

President George W. Bush first signalled his intent to use the events of 11 September to justify American military action against Iraq in his State of the Union address in January 2002. Bush identified Iraq among a trio of states that he characterized as 'an axis of evil'. The other two were Iran and North Korea. A meeting between Bush and the British Prime Minister, Tony Blair, in March 2002 was dubbed in the media a council of war. From documents subsequently published in September 2004, it is evident that by this time both governments were committed to using military force to remove Saddam Hussein from power.[2] Military planning for a swift war to overthrow the Iraqi regime took place in earnest in the United States during the summer months, while efforts to persuade public opinion of the case for the war took place on both sides of the Atlantic during the autumn of 2002. In the United States this coincided with mid-term elections. The Republicans made gains in the election by shamelessly implying that there was a connection between the events of 11 September and the regime of Saddam Hussein.

The concept of terrorism proved invaluable in this context. The overthrow of Saddam Hussein could be said to form a valid part of a war against terrorism on the ground that his overthrow would prevent him from continuing to 'terrorize' the Iraqi people. That case could also be advanced on two other grounds. The first was that Saddam Hussein's Iraq was a 'terrorist state' in the meaning used by the Reagan Administration. That is to say, it was a state sponsor of terrorism by virtue of the support it gave to covert groups that carried out acts of lethal violence across international boundaries. In fact, it was originally in the context of the harbouring of members of the PKK (Kurdish Workers Party) from Turkey that Iraq had been designated a terrorist state by the Reagan Administration. But for members of the Bush Administration, the regime's support for extremist Palestinian factions provided a far more powerful basis for the charge that Iraq remained a terrorist state. Consequently, in response to questions on Saddam Hussein's links with terrorism, the Administration cited the regime's connections to notorious Palestinian figures. Unquestioning support for Israel in the United States made it difficult for any American politician to downplay the significance of the regime's involvement in the Israeli–Palestinian conflict. At the same time, members of the Bush Administration repeatedly justified the overthrow of Saddam Hussein in the context of a war against terrorism forced on the United States by the events of 11 September. Consequently, the American public was left with the clear impression that in some way or other Saddam Hussein had been responsible for the assault on America. To the general public there thus did not seem to be a large distance between Saddam Hussein and Osama bin Laden.

Tony Blair's approach to securing public support for the war against Iraq was scarcely more scrupulous than that of the Bush Administration. In the months leading to the war with Iraq, Blair sought to convey the impression that the British government was seeking to restrain the aggressive intentions of the Bush Administration. He was assisted in this task by differences over whether a mandate for military action should be sought from the United Nations Security Council. Blair's support for recourse to the United Nations put him in conflict with some of the most hawkish elements in the Bush Administration who feared that involving the United Nations would present Saddam Hussein with opportunities to undermine support for war in the United States. The fact that Blair was able to persuade President Bush to follow the UN route boosted his case that his stance of unstinting solidarity with the United States over the war against terrorism had gained Britain influence in Washington. However, what the arguments over the wisdom of referring the issue to the United Nations obscured was that Blair had already committed Britain to go to war, regardless of the outcome of the UN's deliberations or of the findings of weapons inspectors, were Saddam Hussein to cooperate with their reintroduction.

On the issue of going to war with Iraq, as opposed to questions of timing and justification, Blair was in fact as aggressive as the most hawkish neo-conservatives within the Bush Administration. While his approach to using the events of 11 September to secure support for military action against Iraq was by no means as crude as that of Paul Wolfowitz and Dick Cheney who constantly invoked 9/11 as a justification for war against Saddam Hussein, Blair also saw the attacks on America as an opportunity to mobilize public support for the use of force against Iraq. The 9/11 Commission recorded that Blair raised the issue of Iraq when he met with President Bush in the immediate aftermath of the attacks.

> On September 20, President Bush met with British Prime Minister Tony Blair, and the two leaders discussed the global conflict ahead. When Blair asked about Iraq, the President replied that Iraq was not the immediate problem. Some members of the administration, he commented, had expressed a different view, but he was the one responsible for making the decisions.[3]

During the debate on 9/11 in the House of Commons that preceded his visit to the United States, Blair had indicated the drift of his thinking when he declared: 'Our next issue is weapons of mass destruction'.[4] What linked the issue of weapons of mass destruction and the war against terrorism was, in John Kampfner's characterization of Blair's thinking, 'that the world would face a threat of an altogether different scale if Saddam made his chemical and biological weapons available to terrorists'.[5] However, Kampfner also insists that at this point, the autumn of 2001, the British government's priority was the war against the Taliban in Afghanistan and serious consideration was not yet being given to war against Iraq.

By the summer of 2002 war against Iraq was not merely being seen as a possibility. It was regarded as inevitable that America would attack Iraq. A memorandum recording secret discussions in Downing Street on 23 July 2002 set out the British government's position in the starkest terms. It concluded: 'We should work on the assumption that the UK would take part in any military action'.[6] The Foreign Secretary reported to the meeting that in his view Bush had already decided on military action, though not on its timing. He went on:

> But the case was thin. Saddam was not threatening his neighbours and his WMD capability was less than that of Libya, North Korea or Iran. We should work up a plan for an ultimatum to Saddam to allow back in the UN weapons inspectors. This would also help with the legal justification for the use of force.[7]

The issue of legality understandably was the principal focus of the Attorney General's contribution to the meeting. After dismissing regime change as a legal basis for military action, he continued:

> There were three possible legal bases: self-defence, humanitarian intervention, or UNSC authorisation. The first and second could not be the base in this case. Relying on UNSCR 1205 of three years ago would be difficult. The situation might of course change.[8]

In response to these contributions, the Prime Minister expressed the view that 'if the political context were right, people would support regime change'.[9]

Understandably, the first words of this memorandum emphasized the extreme sensitivity of its contents. If it had been leaked prior to the war, it would have been apparent that the objective of recourse to the United Nations was not to secure Iraqi compliance with the demands of the international community but rather to manufacture a legal basis for war if that could be achieved. It is also evident that senior ministers were perfectly well aware that the regime of Saddam Hussein did not pose a threat to international peace though they do seem to have believed that he possessed at least some weapons of mass destruction. And they expected that war would uncover sufficient material to enable a plausible case for the necessity of intervention to be made. They also understood quite clearly that while the Saddam Hussein regime was oppressive, the political situation in Iraq did not constitute a humanitarian emergency. Significantly, the word terrorism appeared in the memorandum only once and then in passing reference to America's justification for military action.

In both the United States and Britain, the public case made by Bush and Blair for war bore little relation to what either knew to be true. This presents the analyst with a difficulty. There is clearly a need to distinguish between the reasons the two put forward to mobilize support for the war and their actual motivation for initiating or contributing to military action. It scarcely requires a flight of fancy to suggest that electoral considerations played a significant role in both cases. The Second Gulf War had made Saddam Hussein a figure of hate in the United States and securing popular support for his removal from office presented the Administration with little difficulty, especially when the connection was made between his regime and the issue of terrorism. Indeed, the prospect of war with Iraq put George W. Bush's domestic political opponents on the defensive. The British case was slightly more complicated. The Leader of the Opposition, Iain Duncan Smith, could be expected to support American action in any circumstances. By supporting Bush, Blair could calculate that he would deny the Conservative Party a political opening. Even more importantly, support for Bush was crucial to Blair's retaining the backing of Rupert Murdoch's media empire. Murdoch had strong neo-conservative political sympathies and his papers around the world were unanimous in their support for war, something which could not even be said of members of the Bush Administration.

It would, however, be a mistake to regard electoral considerations as the sole basis of Bush's motivation. The same was even truer of Blair. In the case of the British government, a significant factor would have been the damage failure to support American military action would have done to Anglo-American relations, especially in the light of previous British support for American policy on Iraq. Much more was obviously at stake for the United States. At its most ambitious, the Bush Administration would have hoped that the overthrow of the Saddam Hussein regime would have enabled the United States to effect the transformation of the Middle East politically and hence of the global international political system itself. Suggestive of American thinking was how its allies perceived the Administration's goals. At the outset of the war, Blair spoke to Bush and according to Woodward's account in his detailed book on the background to the war, spoke the following words:

> I kind of think that the decisions taken in the next few weeks will determine the rest of the world for years to come. As primary players, we have a chance to shape the issues that are discussed. Both of us will have enormous capital and a lot of people will be with us.[10]

Of course, to attribute such megalomania to President Bush is somewhat speculative. One obvious consequence of the manner in which the two governments mobilized support for the war was that the actual reasons for their actions were not subject to public debate or for that matter to critical analysis.

An important implication of the disjunction between the justifications advanced by the two governments for the war and the actual motivations of the two countries' leaders was the corruption and perversion of the machinery of government in both societies. Instead of a process in which decision-making at the top was informed by expert analysis based on the interpretation of data collected at the bottom, the process was reversed. Political decision-makers sought to prevail upon those engaged in expert analysis to find the evidence in the collected data to validate the case already chosen by the decision-makers for political reasons. Its correspondence to reality was not a major concern of the political leaders since its relevance was simply presentational. So common has the practice of searching for the facts to justify a predetermined policy become in Britain that it has come to be encapsulated in a widely quoted mantra, 'what Tony wants'. Assisting the governments in their purposes was a layer of bureaucracy between the government decision-makers and the expert analysts. Bureaucrats could be prevailed upon to do their government's bidding for the usual incentives since they had no personal stake in the integrity of the content of any dossier the government chose to publish or any official briefing given to the media, however far removed these were from the objective judgements of the government's own experts. Understandably, some of those caught in the middle in this perversion of the norms of good governance were deeply frustrated and angered by their exploitation in this way.

An outstanding example of someone who fought back against the Bush Administration's misuse of the machinery of government for its own partisan political purposes is Richard Clarke. His book, *Against All Enemies*, was published in 2004.[11] His criticism of the Bush Administration's conduct of the war in Afghanistan has already been discussed in the previous chapter. As a public servant in successive Administrations, Clarke was convinced of the seriousness of the external terrorist threat to the United States long before the events of 9/11. The attack on America reinforced his convictions. Precisely because of his perception that the al-Qaeda network presented an ongoing threat to the security of the United States, he was deeply offended by the Bush Administration's manipulation of the war against terrorism for its own ideological ends. In his book, he discusses the Bush Administration's obsession with finding a pretext for military action to overthrow Saddam Hussein. Thus, he notes: 'In the new administration's discussions of terrorism, Paul Wolfowitz had urged a focus on Iraqi-sponsored terrorism against the U.S. even though there was no such thing.'[12]

Since Clarke believes the information available to government on the issue of terrorism did not provide the Administration with a reason to give priority to the overthrow of Saddam Hussein, he is left with the need to find other explanations for the Administration's actions. He lists a number of rationales attributed to Cheney, Rumsfeld, Wolfowitz and Bush himself:

- to clean up the mess left by the first Bush administration when, in 1991, it let Saddam Hussein consolidate power and slaughter opponents after the first US–Iraq war;

- to improve Israel's strategic position by eliminating a large, hostile military;
- to create an Arab democracy that could serve as a model to other friendly Arab states now threatened with internal dissent, notably Egypt and Saudi Arabia;
- to permit the withdrawal of US forces from Saudi Arabia (after 12 years), where they were stationed to counter the Iraqi military and were a source of anti-Americanism threatening to the regime;
- to create another friendly source of oil for the US market and reduce dependency upon oil from Saudi Arabia, which might suffer overthrow someday.[13]

Clarke writes that he believes all of these motivations played a part in the decision. He adds a further reason to this list, that President Bush considered that there was a need for him 'to do something big' in response to the events of 11 September. But, of course, because none of these reasons was put forward publicly as a justification for the war, it is difficult to verify Clarke's claims. However, the reasons he puts forward are plausible, though none now appears as sensible reasons for America to have gone to war, given its actual consequences.

A calculation that both Bush and Blair would have made before the war was that a successful outcome of military intervention would silence any critics and the media would lose interest if their reasons for going to war no longer continued to be the subject of political debate. Initially, events appeared to go in their favour. Offensive action by the Coalition of the Willing formed by the United States and its allies in the absence of UN authorization for military intervention began on 20 March 2003. Less than three weeks later on 9 April, Baghdad fell to American forces. By the end of April, mopping up operations had been completed and Coalition forces were in effective military control of the whole of Iraq. A formal declaration of victory was made by President Bush on 1 May 2003 on a warship in the Gulf against the backdrop of a banner emblazoned with the slogan, 'Mission Accomplished'. In the course of the short war, a total of 138 Americans had been killed, fewer than died in Operation Desert Storm in 1991.[14]

However, Bush's triumph proved short-lived. It soon became apparent that military victory had failed to confer on the Coalition either the means or the legitimacy to rule Iraq. The ease with which the Coalition achieved a conventional military victory was somewhat illusory. Once it became apparent that they could not resist the Coalition's forces in a conventional military conflict, Iraqi leaders chose to continue the struggle by other means and that, rather than demoralization of Iraqi forces, accounted for their failure to engage in a last ditch battle to prevent American occupation of Baghdad. The problems faced by the occupiers were compounded by the American determination to dismantle every last vestige of Saddam Hussein's regime. The Americans sought to implement a programme of de-Baathification of Iraq analogous to the policy of de-Nazification imposed on Germany after the end of the Second World War. There was a failure to recognize the vast difference in the political context, including the existence of democratic institutions and parties in Germany prior to Hitler's rule, or the role that the cold war had played in the early consolidation of democracy in the Western half of Germany. At the very moment that Bush was proclaiming victory, the first signs were emerging of development of an insurgency against the occupation. By early November more American soldiers had died as a result of opposition to the occupation than during the war itself. In that month alone, 105 Coalition troops were killed.

The opposition to the occupation took two main forms: resistance from within the country from supporters of the old regime with the addition of Iraqis angered by the conduct of the Coalition of the Willing or fearful of their political future under American tutelage and the violence of foreign jihadists drawn to Iraq by the prospect of taking on American forces in a context in which the American empire lacked international legitimacy and appeared vulnerable. However, jihadist violence was not simply directed against the American presence in Iraq. It was directed at preventing any normalization of the situation. The motive of attacks on the Shi'ite community appeared to be to foment sectarian conflict in the country so as to frustrate the creation of any semblance of political stability. The capture of Saddam Hussein in December 2003 made little difference to the level of violence. And subsequently neither the transfer of power to an Iraqi government in June 2004 nor the relatively successful holding of elections in January 2005 ended the insurgency. The tactic of the suicide bomb was widely used to devastating effect, as a result of which there was a very high toll of civilians killed in the ongoing violence.

By June 2005 American public opinion had turned against the war. The fear of many Americans was that American forces had become bogged down in a quagmire in which there was no end in sight. In an effort to shore up support for the intervention, as well as to underline his Administration's commitment to stay the course, Bush gave a television address to the nation on 28 June 2005 to coincide with the anniversary of the transfer of power to an Iraqi government. The American President explicitly linked the conflict in Iraq to the war against terrorism initiated after 9/11, describing Iraq as 'the latest battlefield in the war against terrorism'. He assured Americans that the troops would stay only as long as they were needed and 'not a day longer'. He explained that the objective of American policy was to turn the fight over to the Iraqis themselves. He justified the war as vital to the country's security and in an echo of the case advanced by successive Presidents in justification of American intervention in Vietnam argued that the strategy was to defeat America's enemies abroad before they could launch an attack on America itself. Aware that a major source of American disquiet was that more than 1,700 Americans had died in Iraq since March 2003, he argued that the sacrifice was worth it and invoked the events of 9/11, declaring that 'the only way our enemies can succeed is if we forget the lessons of September the 11th'.[15] Agreement on a constitution, its endorsement in a referendum and a high turn-out in parliamentary elections in December 2005 eased the domestic political pressure on the Administration somewhat, but Iraqi hostility towards the occupation showed few signs of abating.[16]

Linking the war in Iraq to the events of 11 September has proved politically productive for President Bush. The war on terrorism was the one subject on which Bush maintained a consistent lead over his electoral rivals, including John Kerry, in his successful bid for re-election as President in 2004. The emphasis on terrorism as a justification for the war helped Bush to ride the storm over the failure to uncover any weapons of mass destruction in Iraq after the defeat of the Saddam Hussein regime. Blair's reliance on the argument that Saddam Hussein possessed weapons of mass destruction had been more total than the American President's. Consequently, the absence of any evidence that the regime had possessed any such weapons on the eve of the war proved more damaging to the British Prime Minister. Clumsy handling by the BBC of a fundamentally sound story on the government's deceitfulness over the war helped Blair to deflect some of the criticism, with the aid of an executive-minded judge from Northern Ireland. In the process, considerable damage was done to the BBC and its capacity to sustain a tradition of public service broadcasting independent of the government of the day.

In defence of the war, the government and its supporters in the media relied heavily on the argument that the removal of an evil man from power made the world a safer place. By implication, what mattered was that Saddam Hussein harboured evil intentions and whether or not he currently possessed the capacity to give effect to them was, if not quite irrelevant, less important. This theme was reinforced by emphasizing, as the Americans had from the outset, that the conquest of Iraq constituted liberation not occupation. The difficulty was that the consequences on the ground in Iraq hardly bore out the simple narrative of a grateful people rescued from the clutches of a ruthless dictator. The British government blamed the Bush Administration's mishandling of the war's aftermath for the alienation of Iraqis that dissipated the fruits of liberation. In particular, the British government blamed the failure of the Bush Administration to have a plan for the post-war governance and reconstruction of Iraq.[17]

In addition, the manner in which American soldiers interacted with local communities was unfavourably compared to the conduct of British troops in the south of the country. It was argued that Britain's experience of conducting military operations in Northern Ireland accounted in part for the difference. An alternative explanation was that the Shi'ite population in the south had a much more positive view of the occupation in the light of its treatment under Saddam Hussein than the Sunnis confronting American forces. In any event, the comparison with Northern Ireland was somewhat disingenuous in so far as it implied that the conduct of British troops in Iraq was subject to the same restraints as had been in place in the later stages of the troubles in Northern Ireland. In fact, the same standards were not upheld in Iraq. Specifically, the British government asserted that the troops were not bound by the European Convention of Human Rights in their conduct of operations in Iraq. The obvious implication was that the government did not consider that the ruling of the European Court of Human Rights which had condemned a range of interrogation techniques employed when internment was imposed on Northern Ireland was applicable to Iraq.

Despite the rhetoric of the governments forming the Coalition of the Willing that their actions were motivated by a desire to help the Iraqi people achieve a better future, a significant undercurrent was that the Iraqis had only themselves to blame for the conditions in which they found themselves because at the very least they had acquiesced in the existence of the Saddam Hussein regime. The existence of such sentiments among the Coalition forces, as well as more simply the prevalence of anti-Arab and anti-Muslim attitudes, helped to legitimize the harsh treatment meted out to ordinary Iraqis. It explains the indifference shown during the initial stages of the insurgency to the death toll of Iraqi civilians during the conduct of military operations against the militants. The persistence of the insurgency led to concern that it was being fuelled by collateral damage, but the counter-argument was that the relative quiescence of the Iraqis under Saddam Hussein provided evidence that they could be terrorized into submission.

As the seriousness of the insurgency became apparent, the Americans quickly abandoned their initial interpretation of it as the death throes of supporters of the old regime, especially as they appreciated the extent of coordination and planning that lay behind the attacks by the insurgents. The Bush Administration sought a quick fix to its deficiency in intelligence information on the insurgency. This was to authorize the use of what was euphemistically dubbed 'coercive interrogation', which was distinguished from torture. The difference can be compared to the distinction in the European Convention on Human Rights between 'torture' and 'inhuman and degrading treatment'. However, it is worth emphasizing that both are illegal under the Convention. In January 1978, when the European Court of Human Rights ruled on the use of a number of techniques used by the security forces at the time of the introduction of internment in Northern Ireland in August 1971, it decided that the techniques amounted to 'inhuman and degrading treatment' but stopped short of describing them as torture, as the European Commission of Human Rights had. Headlines in the British popular press at the time put the emphasis on the fact that Britain had been acquitted of torture and played down the fact that the most important aspect of the judgement was that the government had been found guilty of violating the Convention.

The emergency procedures authorized by the British government in Northern Ireland in 1971 included the following: the hooding of detainees, subjecting them to an ear-splitting noise intended to produce disorientation, forcing them to remain standing against a wall for long periods, deprivation of sleep and restricted diet. Such techniques had not previously been authorized in the United Kingdom itself, but they been employed in combating anti-colonial movements in British colonies. Coercive interrogation, as authorized by the Bush Administration in the context of the war against terrorism, encompassed a remarkably similar set of techniques. Its adoption as policy rested on a legalistic distinction between torture and cruel, inhuman or degrading treatment, with only the former being seen as flatly contrary to

America's obligations under the Convention against Torture. At the same time, torture itself was narrowly defined as entailing physical pain 'equivalent in intensity to the pain accompanying serious physical injury, such as organ failure, impairment of bodily function, or even death'.[18]

While the Administration's encouragement of barbaric practices in American detention centres preceded the war in Iraq and is discussed further in Chapter 9, the insurgency prompted their extension to Iraq. An e-mail to personnel of the Federal Bureau of Investigations in Iraq in May 2004 noted:

> (a)n Executive Order signed by President Bush authorized the following techniques among others: sleep 'management', use of MWDs (military working dogs), 'stress positions' such as half squats, 'environmental manipulation' such as use of loud music, sensory deprivation through the use of hoods, etc.[19]

The same e-mail referred to an instruction to FBI personnel to report any abuse they witnessed. It went on: 'We assume that the OGC [Office of General Counsel] instruction does not include the reporting of these authorized techniques, and that the use of these techniques does not constitute "abuse".'[20]

On 28 April 2004 an American current affairs television programme broadcast pictures taken in Abu Ghraib, a prison outside Baghdad. They showed naked prisoners being subject to a variety of forms of sexual abuse by male and female American soldiers. There was an obvious connection between what was happening in Abu Ghraib and the interrogation methods authorized by the Administration. The scandal forced the Bush Administration to temper its encouragement of cruel, inhuman and degrading treatment of detainees. Thus the Executive Order referred to in the FBI memorandum above was withdrawn. But the main basis of the Administration's response was that the abuse stemmed from the aberrant behaviour of a few bad apples. While this was hardly a persuasive explanation of the volume of reports of serious abuses and the telltale statistics of the deaths of prisoners in custody, the

Administration was able to rely on the American public's desire not to believe the worst of their political leaders.

The enormous damage done to the international reputation of the American government by the Abu Ghraib scandal compounded the problems the Coalition of the Willing faced in Iraq. It was reflected in the shrinking of the Bush Administration's ambitions to simply that of avoiding the appearance of defeat in Iraq. That required putting in place Iraqi security forces capable of maintaining order without outside assistance. Even this task did not prove straightforward, given the targeting of recruits to the Iraqi security forces by the insurgents. The jihadist contribution to the violence connected the war to Bush's original aim of a war against terrorism with a global reach. However, that was scant comfort as the link was one that had come about as a result of the Administration's own actions. The Administration's argument that it was better to fight the jihadists in Iraq than anywhere else failed to recognize the role that the occupation of Iraq was playing in recruiting Muslims in different countries to the jihadist cause.

What is worse is that the jihadists may eventually be able to claim that their tactics of suicide bombs and hostage-taking have contributed to the defeat of America's ambitions in Iraq, just as the same tactics had played their part in the withdrawal of French, American and Israeli forces from Lebanon. Indeed, to the extent that America has already been forced to modify its ambitions in Iraq, this has already happened. These wider implications of Bush's war to overthrow the regime of Saddam Hussein in Iraq are considered further below. However, in the next chapter, a step back is taken to examine a conceptualization of violence that arose in response to developments in the years that immediately followed the end of the cold war. The purpose is to determine whether this conceptualization can throw further light on the phenomenon of the global jihadist network.

Notes

1 It is not being suggested that military intervention in another state is never justified in response to a humanitarian emergency. But to describe such intervention as humanitarian intervention is to obscure the nature of the intervention and what it entails. This issue is also discussed further in Chapter 12.

2 See Michael Smith, 'Secret papers show Blair was warned of Iraq chaos', *Daily Telegraph*, 18 September 2004.

3 *The 9/11 Commission Report: Final Report of the National Commission on Terrorist Attacks Upon the United States*, W.W. Norton & Company, New York 2004, p. 336.

4 Quoted in John Kampfner, *Blair's Wars*, The Free Press, London 2004, p. 157.

5 Ibid.

6 The full text of the memorandum is to be found in *The New York Review of Books*, Vol. LII, No. 10, 9 June 2005, p. 71.

7 Ibid.

8 Ibid.

9 Ibid.

10 Bob Woodward, *Plan of Attack*, Simon & Schuster, London 2004, p. 399. By 'issues', it can be taken that Blair did not mean global warming or similar concerns.

11 Richard A. Clarke, *Against All Enemies: Inside America's War on Terror*, Free Press, London 2004.

12 Ibid., p. 264.

13 Ibid., p. 265.

14 James Mann, *Rise of the Vulcans: The History of Bush's War Cabinet*, Penguin Books, New York 2004, p. 359.

15 From text of President Bush's address on 28 June 2005, accessed at http://www.whitehouse.gov.

16 See, for example, Patrick Cockburn, 'Iraq's election result: a divided nation', *Independent*, 21 December 2005.

17 See Kampfner, *Blair's Wars*, p. 335.

18 Justice Department memorandum quoted in Seymour M. Hersh, *Chain of Command: The Road from 9/11 to Abu Ghraib*, Allen Lane, London 2004, p. 5.

19 Quoted in *Guantánamo and Beyond: The Continuing Pursuit of Unchecked Executive Power*, Amnesty International, May 2005, p. 49.

20 Ibid.

CHAPTER 5

Spoiler violence

In 1997, the journal, *International Security*, published an article on the theme of spoiler violence in peace processes.[1] Stedman's article was a timely recognition in an era of peace processes that special security challenges faced societies in the midst of transition from one dispensation to another or engaged in the negotiated settlement of an internal conflict. Stedman's arguments merit consideration in some detail before consideration is given to their relevance in the new international context after 9/11 and to what light they can throw on the global jihadists of al-Qaeda. His primary thesis was a simple one that in peacemaking 'the greatest source of risk comes from spoilers'. These he defined as 'leaders and parties who believe that peace emerging from negotiations threatens their power, worldview, and interests, and use violence to undermine attempts to achieve it'.[2]

With one qualification this is a reasonable definition. Stedman should have added 'the' before peace, since the perspective of spoilers is not that they are opposed to peace as such but to the particular peace emerging from a process they object to or have reservations about. It is the contours of the particular peace that they oppose as a betrayal or sell-out. It is worth underlining that it is perfectly legitimate for anyone to be against a particular peace settlement on all manner of grounds, including that the agreement is poorly designed to achieve its objective of accommodation between previously warring groups. Thus, opponents of a particular peace settlement should not be demonized as the enemies of peace itself. Of course, critics of spoilers often argue, also perfectly reasonably in the given circumstances, that the peace on offer provides the only realistic basis of any sort of peace in the situation in question.

As examples of spoilers that succeeded in destroying the peace, Stedman puts forward the cases of Angola and Rwanda. Civil war followed Jonas Savimbi's rejection of the outcome of elections in Angola in 1992, while the rejection by Hutu militants of the Arusha Peace Accords culminated in genocide in Rwanda in 1994. By contrast, according to Stedman, potential spoilers failed to overturn the peace settlements in Mozambique and Cambodia. He argues that the role of international actors has been crucial as to whether spoilers succeed or fail and that '[w]here international custodians have created and implemented coherent, effective strategies for protecting peace and managing spoilers, damage has been limited and peace has triumphed'.[3] There is a danger of circularity in this argument since it is tempting to treat the outcome of the process itself as the most reliable evidence as to whether international custodians played their proper role. Nonetheless, the argument that the tragedies in Angola and Rwanda might have been averted, had the international community devoted greater resources to the implementation of the peace settlements, does seem persuasive in hindsight. Yet it must also be borne in mind that a large international presence in a society in transition may detract from the legitimacy of a political settlement because of the implication that the agreement was not one freely arrived at by the parties to the conflict themselves. Thus, the difficulties that the Coalition of the Willing have encountered in Iraq stem as much from negative perceptions of the legitimacy of the occupation as they do from lack of resources.

Stedman distinguishes three types of spoiler: limited, greedy and total. He also attaches importance to whether the spoiler is inside or outside an agreement, the number of spoilers and what he calls the locus of the spoiler problem. By this he has in mind whether the impetus for spoiler behaviour comes from the leadership of a party or movement, its followers or both. Next Stedman discusses different strategies that custodians of peace processes can adopt to manage the problem of spoilers. He identifies three main approaches: inducement, socialization and coercion. In fact, these broadly correspond to the three main ways in which governments respond to political violence in general: of accommodation, criminalization and suppression. This is fully discussed in Chapter 9. Stedman then goes on to consider the spoiler problem in relation to five specific cases. All of his case studies date from the early 1990s and he deliberately excluded cases where the outcome of spoiler behaviour remained uncertain. At the time he was writing this included the cases of Bosnia, Northern Ireland and Israel/Palestine. Two of his cases centre on the implementation of the Paris Peace Accords of October 1991 that were intended to bring peace to Cambodia. The others are the Arusha Peace Accords of August 1993 for Rwanda, the Bicesse peace agreement on Angola of May 1991, and the Mozambican peace agreement of October 1993.

Stedman's notion of spoiler behaviour is very wide-reaching. Thus, it encompasses failure to act as required under the terms of an agreement. For example, he treats President Juvenal Habyarimana's stalling on the implementation of the Arusha Peace Accords, notably in failing to establish the broad-based transitional government provided for, as an instance of spoiling and he characterizes Habyarimana as 'a spoiler, but a limited spoiler'.[4] Confusingly, Stedman also includes Habyarimana among the parties of peace that the international community should have done more to protect. Admittedly, Habyarimana's behaviour was far from consistent. However, his fear as to what might transpire with the setting up of a power-sharing government as required by the Arusha Accords was well grounded. When he was finally prevailed upon to accept his obligations, he was killed when his plane was shot down on his return journey to the capital of Rwanda, Kigali. That event provided the trigger for mass killings by Hutu militias of Hutu moderates and the genocide of Tutsis.

The breadth of Stedman's view of spoiler behaviour is driven in large part by his focus on the role of international custodians. The concluding sentence of his article argues for 'a strategy of aggressive management of spoilers' by the international community. In all the cases he examines, external parties played a significant role in putting pressure on reluctant internal parties to arrive at peace settlements. The content of these agreements was dictated at least in part by the external mediators and to that extent reflected their analysis of the conflict rather more than the perspectives of the internal protagonists themselves. Stedman's concern was that the international community should make a greater effort to ensure the success of peace agreements by assisting or pressurizing parties that signed up to these agreements to stay the course and to meet their obligations. This was a laudable purpose, but arguably a narrower definition of spoiler behaviour throws a sharper light on the phenomenon of spoilers that the article helped to highlight.

Spoilers are best seen in the first instance as opponents not of peace, but of the particular peace that forms the base of a political settlement or seems likely to emerge from the negotiations *en train* among the participating parties. It may be the case that the parties involved in a peace process may not fully trust the commitment of their political adversaries and may take steps to protect themselves, as they see it, from potential bad faith by the other side. Even where the behaviour of such parties involves violence or what at least their opponents characterize as the use of violence, such parties are best not seen as spoilers, since they can be expected the support the settlement in question if it takes root. Further, parties opposed in principle to a particular settlement, but which pursue their opposition by constitutional means, are best excluded. So a further characteristic of the phenomenon is the use of violence. The spoiler's goal of destroying a particular settlement is a more limited one than that of the revolutionary who aspires to create a new political dispensation on the ruins of the old regime.

The failure of several peace processes during the 1990s and the first decade of the new millennium, in part as a result of the actions of spoilers, has underlined the importance of the phenomenon. A significant aspect of the spoiler phenomenon has been the way that groups with diametrically opposed political objectives have indirectly combined to frustrate settlements to which they have been opposed for very different reasons. Of course, spoilers are not by any means a new phenomenon and there were numerous cases of spoilers before the era of peace processes in the 1990s. Indeed, any period of transition to a new political dispensation may give rise to spoiler violence, since in periods of transition calculations about the consequences of violence are at their most uncertain. The absence of a settled order provides those who resort to violence with good reason for thinking that their actions can affect the shape of the new dispensation or even whether a new dispensation takes root. However, the ability of those resorting to violence to control the future political development should not be exaggerated. The consequences of violence may not accord with what the perpetrators hope for. Nonetheless, it is evidently the case that, in so far as spoiler violence by its nature is directed towards a negative end, the prevention of the implementation of a particular settlement or the frustration of what the perpetrators perceive as the political designs of others, it is more successful than the use of violence for the achievement of positive ends.

These points are illustrated further through an examination, below, of the role that spoiler violence has played in two different peace processes in Northern Ireland, in South Africa's transition to democracy and in the Israeli/Palestinian peace process. Then, in the concluding section of this chapter, the applicability of the concept of spoiler violence to transnational terrorist networks, such as al-Qaeda, is considered. Before considering Northern Ireland's two peace processes, a brief account of their context is necessary.[5] The creation of Northern Ireland as a separate political entity within the United Kingdom dates back to the 1920 Government of Ireland Act. This unilaterally partitioned the island of Ireland. Admittedly, partition on the basis of a division between six Northern counties and the remaining 26 counties had been foreshadowed by the negotiations that had taken place during the course of the First World War involving the British government, Unionists and representatives of the Irish Parliamentary Party. Nevertheless, both the fact of partition at all and the particular boundaries of the new entity remained contentious. Irish nationalists had expected a Boundary Commission agreed to by the British government in the negotiations on Irish self-rule to recommend a substantial adjustment of the border where there were nationalist majorities adjacent to the Southern state. In the event the Boundary Commission recommended such modest changes to the border that the two political entities in Ireland overrode its conclusions and confirmed the existing division.

Partition was a response to the fact that political divisions over the issue of the transfer of power to an elected government in Dublin coincided with sectarian divisions. Indeed, the creation of Northern Ireland was designed to accommodate Protestant opposition to rule from Dublin by excluding from the transfer the part of the island where most Protestants resided. At the time of partition, Protestants outnumbered Catholics by roughly two to one within the borders of Northern Ireland. From a Unionist perspective, maintaining Protestant unity appeared to represent the safest way of ensuring the continuance of the union with the rest of the United Kingdom and this was the strategy adopted by successive Unionist governments from 1921 until the early 1960s. The consequence was a further reinforcement of the divisions between Protestants and Catholics that had consolidated into an ethnic divide during the course of the nineteenth century. During the period, 1921–63, the Unionist government defeated a succession of violent challenges to its rule by the Irish Republican Army (IRA). It did so with local security forces.

Pressure for reform in the 1960s proved more difficult for Unionists to handle. Reformist rhetoric raised but failed to satisfy Catholic expectations. The result was increasing Catholic mobilization behind a civil rights movement pressing for an end to discrimination in imitation of the civil rights movement in the United States, a Protestant backlash and violent clashes on the streets. This culminated in the onset of what is known in Northern

Ireland as the troubles, the term used to describe a prolonged period of violent disturbances. The troubles are generally dated from 5 October 1968 and clashes in the city of Londonderry/ Derry between civil rights demonstrators and the police after the banning of the demonstration by the Stormont Minister of Home Affairs. It is worth emphasizing that this violent breakdown of the political system preceded the deployment of British troops in aid of the civil power. This followed in August 1969. It also preceded the formation of what was to become the main Republican paramilitary organization in Northern Ireland, the Provisional IRA. This was formed in December 1969. The main Loyalist paramilitary organization, the Ulster Defence Association (UDA), was formed in September 1971.

The term, paramilitary, is used in Northern Ireland to describe private armies, not official agents of the state. Indeed, paramilitary organization can be regarded as a less pejorative way of referring to terrorist groups, though it should be said that some of the activities engaged in by paramilitary organizations during the early years of the troubles, such as patrolling their own neighbour-hoods, did not amount to terrorism. The terms, Republican and Loyalist, are used to refer respectively to militant nationalists and militant Unionists, though the peace process has tended to under-cut the implication that a readiness to use physical force or engage in actions of communal deterrence distinguishes them from their less militant counterparts. In the early years of the troubles, the British government sought to limit its involvement to reform of the security forces and to maintain the Unionist government while pressing it to introduce reforms. This approach failed. It led to a radicalization of Catholics who were fearful that after the limited reforms, the situation in Northern Ireland would disappear from the international limelight and they would be left to face contin-uing Unionist domination of the political system.

Following further violence in response to the introduction of internment without trial in August 1971, the British government introduced direct rule from London in March 1972. Direct rule paved the way for a major political initiative by the British government to reshape government in Northern Ireland. This culminated in the Sunningdale Agreement of December 1973. It led to the establishment of a power-sharing government in Northern Ireland, which took office in January 1974. The Sunningdale Agreement was so called because the negotiations that led to the accord took place at the Civil Service Staff College situated in Sunningdale Park in Berkshire near London. Deliberations involving the British and Irish governments and the parties in Northern Ireland that were committed to power-sharing resulted in agreement on the establishment of a Council of Ireland to encourage functional cooperation between the two parts of Ireland. For many Unionists this Irish dimension to the experiment in power-sharing represented a step too far.

That was reflected in the formation of the Ulster Army Council by Loyalist paramilitaries as an umbrella organization for opposition to the Sunningdale Agreement and by a vote of the Ulster Unionist Council against the deal. At the same time, the Provisional Irish Republican Army (IRA) continued its violent campaign against British rule in any part of Ireland. But whereas Loyalists viewed the settlement as the slippery slope to a united Ireland, proclaiming that Dublin was a Sunningdale away, Republicans viewed it as entrenching partition and the British presence. Despite the conflicting basis of their opposition to the Sunningdale Agreement and the formation of the power-sharing Executive, the fact that they shared the common objective of destroying the settlement created the temporary basis for a tactical alliance of the extremes. Thus the weekly paper of the Provisional Republican movement, *An Phoblacht*, enthusiastically reported on what it perceived as common ground in the proposals being put forward by Loyalists and Republicans under the headline: 'Loyalists and Republicans on the way to peace'.[6]

Shortly after the power-sharing Executive began its work, there was a British general election in February 1974. It was called by the British government over a strike by mineworkers in Britain. However, there were no coal mines in Northern Ireland where it provided Unionist opponents of the Sunningdale Agreement with the opportunity to demonstrate the strength of Protestant opposition to its provisions. The victory of anti-Agreement Unionists in 11 of Northern Ireland's 12 parliamentary constituencies was a massive blow to the legitimacy of the settlement. The end came after a general strike by Protestant workers in May 1974, enforced by the muscle of Loyalist paramilitaries, persuaded the Unionist members of the power-sharing Executive to resign. In the midst of the strike, Loyalist paramilitaries carried out bomb attacks in the Republic of Ireland in which 33 people died. Republicans as well as Loyalists welcomed the collapse of the Sunningdale Agreement, but their success as spoilers did not create the basis for any cooperation between the two sides thereafter. The illusion that a settlement could be achieved which was based on an alliance of the extremes was rapidly dispelled.

One of the lessons that the British and Irish governments derived from the failure of Sunningdale, when the opportunity for a new peace process arose in the 1990s, was that any political settlement should be as inclusive as possible. Another was that popular endorsement of any settlement in a referendum was necessary to underwrite its legitimacy ahead of its implementation. Thus, in the negotiations that followed the paramilitary ceasefires in 1994, the British government took steps to ensure the widest possible participation of parties in the negotiations, as well as declaring that any settlement to emerge from the negotiations would be submitted to a referendum of the people of Northern Ireland. In fact, the Good Friday Agreement was submitted to referendums in both Northern Ireland and the Republic of Ireland on the same day.[7] There was a need for a referendum in the Republic of Ireland to authorize the changes to Articles 2 and 3 of the Irish constitution to which the Irish government had agreed as part of the Good Friday Agreement. In addition, holding referendums in both parts of Ireland simultaneously lent credibility to the claim that the endorsement of the Agreement would constitute an authentic act of self-determination by the people of Ireland as a whole, undercutting the notion that the continuing partition of the island represented a denial of that right.

Support for the Good Friday Agreement by Sinn Féin, the political wing of the Provisional IRA, and by the political wings of the main Loyalist paramilitaries vindicated the approach of the two governments, especially when on an unusually high turnout of voters, over 70 per cent of those voting supported the Agreement. However, the very different interpretations of the Agreement by pro-Agreement Unionists and Sinn Féin pointed to difficulties ahead. At the same time, there were from the outset a number of small paramilitaries on both sides of Northern Ireland's sectarian divide opposed to the Agreement. The main dissident group among the Loyalists was the Loyalist Volunteer Force (LVF), while the Real IRA and the Continuity IRA championed opposition to the Agreement among Republicans. All three of these groups were responsible for a number of acts of violence during the first half of 1998. Then on 15 August 1998, the Real IRA placed a bomb in the centre of the town of Omagh in which 29 people were killed and 360 wounded as a result of a misdirected warning.

The Omagh bomb was the most lethal atrocity in Northern Ireland's history. It was widely interpreted as demonstrating that dissident groups were willing to be even more indiscriminate in their use of violence than the mainstream groups had been during the course of the conflict. Among the dead in Omagh were two Spanish tourists from Madrid. As a consequence there was wide coverage of the Omagh bomb in the Spanish media. This proved significant in 2004. The Omagh precedent formed part of the Spanish government's case that ETA could have been responsible for the multiple train attacks that caused hundreds of casualties and killed 191 people in Madrid in March 2004. In particular, in response to the argument that causing such indiscriminate carnage had not been a hallmark of ETA's campaign of violence, the government posited the possibility that the attack had been carried out by an extreme faction within ETA and reflected the ruthlessness of which such splinter groups were capable. However, this analysis was based on the dubious premise that the Real IRA's misdirected warning at Omagh was not a mistake, but that the group had actually intended to cause indiscriminate slaughter. In fact, the pattern of previous attacks by the Real IRA suggested that Omagh was part of a campaign of attacks on town centres across Northern Ireland, the primary purpose of which was to cause maximum disruption rather than death.

Whatever the intentions of the perpetrators of the Omagh outrage, its initial political effect was to advance rather than retard the peace process in Northern Ireland. In particular, the strength of the public backlash against the bombers forced the Real IRA to declare a ceasefire. While both pro-Agreement and dissident paramilitaries continued to engage in various forms of violence, there was a decline in acts of violence that endangered the general public and after Omagh there was a fall in the number of fatalities as a result of political violence. Only five people died as a result of political violence in 2004. However, the threat of violence by no means disappeared and played its part in the crises that beset the political process. As a result of the slow progress of the decommissioning of IRA weapons, Protestants lost confidence in the Good Friday Agreement and that was reflected in the victory of the radical Democratic Unionist Party (DUP) over its more moderate rival, the Ulster Unionist Party (UUP) in elections to the Northern Ireland Assembly in November 2003. By this time the actual institutions of devolved government created under the Good Friday Agreement were not functioning. They had been suspended in October 2002 as a result of allegations of IRA spying.[8]

Accusations by Unionists that the Provisional Republican movement had been acting in bad faith had been a constant feature of the peace process from the very outset, even before they could be related to specific obligations under the Good Friday Agreement. Such accusations, which may or may not be well founded and which may also stem from conflicting interpretations of agreements which the parties have signed up to, are commonplace in peace processes. Bad faith in peace processes, however, should be distinguished from spoiler behaviour that is directed at the destruction of a particular settlement. Admittedly, the intentions of parties in a peace process, as in a conflict, may not be straightforward and it may be the case that parties shoehorned reluctantly into an agreement may actually seek to undermine the settlement of which they are a part. Here the distinction between spoiling and bad faith is moot. More commonly, parties may turn against agreements as a result of developments contrary to their interests and expectations. Ultimately, of course, the behaviour of a party seeking an exit from a settlement it initially signed up to may come to resemble that of a spoiler.

Bad faith itself typically arises as a result of a power struggle among parties to an agreement to tilt the implementation of a settlement in their favour. Even more commonly, parties in this situation will trade accusations of bad faith to justify their own failures to adhere to the letter and spirit of the agreement. However, it seems perverse to label a party as a spoiler that wishes to see an agreement implemented, albeit as far as possible on its terms, even if the result of this behaviour may inadvertently destroy the settlement. Instances of bad faith in the implementation of settlements for partisan advantage should also be distinguished from what might be called bad faith interpretations of peace processes in general, the view that bad faith is inherent in the nature of peace processes.[9] What can be concluded about the Northern Ireland case from the perspective of spoiler violence is that the Good Friday Agreement has proved more successful in curbing this phenomenon than was the Sunningdale Agreement and that this was in part due to its inclusive character.

Between Mandela's release from prison in February 1990 and his inauguration as the first President of a democratic and non-racial political dispensation in South Africa in May 1994, approximately 20,000 people died in political violence inside South Africa. In fact, the transition to democracy proved to be the most violent period in the country's history.[10] By releasing Mandela and removing the ban on the African National Congress (ANC), the Pan-Africanist Congress (PAC) and the South African Communist Party (SACP), President F.W. de Klerk signalled his intention to enter into negotiations on the creation of a new political dispensation. This amounted to an acknowledgement that apartheid had failed, both as its architect, H.F. Verwoerd, had envisaged its development and in the modified form that P.W. Botha had established. To put the point another way, De Klerk recognized that the days of white minority rule in South Africa were numbered. The campaign of the ANC's military wing, *Umkhonto we Sizwe*, had played an insignificant role in the failure of apartheid. Nonetheless, the ANC's international and domestic standing created the expectation that the organization would play a leading role in the negotiations.

At the outset, a major objective of the ruling National Party was to weaken the ANC during the transition, so that the National Party would be in a better position to compete for a share of power with the extension of the franchise to the whole of the country's adult population. In this context, the main goals of the National Party were to prevent the outcome of simple majority rule and to ensure the new dispensation made provision for group or minority rights in such a way that the National Party would be guaranteed a place in government after the holding of democratic elections. By contrast, the goal pursued by the extreme right was altogether simpler. It was to abort any transfer of power from white minority rule.

A dilemma for the extreme right was whether to pursue its opposition to such a transfer of power by constitutional means through the existing political institutions established under apartheid or through spoiler violence. In the initial stages of the transition, the emphasis was on constitutional political means, with the extreme right seeking to demonstrate, in particular, that De Klerk had no mandate from the white electorate for abandoning apartheid. And, in fact, pressure from the extreme right prompted De Klerk to hold a referendum among whites in March 1992 to secure support for the continuance of the negotiations. De Klerk's victory in the referendum defeated the extreme right's effort to block any transfer of power through conventional political means. Use of spoiler violence by the extreme right followed. There were four major episodes of such violence during the course of the South African transition. They were the assassination of the popular SACP leader, Chris Hani, on 10 April 1993, the invasion of the venue for the Multi-Party Negotiating Process on 25 June 1993, intervention by armed elements of the extreme right in Bophutswanan crisis in March 1994, and a bombing campaign during the holding of South Africa's first democratic elections in April 1994.

None of these actions achieved the extreme right's objective of disrupting the transition. Indeed, the first three proved counter-productive from this perspective, while the fourth was ineffective in disrupting polling in the elections. The assassination of Chris Hani caused a wave of anger in South Africa's townships hous-ing the country's urban African population that threatened to engulf the country in violence. Mandela intervened to urge calm. Recognition of his indispensability to the country's social stability enhanced his personal authority, as well as increasing the bar-gaining power of the ANC in the negotiations. The crisis over Hani's assassination prompted the parties in the negotiations to agree to the setting of a date in April 1994 for South Africa's first democratic elections, thereby limiting the time available for the parties to reach agreement over a provisional constitution to see the country through the elections. The invasion of the World Trade Centre by armed members of the extreme right militia, the *Afrikaner Weerstandsbeweging* (AWB – Afrikaner resistance movement), was intended to dissuade the negotiators from formally endorsing a date for the elections. It not merely failed in this endeavour but through the racist behaviour of some of those who participated in taking over the World Trade Centre caused divisions in the political alliance that the extreme right had forged with other parties hostile to the domination of the negotiating process by the National Party and the ANC.

The intervention in Bophuthatswana was intended to disrupt the transition by assisting Chief Mangope in his objective of maintaining his homeland's independence in the face of internal opponents, many of whom were fearful that the homeland would be unable to honour pension and other financial commitments as an independent state. However, the actions of the AWB members in killing black civilians in the course of their intervention prompted the defection of Mangope's army. That ensured the homeland's incorporation into South Africa enabling its residents to participate in the elections. A total of 21 people were killed in the extreme right's election bombing campaign, but the campaign had no discernible impact on the turnout of voters. This failure was compounded by the fact that after the Bophuthatswanan debacle a section of the extreme right had opted to participate in the elections to enhance the extreme right's influence on the drawing up of the final constitution that would follow the elections.

While the impact of extreme right violence was considerable in terms of the media coverage it received, it was responsible for only a very small proportion of deaths from political violence in the course of the transition. Most of the violence was carried out by groups seeking to affect its outcome and thereby to shape the nature of the country's post-apartheid political institutions. Admittedly, the objectives of radical Pan-Africanists included preventing a negotiated settlement in the belief that only a revolutionary transfer of power would ensure the country's transformation along Africanist lines. Thus, the attacks on whites by the Azanian People's Liberation Army (APLA) seem clearly to have been designed to provoke inter-racial conflict, but the numbers killed in such attacks were relatively small and failed in this objective. By far the largest numbers of fatalities were caused by conflict between the ANC and the Inkatha Freedom Party (IFP). The IFP enjoyed solid support among the rural population of the KwaZulu homeland and this extended to Zulus who maintained links with the homeland. Its attempts to challenge the ANC's dominance of townships with such links outside Johannesburg, Durban and Pietermaritzburg was supported by the National Party government in the first two years of the transition as part of its strategy of weakening the ANC.

The National Party abandoned this strategy in 1992. The turning point was the Record of Understanding between the government and the ANC in September 1992. At this point, the IFP leader, Chief Mangosuthu Buthelezi, arguably became a spoiler, since his objective became one of seeking to disrupt the transition now that it was taking place in circumstances of cooperation between the National Party and the ANC. IFP plans included boycotting and active disruption through violence of the elections in April 1994. However, violence in the centre of Johannesburg by IFP supporters in late March caused a rift with the King of the Zulus. The potential threat this represented to Buthelezi's support among traditionalist Zulus persuaded the IFP leader to relent and the party took part after all in the elections. While there is room for debate over whether APLA and IFP violence during the transition should be included in the category of spoiler violence, its results were similar to the spoiler violence of the extreme right. That is, the main effect of the violence was to strengthen the position of the ANC, contributing to its emergence from the transition to a position of political dominance.

The case that contrasts most sharply with that of South Africa is Israel/Palestine. In Israel/Palestine spoiler violence was a major factor in the breakdown of the peace process. The breakdown itself and its implications for global terrorism are considered in the next chapter. This chapter focuses on the impact of spoiler violence in the period from the Declaration of Principles between the Israeli government and the Palestine Liberation Organization (PLO) in September 1993 to the Israeli general elections of May 1996. The first major act of violence after the formal launch of the Oslo peace process was by carried out by a lone Israeli settler. This was the massacre by Baruch Goldstein of 29 Muslims at a mosque in Hebron on 25 February 1994. It was followed by major acts of violence by Palestinian opponents of the Oslo process. On 6 April 1994 a Hamas suicide bomber detonated explosives at a bus stop in the northern Israeli town of Afula, killing seven Israelis. This was the first use of the tactic of the suicide bomb within Israel. There was another such bombing on a bus in the coastal town of Hadera a week later on 13 April, in which five Israelis died. There were further suicide bomb attacks by Hamas in the course of 1995. On 24 July a suicide bomb attack on a bus in a Tel Aviv suburb killed six civilians and injured 30. A further attack on a bus in West

Jerusalem in August killed five people and injured 107. The bombings in 1994 and 1995 prompted demonstrations against the peace process in Israel. There was a sharp fall in the numbers supporting the peace process according to the opinion polls. However, they did not prevent the progress in the peace process. In September 1995 the Israeli government and the PLO signed an interim agreement on Palestinian self-determination in September 1995 (Oslo II).

The next major act of violence was the assassination of Prime Minister Yitzhak Rabin at a peace rally on 4 November 1995. The perpetrator was a 25 year-old student from Bar Ilan University and opponent of the Oslo process, Yigal Amir. In an analysis of the outcome of the Israeli general election in May 1996, Benny Morris began his article by arguing that Amir was the real winner of the Israeli general election. According to Morris, Amir had calculated accurately that Rabin 'was the only Labor Party leader capable of carrying the nation with him through the peace process'.[11] However, in the immediate aftermath of the assassination, there was a strong backlash against the rightwing opposition and its candidate for the premiership, Benyamin Netanyahu, and in fact, Morris himself alluded to this in his discussion of why Rabin's successor, Shimon Peres, failed to exploit it by calling swift elections, as was being urged by many of his followers. He argued that Peres hoped to go to the electorate with a draft peace treaty with Syria achieved and only decided to call elections in May (ahead of the final date for the elections of November 1996) when he reached the conclusion that no deal was possible with the Syrian leader, President Assad, ahead of Israeli general elections.[12]

The delay reduced the impact of the shock of Rabin's assassination on the election campaign, though from the outset of the campaign the Labour Party signalled that it intended, as David Horovitz put it, 'to make maximum use of one definite election asset: the ghost of the much-mythologised murdered prime minister, Yitzhak Rabin'.[13] A comparison might be drawn between the assassination of Rabin and that of Chris Hani in South Africa in April 1993. In that case, Hani's assassination proved entirely counter-productive for its extreme right-wing perpetrators, strengthening the ANC's position at an important point in the transition. However, in the event, the backlash in Israel against rightwing opponents of the peace process proved temporary. One reason for the difference was the resumption of Hamas's campaign of suicide bomb attacks ahead of the Israeli elections. On 25 February, there was a suicide bomb attack on a bus in Jerusalem and another such attack at a hitch-hiking post at Ashkelon. There was a further attack on a bus in Jerusalem on 3 March and that was followed by an attack on a shopping mall in Tel Aviv on 4 March. A factor in the resumption of the attacks was calls for vengeance among Palestinians in response to a targeted assassination by the Israeli security forces. On 5 January 1996 Israeli agents had managed to use a booby-trapped mobile phone to kill Yehiya Ayash (a reputed bomb-maker known as 'the Engineer').

In his successful campaign for the premiership, Netanyahu focused on the continuing threat that suicide bombers posed to Israel as a reason for rejecting the Oslo process. He made effective use of the issue in his debate with Shimon Peres a few days before polling, as is evident from contemporary reports. 'Five, six, seven times he [Netanyahu] charged that the people of Israel were "living in fear" of further Islamic extremist suicide bombings, ridiculing Mr Peres's vision of a new Middle East peace in the context of such harsh realities.'[14]

This issue overwhelmed positive developments in the peace process, such as the holding of elections for the Palestinian Authority on 20 January 1996 in which Arafat had secured 87 per cent of the vote in the Presidential elections and Fatah and Fatah-aligned independents had won an overwhelming majority in the legislative council. Another factor that proved damaging to Peres was the alienation and consequent abstention of some Israeli Arab voters as a result of military operations in Lebanon designed to shore up Peres's support among the Jewish majority, but this was clearly a much less significant factor than the impact of Hamas's violence on attitudes to the peace process. An article in the *Financial Times* described the economic performance of the government as one 'with which any western government would gladly face its electorate'.[15]

Netanyahu's election as Prime Minister of Israel was a huge blow to the Oslo peace process, though it did not cause its immediate breakdown. That is examined in the next chapter. The narrowness of Netanyahu's victory and the centrality of the issue of Hamas's violence to the election campaign underscored the decisive role played by spoiler violence in the outcome. The Israeli/ Palestinian case shows that there are circumstances in which spoiler violence can have a profound effect on the course of political developments. The number of episodes of spoiler violence on both sides of the conflict, the scale of the violence and its significance distinguish it from that of Northern Ireland. The South African transition was less vulnerable to spoiler violence, because no amount of violence obviated the need to create a new dispensation to replace the failed system of apartheid. However, violence in Israel/Palestine made a mockery of what gave the Oslo process legitimacy, the promise of peace between Israelis and Palestinians.

The final question to be considered in this chapter is whether the concept of spoiler violence is a fruitful one for examining the phenomenon of violence emanating directly from the al-Qaeda network or from other smaller jihadist groups through imitation. Spoiler violence is essentially negative in so far as the principal concern of its users is to prevent negotiations from succeeding or a new dispensation from taking root. Because the purpose is to disrupt, all manner of unholy alliances may come into existence. Groups with diametrically opposed long-term objectives may tacitly work together to destabilize the situation. Further, because the success of spoiler violence can be judged in a much shorter timeframe than violence for a revolutionary or nationalist purpose, it tends to be employed with fewer restraints than either of these two other types of violence. They typically conduct their campaigns of violence under the constraint of some notion of what constitutes legitimate targets in their struggle.

However, while the Western media have had little difficulty in fitting the violence of Hamas during the Israeli/Palestinian peace process, or, for that matter, jihadist violence in post-Saddam Iraq, into a spoiler framework, the events of 11 September, the Bali bombs and the attacks on Madrid and London have generally not been interpreted in this way. This is because the relationship between means and ends is far from clear in these cases. That has made it difficult for commentators to fit the attacks into any framework, other than one that stresses the religious motivation of the perpetrators of these acts. Generally, such explanations are accompanied by emphasizing that such acts are not permissible in terms of any of the mainstream interpretations of the Muslim religion. That ultimately suggests that al-Qaeda and its associates constitute a violent religious sect or cult not altogether dissimilar from the Aum Shinrikyo sect in Japan that carried out a Sarin gas attack on the Tokyo subway rail system.

To fit the attacks of al-Qaeda and its associates into a spoiler framework, it is necessary to view the world through their eyes. A common theme of statements by the leaders of al-Qaeda has been that the Muslim world is under attack from non-Muslims. An example is the florid account of the contemporary situation to be found in al-Qaeda's founding statement of 1998.

> The Arabian Peninsula has never – since God made it flat, created its desert, and encircled it with seas – been stormed by any forces like the crusader armies spreading in it like locusts, eating its riches and wiping out its plantations. All this is happening at a time in which nations are attacking Muslims like people fighting over a plate of food. In the light of the grave situation and the lack of support, we and you are obliged to discuss current events, and we should all agree on how to settle the matter.[16]

The same theme recurs in numerous pronouncements that al-Qaeda leaders have made since the events of 11 September. Osama bin Laden's deputy, Ayman al-Zawahiri, used the example of Algeria to underscore his contention that Islamists would never be allowed to come to power by democratic means and had no alternative to jihad. In this piece published in December 2001, he argued that to prevent Islamists from exercising power, what he called 'the Jewish–Crusader alliance' would open a battlefront that would include the whole world.[17]

From this perspective, the violent campaign of transnational terrorism conducted by al-Qaeda and its associates can be seen as a defensive reaction to a new era of aggressive policies by non-Muslims towards Muslim lands. At the same time, the unrestrained and indiscriminate nature of jihadist violence, as well as the minimal efforts made to justify it, might be seen as further characteristics that it has in common with spoiler violence. Thus, the attacks on Madrid and London might be regarded as designed to disrupt the Coalition of the Willing in its occupation of Iraq, by targeting respectively, Spanish and British citizens. It is possible that Australian foreign policy was the main target of the Bali bombs. However, the spoiler framework is much less successful in accounting for by far the most significant of al-Qaeda's actions, the events of 11 September. It seems more plausible to regard the attack on America as a calculated effort to provoke an aggressive response from the United States so as to revive the fortunes of the jihadist cause than as a response to American 'aggression', even bearing in mind the jihadists' perspective on the world.

Of course, the global order, in so far as it exists and is not simply an abstraction from the reality of the world of states, is quite different from political dispensations within states, so the objective of disrupting the global order is by no means the same as destabilizing the governance of a particular state. Waging a war against the global order, against imperialism or for that matter against terrorism is unlike battling against a specific regime or group. Such a war is potentially limitless in its scope. Further, victory or defeat in such a war is hard to measure. In this context, it is significant that al-Qaeda's pronouncements gravitate wildly between characterizing the conditions facing righteous Muslims as catastrophic and the interpretation of events such as Israel's withdrawal from Lebanon or the American abandonment of Somalia as victories along the way to the ultimate triumph of a global jihad.

The major point in common in these widely contrasting representations of reality is the centrality accorded to Muslim identity. In the next chapter, the breakdown in 2000 of the Israeli/ Palestinian peace process is examined. The importance of the Muslim holy places in Jerusalem in that process gave further impetus to the construction of a jihadist Muslim identity that is simultaneously victimized and assertive, not just among Palestinians, but globally.

Notes

1 Stephen John Stedman, 'Spoiler Problems in Peace Processes', *International Security*, Vol. 22, No. 2, Fall 1997.

2 Ibid., p. 5.

3 Ibid., p. 6.

4 Ibid., p. 25.

5 For a solid history of the problem, see Jonathan Bardon, *A History of Ulster*, The Blackstaff Press, Belfast 1992.

6 *An Phoblacht* (Dublin), 18 January 1974.

7 For analysis of the Agreement, see Rick Wilford (ed.), *Aspects of the Belfast Agreement*, Oxford University Press, Oxford 2001.

8 Bizarrely, it transpired that Denis Donaldson, who was at the centre of the allegations of the existence of an IRA spy ring, had been working for British intelligence for 20 years. *Irish Times*, 17 December 2005.

9 See, for example, Michael A. Ledeen, 'Why Peace Processes Do Not Work: A Machiavellian View' in L. Sergio Germani and D.R. Kaarthikeyan (eds), *Pathways out of Terrorism and Insurgency: The Dynamics of Terrorist Violence and Peace Processes*, New Dawn Press, New Delhi 2005, pp. 50–4. Ledeen's sceptical view of peace processes in general is common among American neo-conservatives who prefer the use of military force to negotiations. Ledeen is a fellow of the American Enterprise Institute.

10 For an account of the transition, see Adrian Guelke, *South Africa in Transtion: The Misunderstood Miracle*, I.B. Tauris, London 1999.

11 Benny Morris, 'Israel's elections and their implications', *Journal of Palestine Studies*, Vol. XXVI, No. 1, 1996 (Issue No. 101), p. 70.

12 Ibid., p. 74.

13 David Horovitz, 'Peres leans on Rabin in election bid', *Irish Times*, 11 May 1996.

14 David Horovitz, 'Netanyahu outperforms Peres in Israel's television debate', *Irish Times*, 27 May 1996.

15 Julian Ozanne and David Gardner, 'Peace path's deep divide', *Financial Times*, 28 May 1996.

16 Quoted in Halliday, *Two Hours that Shook the World*, p. 217.

17 Al-Zawahiri's publication, *Knights under the Prophet's Banner*, is quoted extensively in Richard Bonney, *Jihad: From Qur'an to bin Laden*, Palgrave Macmillan, Basingstoke 2004, especially p. 356 and p. 362.

CHAPTER 6

Breakdown

The prime example of the breakdown of a peace process is the case of Israel/Palestine. The breakdown preceded the events of 11 September. Inevitably, it formed a significant element both in the interpretation of the assault on America and in how Americans and their government responded to the attacks. However, the connection between the conflict between Israelis and Palestinians and the transnational terrorism of al-Qaeda and its affiliates is not merely a complex issue analytically, but also a point of considerable political contention and sensitivity.[1] So too is the broader issue of the connection of the Israeli–Palestinian conflict to terrorism in general and to its conceptualization. In the course of an interview with the BBC following the bomb attacks on London in July 2005, the British Prime Minister, Tony Blair, argued that while security was the obvious priority in the circumstances, 'the solution cannot be only security measures' and that the causes of terrorism needed to be addressed. He highlighted in this context the importance of progress in the promotion of peace in the Middle East between Israelis and Palestinians. A columnist in an Israeli paper picked up his words arguing that Blair's words 'turned Israel from a partner to a common fate to a partner in blame'.[2] (From other remarks made by the British Prime Minister, it was evident that his intention was to deflect any implication that any of *his* policies had played a role in the bombers' motivation.)

Of course, to argue that the violence between Israelis and Palestinians was one of the factors that may have motivated the suicide bomb attack on London is very far from blaming Israeli policies as even indirectly contributing to the terrorism suffered by Londoners. Similarly, the rather more plausible argument that British policies, and most particularly the government's participation in the Coalition of the Willing in Iraq, were a factor in the motivation of the bombers, is separable from the issue of whether any blame should be attached to the British government as a consequence. However, in the initial aftermath of the London bombs, it was evident that British commentators were extremely reluctant to suggest any connection between the war in Iraq and the outrage in London, out of a fear of being accused of blaming the Prime Minister and/or of exculpating the bombers. Given the Pakistani connections of the bombers, it is conceivable that another conflict, the war in Afghanistan immediately after 9/11, loomed larger in their motivation than either Israel/Palestine or Iraq.[3] But since the war in Afghanistan was less contentious in Britain, making this point would be less likely to be interpreted as indicating a critical attitude to military intervention in Afghanistan in 2001. Another quite different response to the London bombs came from opponents of the Israeli government's policy of withdrawal from Gaza who argued that the London bombs highlighted the danger that the establishment of a 'PLO Islamic State' in Gaza could represent to Israeli, American and Western interests.

The history of the area ruled over by the modern Israeli state plays an important role in the discourse not just of the protagonists in the Israeli–Palestinian conflict but also in that of al-Qaeda. It also plays a significant role in these parties' actual interpretation of current events and in their expectations and aspirations. Much of the basic elements of this history will be well known to readers, but a brief reprise of some of its most salient points may be helpful in illuminating the perceptions of the parties in their responses to current developments. Jewish settlement of ancient Palestine, the name deriving from another of the ethnic groups that settled in the area, the Philistines, dates back to well before 1200 BC.

Politically, Jewish settlement of the area gave rise to the establishment of a number of kingdoms, the most important of which made
Jerusalem its capital. This kingdom was ultimately swept aside
by the Babylonians who conquered Jerusalem and destroyed its
temple. However, a second temple was built in its place, after the
era of the Babylonian captivity came to an end. The second temple
was eventually destroyed by the Romans in AD 70 following a
Jewish revolt against their impositions. This revolt culminated
in the Romans' defeat of the Zealots at Masada. Rather than
surrender, the Zealots committed suicide on the plateau of the
rock that formed their stronghold. The ending of the revolt was
followed more than half a century later by the enforced dispersal
of Jews from the area. Notwithstanding this diaspora of the Jewish
people, small numbers of Jews continued to live in the area,
though at times their numbers fell to the low thousands.

Both the destruction of the temples and what happened to the
Zealots on the Masada plateau resonate in the modern state of
Israel. In particular, fringe Jewish groups exist which harbour
the ambition to rebuild the temple where the second temple once
stood. They also have the support of some Christian fundamentalist groups that regard the rebuilding of the temple as a
fulfilment of Biblical prophecy. The building of a third temple
would, not accidentally, involve the destruction of a site of major
religious significance for Muslims in the old city. The capacity of
the fringe groups to fulfil their ambition is, practically speaking,
nil, but the provocative nature of such a threat to the Muslim holy
places on the Temple Mount or Haraam-al-Sharif has proved
sufficient from time to time to be a cause of major disturbances
among Palestinians. For example, in September 1996, the opening
of a tunnel to the Western Wall was perceived as a threat by
the Palestinians to the Muslim holy places and prompted violent
conflict, including clashes between Palestinian police under the
control of the Palestinian Authority and Israeli security forces.

The last stand of the Zealots on Masada has been used as
a metaphor by Israeli governments for the readiness of Israelis to
fight to the end. In the 1970s, the term, Masada complex, was

coined to underscore the psychological significance of this siege mentality. It was also used to explain the thinking behind the country's possession of an undeclared, but widely known, nuclear arsenal. The implication was that Israel would use its nuclear weapons capability if the country was ever threatened with being overrun by conventional armies. Admittedly, this had much greater relevance in the era of inter-state conflict between Israel and the neighbouring Arab countries than it does today. The transformation of the conflict into an internal one between Israeli Jews and Palestinian Arabs limits the continuing significance of such a posture, though that has not hitherto persuaded any Israeli government to disavow the possession of weapons of mass destruction. In recent times, the notion of a Masada complex has been applied to Israeli politicians who have declared that the withdrawal from any part of the West Bank or Gaza would be tantamount to surrender.

The emergence of Islam in the seventh century was accompanied by the creation of a vast theocratic empire that encompassed the Middle East stretching as far as India, North Africa and much of Spain. At the heart of the empire, which included Palestine, there was a fusion between conversion to Islam and the spread of the Arabic language, forming the basis for the emergence of a new predominant culture in the area. For reasons that had far more to do with conditions in Europe than those in the Middle East, attempts were made by Christian armies to challenge Muslim rule of Palestine, and most particularly, Jerusalem, from the eleventh to the thirteenth centuries. These attempts were known collectively as the crusades. Analogously, jihad has come to be associated with the aggressive waging of holy war by Muslims against the non-Muslim world, so much so that the term, jihadist, provides a convenient shorthand for describing Islamists ready to use violence to forward their cause.

This is not to say that the term jihad is not susceptible to more pacific interpretations within Islam. Indeed, jihad may be translated to mean not holy war, implying the use of force or violence, but more generally a struggle, which is compatible with the pursuit of one's political objectives by perfectly legitimate means.

Similarly, within the Muslim world, the term, crusade is associated with unprovoked Christian aggression and violence towards Islam. In fact, the notion has much the same meaning for Muslims as jihad has for the non-Muslim world. And the way in which some Islamists use the term, crusader, is similar to the usage of jihadist as shorthand for Islamists pursuing their objectives by violent means and carries just as strong negative connotations. Indeed, it might be said that one person's jihadist is another person's crusader. Yet what is clearly ahistorical in al-Qaeda's evocation of a continuous history of aggression against Muslims since the crusades is its inclusion of Israel in this picture since in reality the medieval crusades were marked by an upsurge of Christian intolerance towards other religions, but most especially Judaism. At the same time, the ugly dimensions of the medieval crusades have little resonance in Europe today where the crusades are chiefly remembered in terms of the stories of a few heroic figures such as Richard the Lionheart and Frederick Barbarossa.

The modern history of the Israeli–Palestinian conflict dates from the late nineteenth century.[4] By this time, Palestine had long been part of the Ottoman Empire. Even before the waves of Jewish immigration known as *aliyas* had started with the emergence of Zionism, an ideology promoting the concept that Jews should establish a national home of their own, the size of the Jewish community in Palestine had begun to increase. A facilitating factor was a change in the law in 1867 that permitted foreigners to purchase land in Palestine. Further impetus was given to Jewish immigration to Palestine by the failure of the 1905 Russian revolution. During the First World War, Turkey was allied to Germany. Its empire became a significant arena of conflict between the two coalitions of states that fought the war. The *entente* powers as part of their war effort gave encouragement to an Arab revolt against Turkish rule in Palestine and other Arab territories that formed part of Turkey's empire. The British government, in particular, held out the promise of independence to encourage the revolt. The British also, however, entered into an agreement with the French on a post-war division of the spoils.

In addition, the British foreign secretary wrote a letter to Lord Rothschild that declared that the government 'viewed with favour the establishment in Palestine of national home for the Jewish people'.[5] Though the Balfour Declaration qualified this statement by affirming that 'nothing shall be done that which may prejudice the civil and religious rights of the existing non-Jewish communities in Palestine',[6] it was widely interpreted as British support for the realization of the Zionist project in Palestine.

While Arab guerrilla warfare played its part in the defeat of the Turks, Jerusalem was captured by regular forces under General Allenby who entered the city in December 1917 and Palestine came under British military occupation. This lasted to July 1922. Thanks to President Wilson's insistence that the war should not be followed by wholesale annexations of enemy territory, Palestine was transformed into a League of Nations mandate, albeit with Britain as the mandatory power. The British government divided the area it had been given responsibility for by creating an Arab emirate, Transjordan, in the part of the territory to the East of the Jordan River. Whereas there had been a relatively muted reaction from the Arab population between the Jordan and the sea to pre-war Jewish immigration, the substantial post-war immigration gave rise to a series of disturbances. The change was a reflection not merely of the increased scale of the immigration but its connection with the credible political objective of establishing a Jewish state in the area.

By 1936, the Yishuv (i.e. the Jewish community) constituted 30 per cent of the population West of the Jordan River. In the same year an Arab revolt against British rule was initiated that was to last three years. In response to the Arab revolt, a commission established by the British government proposed partition of the territory. It also recommended restrictions on Jewish immigration. Partition was rejected by the leaders of the Arab community, as well as by subsequent commissions set up by the British government that argued that partition was not a practicable solution. The outbreak of the Second World War delayed further consideration of Palestine's future. During the war itself, the issue of restrictions on Jewish immigration prompted a wide measure of hostility within the Yishuv towards the British authorities but it was kept in check by the greater importance of the outcome of the global conflict. However, once the war was over, the tensions erupted into violence.

The most lethal act of violence in this context was a bomb attack on the British army's headquarters in the King David's Hotel in Jerusalem on 22 July 1946. The attack in which 90 people died and hundreds were injured was carried out by a rightwing terrorist organization, Irgun. It stands out as one of the most widely cited acts of terrorism in the literature on the subject before the wave of terrorist attacks that took place in the late 1960s at the start of what has commonly been referred to as an age of terrorism. With the League of Nations defunct, the British government did not envisage the continuance of its mandate in Palestine and referred the future of the territory to the United Nations. In November 1947, in a vote that was seen as a victory for supporters of the establishment of a Jewish state and a defeat for the Arab states, the General Assembly voted in favour of a partition plan that divided the territory into two states, one Jewish and the other Palestinian Arab. The division was problematic as at the time Jews were a minority of the population within the proposed Jewish entity. The plan was not supported by the mandatory power, Britain. The British government opted for a policy of withdrawal that amounted to a disavowal of any responsibility for the area's future governance. At the time such action had few precedents, but it was to be repeated by Britain in the case of Aden in 1967 and by Portugal in the case of Angola in 1975. The result in the latter cases was civil war, and in the former, war between the emerging state of Israel and the country's Arab neighbours.

The year 1948 has very different meanings for the protagonists. For the Jewish community in Palestine it was a triumphant watershed. War might have extinguished the very existence of the Yishuv but instead it made possible the creation of a viable Jewish state within a larger area than had been proposed by the General Assembly, and by the movement of population it brought about, seemed to remove any possible demographic threat in the future to the Jewish character of the new state. For the Palestinians, 1948 was a catastrophe and is referred to as the *naqba*, meaning calamity. The new state of Israel confiscated the land and property not just of those who fled the country but also of those who suffered internal displacement as a result of the fighting. Two consequences of the war were that the boundaries of Israel were based on the armistice lines at its conclusion and that the Palestinian state envisaged in the General Assembly's partition plan failed to materialize.

For almost two decades after Israel's independence, the conflict between the dominant community and the Palestinian minority within the borders of the new state was submerged by the threat and reality of war between Israel and the neighbouring Arab states. There were wars between Israel and Egypt in 1956 and between Israel and Egypt, Syria and Jordan in 1967. Israel's victory in the six-day war of June 1967, resulting in the occupation of the West Bank and Gaza, multiplied the number of Palestinians subject to Israeli rule. But the regional framework remained the main focus of Israel's security concerns. It was only after another war with Egypt and Syria in 1973 and a peace process with the Egyptians that relations between Israelis and Palestinians came to be seen as the core of the Middle East conflict. Thus, Israel's controversial intervention in Lebanon in 1982 was directed less at the regional strategic environment than at the Palestinian presence in Lebanon and violence across Israel's border from Lebanon. Israel was successful in securing the removal of the PLO from Lebanon, but the government's reputation was tarnished by the massacres by Christian militias allied to Israel of Palestinian refugees in Sabra and Chatila outside Beirut.

The centrality of the Palestinian issue was underscored by the outbreak of the intifada in December 1987.[7] The Israeli state's attempts to crush the uprising by military force not merely failed to quell the intifada but engendered considerable sympathy for the Palestinian cause internationally. Though the methods used in the course of the intifada were by no means wholly non-violent, Israel was unable to persuade even its closest ally, the United

States of America, to label the intifada as a form of terrorism. This was despite the extent to which the Palestinian cause had come to be associated with terrorism as a result of hijackings by Palestinians in the 1960s and 1970s and outrages such as the attack on Israeli athletes at the Munich Olympics in 1972.

Ending the intifada was one of the motivations for the Israeli Labour government elected in 1992 seeking a dialogue with the PLO. Other factors included the change of the overall strategic environment as a result of the end of the cold war and the repercussions of Iraq's defeat in 1991 following its occupation of Kuwait. Both were perceived as weakening the PLO and making it more amenable to a negotiated settlement. At the same time, the government believed that an end to the conflict could not be achieved solely by military means. They also recognized that Israel's occupation of the West Bank and Gaza was fuelling the conflict. Addressing this issue was encapsulated in the phrase, 'land for peace'. The implication was not merely that Israel's withdrawal from these areas would be a central feature of the peace process, but that ultimately it would lead to the creation of a Palestinian state alongside Israel. Where the approach of the government led by Rabin differed most clearly from its predecessors was its belief that through a phased process a final settlement could be reached with the PLO that would end the conflict. This assumption underwrote the Oslo peace process, from the perspective of the Israeli government.

From the outset there was considerable opposition within the dominant community in Israel to the Oslo peace process from those who were against the creation of a Palestinian state and favoured the eventual incorporation of substantial parts of the occupied territories into Israel. But some opponents of Oslo questioned the process more than the government's ultimate objectives. In particular, they queried the government's strategy of negotiations in stages and doubted the PLO's commitment to accept a peace within the parameters determined by Israel. As described in the previous chapter, spoiler violence by both Israeli and Palestinian opponents of the peace process between 1994 and

1996 undermined confidence in the Oslo process and resulted in the election of Benyamin Netanyahu as Prime Minister of Israel. Netanyahu had been an opponent of the Oslo process. However, his election did not bring about the immediate collapse of the peace process, particularly as the government of Israel's principal ally, the United States, remained strongly committed to it. In fact, some neo-conservative supporters of the Israeli right in the United States, were disappointed that Netanyahu failed to oppose the Clinton Administration openly on the issue of the Oslo peace process.

Pressure from the Clinton Administration was largely responsible for Netanyahu's acceptance of the Wye River memorandum of October 1998. However, as with other aspects of the peace process during this period, little progress was made in implementing the accords. Sporadic violence by militant Palestinian groups, including a suicide bomb attack in Jerusalem in September 1997, justified the government's stalling while also underscoring the extent of Palestinian disillusionment over the failure of the peace process to transform the conditions under which they lived. In the Israeli general election of May 1999, Netanyahu was defeated by Labour's candidate for the premiership, Ehud Barak. His election raised hopes outside Israel of a revival of the peace process. But while Barak's objectives included arriving at a final settlement with the Palestinian Authority, his immediate priorities lay elsewhere. He believed that addressing the regional context first would make it easier to reach an agreement with Arafat. His priorities in this context included the promised withdrawal of Israeli forces from Lebanon and the exploration of a possible deal with Syria.

Barak's approach to a settlement with the Palestinians was governed by three assumptions. First, Barak believed that small steps should be avoided as expending political capital for little gain and he therefore held back on implementation of the Wye River memorandum. Second, he believed that the Palestinian leadership would only accept a final settlement if the leaders believed that they had no alternative, an assumption that drove his desire to cement Israel's position in the region ahead of dealing with the

Palestinians. Third, Barak believed that calm was required to secure the Israeli public's support for concessions to the Palestinians and that consequently nothing should be done, such as curbing the growth of settlements that would excite rightwing opposition ahead of the final set of negotiations. Barak's focus on the regional framework was reflected in an ultimately fruitless pursuit of a peace agreement with Syria and the fulfilment in May 2000 of his promise to achieve a complete Israeli withdrawal from Lebanon. Further, little effort was made by Barak to develop a relationship with the Palestinian leadership ahead of final status negotiations. By this time the standing of the Palestinian Authority among the Palestinian population in the occupied areas had weakened as a result of pervasive allegations of corruption, as well as its incapacity to prevent the continuing expansion of Israeli settlements. However, it was a period of economic growth in the Palestinian areas. The level of political violence was also low, though clashes involving Israeli and Palestinian security forces on Naqba day, 15 May 2000, underscored the potential for conflict, as well as the extent of distrust at an official level between the two sides.

The critical negotiations that formed the backdrop to the breakdown of the peace process and the resumption of violence on a large scale took place in the United States at Camp David between 11 and 25 July 2000. What happened at Camp David has been the subject of extensive debate and analysis.[8] However, the broad outlines of what occurred are not in dispute. A deal was put to the Palestinian side by President Clinton under which Israel would acquire approximately 9 per cent in area of the West Bank, encompassing the principal Israeli settlements, but would withdraw from the rest. At the same time, the Palestinian Authority would acquire 1 per cent of pre-1967 Israel in part exchange. Not merely was this deal rejected as a whole by the Palestinian negotiators, but there was little effort on their part to engage with the details of the proposals. Much of the coverage and commentary on Camp David highlighted just how much of the occupied territories the Israeli government was indicating its willingness to give up and glossed over the issue as to whether Israel had any right to acquire any part of the occupied territories in the light of Security Council resolutions. The generosity of the Israeli stance during the talks was stressed, with the clear implication that the Palestinian negotiators and Arafat personally were to blame for the failure of the negotiations. This was the position taken up not just by the Israeli government but also by the Clinton Administration.

Both the Barak government and the Clinton Administration seemed to have believed that by challenging Arafat's commitment to the peace process they could pressurize him into acceptance of what was on offer, despite the repeated warnings they had received that the Palestinian leadership was not ready to conclude a comprehensive settlement in the absence of much more extensive preparation of the ground for such a deal. The Clinton Administration showed an understanding of the domestic political difficulties that shaped the approach of the Barak government to the negotiations, but appeared blind to the impact that Barak's manoeuvring had on the Palestinian leadership's confidence in his commitment to the peace process. It also showed scant appreciation that if a final settlement was not to undermine the position of the Palestinian leadership, it had to satisfy the requirement of being seen to be internationally legitimate. The deal on offer to the Palestinian leadership at Camp David palpably did not satisfy this criterion. By questioning Arafat's good faith at the conclusion of the Camp David talks, Barak and Clinton turned the failure of these negotiations into a watershed in the whole Oslo peace process. Though Clinton put forward new proposals, the Clinton parameters, in December 2000 and there were further negotiations between representatives of the Israeli government and the Palestinian leadership in Taba in Egypt in January 2001,[9] these were desperate efforts to revive a process that had already broken down as a result of the Clinton Administration's mishandling of the Camp David negotiations.

The Camp David negotiations were not followed immediately by extensive violence. That was triggered by an event that was to give its name to a new Palestinian intifada. This was the provocative tour of the Temple Mount or Haraam-al-Sharif by the leader of Likud, Ariel Sharon, on 28 September 2000. This triumphal display ran counter to Israeli practice since the six-day war in 1967 to respect the wishes of the Muslim religious authorities, a position reinforced by a message from the Chief Rabbi placed at the Western Wall urging observant Jews not to visit the Temple Mount. Sharon's intent was to underline his commitment to the retention of Israeli sovereignty over the whole of the old city, while also shoring up his leadership of his party. Barak facilitated Sharon's provocative behaviour in the belief that Sharon's continuing leadership of Likud was in his (i.e. Barak's) electoral interest. Palestinian protests at Sharon's visit were brutally suppressed by the Israeli security forces and resulted in a large number of deaths among the protestors in the days that followed. A factor in the extreme harshness of the Israeli response to the protests was the belief that the failure of Camp David would lead to violence from the Palestinians, coupled with the conviction of the government that the Palestinians needed to be taught a lesson that violence would not improve their bargaining position. The affront that Sharon's visit was seen as representing to the Muslim holy places on the Temple Mount was reflected in the dubbing of the intifada that followed his visit as the al-Aqsa intifada, after the principal mosque situated on the Temple Mount or Haraam-al-Sharif.

Worse was to come. The Israeli army characterized the remaining period of Barak's premiership up to his defeat by Sharon in elections in February 2001 as a stage of containment. The army's characterization of subsequent stages in the conflict charts the escalation of violence under Sharon. These were:

> the stage of leverage or ongoing continuous pressure (2001); the stage of the systematic dismantlement of terrorism infra-structures (January–March 2002); the stage of the counter-blows of Operation 'Defensive Shield' (March–April 2002); the stage of security control of Operation 'Determined Path' (June 2002–May 2003); and the stage of regularization and operational stabilization (second quarter of 2003 and after).[10]

The period from March to December 2001 established a cycle of violence as each side responded to the violence of the other. There were Israeli military incursions into areas under the control of the Palestinian Authority, as well as targeted assassinations of militants. There was a spate of suicide bombings by Palestinian groups. In the period a total of 35 attacks took place with a further 16 being thwarted. Sharon, like Netanyahu, was opposed to the Oslo peace process, but unlike Netanyahu he came under no pressure from the American government to try to preserve the process or to exercise restraint in responding to Palestinian violence.

The posture taken by the Bush Administration was that it was up to the parties in the conflict to recognize that their interests would be better served by negotiations. This stance was in part motivated by the desire of the new Administration to establish that the style of its diplomacy would be different from that of its predecessor and it would eschew involvement in conflicts where American interests were not directly affected. Further, the Bush Administration did little to challenge the interpretation that Sharon placed on the escalation of Palestinian violence. This explained the violence as Arafat's response to his failure to get his way during the Camp David negotiations. Verisimilitude was given to this proposition by the involvement in the violence of groups connected politically to the Palestinian leadership. This gave rise to a new mantra, that Israel could not pursue a peace process because it lacked a Palestinian partner for peace.

By the summer of 2001, the Bush Administration had begun to rethink its attitude towards the Israeli–Palestinian conflict as it came to recognize that the appearance of American impotence in the face of the escalating violence was damaging American interests. Despite opposition from neo-conservatives inside and outside government, preparations were made for an American initiative to revive negotiations between the parties. Then the events of 11 September happened. Al-Qaeda's assault on the United States did not immediately cause President Bush to abandon his plans and this prompted a bitter attack on Bush by Sharon in which he implicitly compared the American President to Neville

Chamberlain as an appeaser. At this point, the Bush Administration changed tack, accepting that the wide use by the Palestinians of suicide bombings made it impossible to persuade the American public that there was any fundamental distinction to be drawn between the terrorism of al-Qaeda and that of Palestinian groups.

This is an appropriate point to consider in greater depth the connections between the Israeli–Palestinian conflict and the attacks on 11 September, not just as a particular set of actions, but rather as representing the full emergence of super-terrorism or terrorism with a global reach, to take just two of the commoner characterizations of the violence of the al-Qaeda network in the wake of the assault on America. A basic if somewhat obvious point should be made at the outset. While it is possible to identify a number of individual Palestinians in the al-Qaeda network, relatively speaking, few Palestinians joined the network. To start with, very few Palestinians were to be found in the ranks of those who joined the jihad against the Soviet occupation of Afghanistan, the Arab Afghans, from whom many of al-Qaeda's recruits were drawn. From the perspective of the main Palestinian organizations at the time, the Soviet Union was an ally, so joining a jihad against the Soviet Union would have seemed contrary to their own interests. But even leaving aside the influence of the political alignments prevailing during the last decade of the cold war, Palestinians had little motivation to look beyond their own situation. Further, groups such as Hamas provided an outlet for Palestinians who placed an Islamist interpretation on their own conflict.

However, the absence of Palestinians within the al-Qaeda network did not mean that the Israeli–Palestinian conflict was not important to the network. The highly visible character of the al-Aqsa intifada with the daily relaying of television pictures to the outside world of death and destruction was of huge significance as a mobilizing factor for recruitment into the network. The Palestinian victims of the conflict were for the most part Muslims and the high number of deaths among Palestinians in the context of the Israeli response to suicide bombings fuelled perceptions of the conflict as an injustice to Muslims in which their lives were seen as of little account. Even if the scale of killings in the conflict was not as great as that in many less visible conflicts, with close to 1,000 Israeli deaths and over 3,000 Palestinian deaths from September 2000 to the end of 2004, it was proportionately high, given the population of Israel/Palestine. Further, the origin of the conflict in what was widely seen in the Muslim world as an insult to, if not desecration of, the third most holy place in the Islamic religion, ensured that Islamists placed the blame for the conflict entirely on Israel.

Of course, the impact of the Israeli–Palestinian conflict was greatest within the Arab world where there was identification with the Palestinians as fellow Arabs as well as Muslims. However, Muslims outside of the Arab world were by no means indifferent to the conflict. When a radical Islamist party, *Mutahidda Majlis e Amal* (MMA), emerged as the strongest party in North-West Frontier Province and Baluchistan in elections to Pakistan's national assembly in October 2002, it caused some disquiet in the West. The leader of the party was interviewed by the *Observer* and declared: 'We are not extremists. We would like to make bridges with the West – but we want justice. Injustice is being done to Muslims in Palestine and Kashmir.'[11] A distinction is sometimes made between the objectives of al-Qaeda and its leader, Osama bin Laden, and the means used by al-Qaeda to attract recruits willing to engage in suicide attacks and supporters willing to propagate its radical message of Islamist militancy. In particular, it is argued that Osama bin Laden has used the emotive power of the images of violent death from conflicts involving Muslims essentially for propaganda purposes and in this context has made use of a number of conflicts, including those in Israel/Palestine, Bosnia, Kosovo, Chechnya, the Philippines and Kashmir. In a number of these cases, the Muslim identity of the insurgents is or was less important to their struggle than a more local ethnic identity and the objective of many of those engaged in these struggles has not been to establish an Islamist state but simply a separate state.

While it is indeed important that the nationalist dimensions of these conflicts should be understood, from al-Qaeda's perspective it is possible to fit all of them into its larger worldview of a global Muslim community at war with non-Muslims. It may be true that Osama bin Laden personally cared more about the affront to Islam, as he saw it, of the American presence in Saudi Arabia than about the Israeli–Palestinian conflict at the time of 9/11. But it is questionable whether this was true of Islamists in general. In any event, what would have mattered more to bin Laden was whether recruits shared his worldview than how they were drawn to this view of events. Further, in so far as al-Qaeda has ceased to operate as a centrally directed organization since the fall of the Taliban in Afghanistan, the views of its leaders have become less important in determining actions carried out in its name or inspired by its example. But the role of the Israeli–Palestinian conflict within the ideology of al-Qaeda before and after the events of 11 September or, for that matter, before or after the start of the al-Aqsa intifada in the days after 28 September 2000, is of less significance than its influence on recruits to the al-Qaeda cause and on their readiness to carry out horrific acts of lethal violence, often involving their own death. From what is known about the willingness of individuals to participate in the clandestine violence of small groups, witnessing or experience of violence is a crucial motivating factor. Admittedly, in most cases, this is likely to result in the individual's participation in the conflict in question, so a further step is involved in the case of violence directed at a party not directly engaged in the conflict. This important issue, which has a fundamental bearing on how 9/11 is characterized, is addressed in the next chapter.

The American response to the events of 11 September was encapsulated in the question: 'why do they hate us?' For some, this was to pose a genuine puzzle for which there was no obvious answer. For others, the question simply was a way of saying that only immense hatred could explain the events of 11 September, but did not imply any especial interest into delving into its unreasonable or irrational source. But for still others, the answer to the question scarcely required much investigation since they regarded it as axiomatic that America's offence in the eyes of the perpetrators of 9/11 was the country's support for Israel. This assumption is well described by James Bovard.

> In the aftermath of 9/11 'We are all Israelis now' was the chorus of Americans ranging from *New Republic* editor-in-chief Martin Peretz to *Washington Times* columnist Larry Kudlow, to *USA Today* commentator Samuel Freedman to *Arkansas Democrat-Gazette* editorial page editor Paul Greenberg, to former drug czar and conservative moral eminence Bill Bennett. Many Americans believed that the attack by Arab terrorists proved once and for all that the destinies of the United States and Israel are intertwined.[12]

As Bovard noted further, this reaction did not go unnoticed in Israel. 'Prominent Israelis also promptly linked the attacks to their country's plight. Former Israeli Prime Minister Benjamin Netanyahu, speaking of the terrorist attacks, told Israeli radio on September 12, 2001: "This was a very good thing for Israel's relationship to the United States."'[13]

As Netanyahu correctly surmised, the events of 11 September reinforced support for Israel in the United States. It became harder for the case to be made that the Bush Administration should have acted to restrain the aggressive approach of the Sharon government, since it might be seen as the advocacy of a policy of appeasement towards the threat posed by al-Qaeda or a rationalization for the horrors perpetrated on 11 September. Indeed, far from prompting critical questions about Israel's policies, the events of 11 September prompted American emulation of the counter-terrorist policies of Israel. The debate that took place in the American media on the legitimacy of extreme steps, such as the use of torture to extract information and the assassination of suspected terrorists, i.e. what was known as targeted assassinations, was premised on the assumption that Israeli policies provided the limits of what any democracy might do in the face of such an emergency. Of course, this depended on viewing Israel as a democracy, but that was practically an American article of faith.

The characterization of Israel as an imperfect, ethnic democracy or an ethnic constitutional order that is common in the scholarly literature on the country's politics has scarcely penetrated public consciousness in the United States.[14] Admittedly, it might be argued that what is most salient in this context is that Israel is a constitutional state and that this places some legal restraints on the conduct of the Israeli government, particularly within the country's legal borders.

Attitudes towards Israel in Europe, both among governments and the populace at large, differ substantially from those prevailing in the United States. There tends to be much more awareness in Europe that Israel is a deeply divided society and that its government represents the country's dominant community. There also tends to be more appreciation of the denial of the political rights of Palestinians in the occupied territories and the limited influence of the Palestinian minority inside Israel on the country's policies. These differences were not reflected in the initial responses of European governments to the events of 11 September, which was one of unconditional solidarity with the United States. Arguably, they were a factor in both popular and governmental opposition in Europe to the targeting of Iraq by the Bush Administration after the broadly successful first phase of the war against terrorism during which the Taliban regime in Afghanistan was overthrown.

Nevertheless, there remained considerable reluctance within Europe to connect the assault on America to the violent breakdown in the Israeli–Palestinian peace process, let alone to the Bush Administration's apparent indifference to the breakdown. In part, that was due to the accurate perception that al-Qaeda's violence was not solely driven by the Israeli–Palestinian conflict, a point underlined by the fact that the al-Qaeda leadership's planning of an attack on the American mainland preceded the start of the al-Aqsa intifada.[15] Another factor that inhibited European governments from connecting these issues in a manner that might have been perceived as critical of American policy was the fear that in the light of the tragic fate of millions of European Jews during the Second World War, such criticism might have raised the spectre of European anti-Semitism. In the case of a number of European governments, an additional factor was at work. This was that they wished to enhance the legitimacy of their own efforts to combat political violence within their own boundaries by its characterization as terrorism falling within the scope of the global war against terrorism. This was most obviously a strong motivation in the case of the conservative government in Spain which sought to portray the violence of Basque separatists in a similar light to that of al-Qaeda.

From the Israeli government's perspective, the effect of the events of 11 September was to reduce the constraints on its military response to Palestinian violence. As Bar-Siman-Tov, Lavie, Michael and Bar-Tal put it, 9/11 'was of crucial importance in providing domestic and international legitimacy for an expanded, unrelenting, systematic mode of operation which was intended to vanquish Palestinian terrorism by military means'.[16] They describe the consequences further as follows:

> Thus the Palestinian Authority, already perceived as not being a potential partner to renew the political process, was, as of December 2001, defined as a supporter of terrorism which used its security organizations for terrorist missions. Even though at this very time Arafat ordered a cease-fire and also managed to begin implementing it in practice, the Israeli government placed no credence in his efforts and decided to dismantle the PA's security apparatuses.[17]

The escalation of the conflict was accompanied by the demonization of Yasser Arafat as a twin to Osama bin Laden. While not endorsing this view in so many words, the Bush Administration also placed the blame for the conflict on Arafat and in June 2002 President Bush called on Palestinians to replace Arafat as their leader by someone not compromised by an association with terrorism. The effect of this pronouncement was to scupper any prospect of negotiations on the roadmap or any other of the initiatives for the restarting the peace process while Arafat was alive. This left the Sharon government free to pursue its own course.

Military suppression of the intifada was the priority in the first years of Sharon's premiership. The violence reached a peak in 2002. The scale of violence fell in 2003 and dropped further in 2004. However, the threat (and reality) of further suicide bombings was by no means eliminated by Israeli military action. In May 2003 Sharon gave a speech in which he declared that occupation of Palestinian territories could not continue indefinitely. By the time of Arafat's death on 11 November 2004, the Sharon government was committed to unilateral withdrawal from Gaza. While Sharon's objective was that the withdrawal should strengthen Israel's hand in negotiations on the future of the West Bank, the commitment divided the Israeli right. Opponents of the withdrawal feared that it would create a precedent of the dismantlement of settlements on the West Bank, as the Gaza withdrawal entailed the evacuation of some 8,500 settlers who had established homes there. The consequence was a partial realignment of Israeli politics, with Sharon dependent on support from the Israeli left to implement his policy. The withdrawal from Gaza split Likud and ultimately persuaded Sharon to leave Likud and form his own party, further realigning Israeli politics, with unpredictable consequences for the revival of the peace process.

The controversy over the Gaza withdrawal overshadowed two other important developments, the election of Mahmoud Abbas (also known as Abu Mazen) as Palestinian President in succession to Arafat in January 2005 and the construction by the Israeli government of a security fence to separate the major centres of Palestinian population in the occupied territories and Israel. Even before Arafat's death, Abbas had expressed the opinion that the al-Aqsa intifada had been a mistake. In the same interview, Abbas also underlined his strong opposition to the offer that had been presented to the Palestinians at the Camp David summit in 2000.[18] Work on the construction of the security fence started in 2003. Its routing was highly controversial since it appeared to indicate the government's intention to incorporate parts of the West Bank on a permanent basis, as well as providing a further barrier to the movement of Palestinians within the occupied territories. Abbas's election has revived the prospect of substantive negotiations between the Israeli government and the Palestinian Authority. At the same time, there are hopes among European governments, including the British, that movement back towards a peace process may be facilitated by a re-elected Bush Administration less fixated on domestic electoral considerations. However, the wide gulf in the positions of the parties provides ample grounds for caution in predicting any early end to the conflict.

The breakdown of the Israeli–Palestinian peace process is a striking example of how a collapse of trust between parties engaged in such a process can lead to an explosion of violence on a scale even greater than that which existed prior to negotiations between the two sides. A campaign of violence, the ultimate objective of which is the initiation of a political process, may be conducted with greater restraint than are acts of violence which are conceived as retaliation for the other side's bad faith or which are directed towards forcing the other side to change its position. Further, violence that occurs in the context of the breakdown of a peace process is less likely to be conducted with a view to sustaining a campaign of violence over a long period. In the case of the breakdown of the Israeli–Palestinian peace process, two external factors played a significant role in the escalation of the conflict. Israel's withdrawal from Lebanon in May 2000 could be interpreted by Palestinians as further proof of the utility of the tactic of suicide bombings that had already been instrumental in the rapid withdrawal of French and American forces in the 1980s. At the same time, the events of 11 September and the ensuing war against terrorism encouraged the Israeli government to believe that in this atmosphere it had little reason to fear international condemnation of its use of extreme measures to suppress the intifada.

Notes

1 A striking example of a politician explicitly linking the issue of the Israeli–Palestinian conflict to the threat posed by al-Qaeda was a

statement made by Robin Cook in March 2004, in which he declared: 'We would have made more progress rolling back support for terrorism if we had brought peace to Palestine rather than war to Iraq'. Cook's opinion piece was reproduced on the front page of the *Independent* on 8 August 2005 following the politician's sudden death that month.

2 Akiva Eldar, 'Blair's responsibility', *HAARETZ.com*, 11 July 2005.

3 One of the bombers, Mohammed Sadi Khan, pre-recorded a video that was ultimately broadcast on 1 September 2005. He spoke in general terms about atrocities by Western governments against 'my people' as his motivation. Text of broadcast published on http://news. bbc.co.uk on 1 September 2005.

4 There are numerous histories of the conflict. See, for example, Mark A. Tessler, *A History of the Israeli–Palestinian Conflict*, Indiana University Press, Bloomington 1994.

5 Quoted in Leonard Stein, *The Balfour Declaration*, Valentine-Mitchell, London 1961, p. 548.

6 Ibid.

7 For an account of this first intifada, see Zachary Lockman and Joel Beinen, *Intifada: The Palestinian Uprising against Israeli Occupation*, I.B. Tauris, London 1990.

8 See, for example, Robert Malley and Hussein Agha, 'Camp David: The Tragedy of Errors', *New York Review of Books*, Vol. XLVIII, No. 13, 9 August 2001.

9 See 'The Taba Negotiations (January 2001)', *Journal of Palestine Studies*, Vol. XXXI, No. 3, Spring 2002.

10 Yaacov Bar-Siman-Tov, Ephraim Lavie, Kobi Michael and Daniel Bar-Tal, *The Israeli–Palestinian Violent Confrontation 2000–2004: From Conflict Resolution to Conflict Management*, The Jerusalem Institute for Israel Studies, Jerusalem 2005, p. 48.

11 The *Observer*, 13 October 2002.

12 James Bovard, *Terrorism and Tyranny: Trampling Freedom, Justice and Peace to Rid the World of Evil*, Palgrave Macmillan, Basingstoke 2003, p. 257.

13 Ibid.

14 See, for example, Ilan Peleg, 'Transforming Ethnic Orders to Pluralist Regimes: Theoretical, Comparative and Historical Analysis' in Adrian Guelke (ed.), *Democracy and Ethnic Conflict: Advancing Peace in Deeply Divided Societies*, Palgrave Macmillan, Basingstoke 2004, pp. 8–9.

15 See Jason Burke, *Al-Qaeda: The True Story of Radical Islam*, Penguin Books, London 2004, p. 248. Burke argues that the decision to attack America was made between the end of 1998 and late 1999.

16 Bar-Siman-Tov *et al.*, *The Israeli–Palestinian Violent Confrontation 2000–2004*, pp. 49–50.

17 Ibid., pp. 50–1.

18 The Middle East Media Research Institute (MEMRI), *Special Dispatch N.793*.

CHAPTER 7

Revenge and spill-over

Cinna, the Poet: I am not Cinna the conspirator.
Second Citizen: It is no matter, his name's Cinna; pluck but his
name out of his heart and turn him going.[1]

Revenge is a common motivation for violence. It is also a characteristic of revenge that those engaged in exacting revenge are not
especially particular about choice of targets, as the quotation from
Shakespeare's play, *Julius Caesar*, illustrates well. In the context of
violent conflicts, fear of 'tit for tat' killings is a realistic concern
since cycles of violence, in which revenge forms a significant motivating force for the perpetrators of violence, often arise in such
situations. In fact, it may come to loom larger than the original
causes of the conflict. A related fear is that violence will spill over
the boundaries of the conflict in the form of clandestine violence,
due in part to the operation of revenge, whether such violence is
carried out by sub-state groups or agents of a particular state. For
example, at the time of the Gulf War in 1991, that is, the war to
expel Iraq from Kuwait, there were such widespread fears that the
regime of Saddam Hussein would resort to terrorism outside
the arena of conflict that the profitability of airlines on the transatlantic route was affected by a fall in the number of American
passengers willing to travel to Europe during this period.

A theory canvassed at the time of the murder of a popular BBC
presenter, Jill Dando, in 1999 was that the perpetrator was a Serb

seeking revenge for Britain's involvement in the war over Kosovo. This proved not to be the case. Another instance in which it was long assumed that the motive was revenge was the downing of Pan Am flight 103 in Lockerbie in Scotland in 1988 in which 259 passengers and crew and 11 local people were killed. In this case, the assumption was that the placing of a bomb on the airliner was motivated by the desire of the authorities in Tehran for revenge over the shooting down of an Iranian passenger airliner over the Gulf by an American warship. However, the subsequent conviction of a Libyan agent in connection with Lockerbie failed to validate this theory, though it did not entirely dispel it. The clearest example of a terrorist atrocity motivated by revenge was the placing of a bomb on Air India flight 182 from Montreal to London in June 1985 killing 329 people. Though only one person was convicted for involvement in this atrocity, this established what had long been suspected. This was that the bomb had been placed on the airliner by Sikh militants seeking revenge for the Indian government's actions against Sikh separatists in Punjab, including the sending of troops into the Golden Temple in June 1984 where separatist militants had taken refuge. According to the official figures, 576 people died in the storming of the Golden Temple. This includes 83 troops. However, Patricia Gossman argues that the official figures underestimate the number of innocent bystanders killed in this episode.[2] A characteristic of revenge is that perpetrators of violence may feel less need to advertise their motive than where violence is being used to communicate a set of political demands. Further, because revenge is often seen as having less legitimacy than other motives, there tends to be less readiness to claim responsibility for such acts.

A complicating factor in the case of the current wave of transnational jihadist terrorism is that even when claims of responsibility have been made through the posting of information on an internet site, it has been hard to judge the authenticity of the claim and hence whether the motive ascribed to the act was actually shared by the perpetrators. For example, following the London bombings on 7 July 2005, information posted on an internet site claimed that the bombings had been carried out in retaliation for British military intervention in Iraq and Afghanistan, but while this was widely reported, it was not treated as a definitive explanation of the motives of those who carried out and planned the bombings. In the case of transnational terrorism in general, there tend to be more reservations in accepting the motives claimed for acts of violence, in part because of the difficulty in relating the often indiscriminate nature of the violence to specific motives. Consequently, there is frequently a reluctance to accept what is retrospectively claimed at face value.

The role that revenge plays in cycles of violence within societies engulfed in conflict is easier to chart than it is to identify in the violence of transnational networks such as al-Qaeda, though this is not to dismiss the significance of the factor of revenge in the case of jihadist violence and this will be explored further below. Both the Northern Ireland conflict and the Israeli–Palestinian conflict are replete with examples of 'tit for tat' violence, where particular actions are justified as a response to the violence of the other side. In the Israeli–Palestinian conflict, there have been a number of examples of suicide bombings being followed by targeted assassinations and also of the converse, targeted assassinations being followed by suicide bombings. Admittedly, the justifications advanced for action in response to the violence of the other side is not generally revenge as such, but more typically the claim is put forward that the other side must be made to pay a price for its violence or must be taught that it will gain no advantage from the use of violence. Alternatively, the response is justified on the basis of deterring the other side from carrying out any further such actions. In the case of Northern Ireland, the motive of revenge or retaliation has tended to be more explicit. However, recognition by paramilitaries that revenge provided a dubious justification for lethal violence commonly directed indiscriminately at the other community at large led them to carry out such acts in the names of fictitious organizations, such as the Protestant Reaction Force and the Catholic Reaction Force.

In discussing the propensity of deeply divided societies such as Northern Ireland to become trapped in cycles of violence, Frank Wright coined the expression 'representative violence' in a book published in 1987. He explained the context as follows:

> Very few people in Northern Ireland today would try to claim that the victims of violence are chosen because of their individual characteristics; they are attacked because they are identified as representing groups of people. The point is so obvious that few people dwell on it: it is treated as an 'aspect' of the situation rather than the core of it.[3]

But Wright pointed out that the implications of the existence of representative violence were far-reaching, notwithstanding the tendency in deeply divided societies to take it for granted.

> This condition of representative violence is very simple. If anyone of a great number of people can be 'punished' for something done by the community they come from, and if the communities are sufficiently clearly defined, there is a risk that anyone attacking a member of another community can set in motion an endless chain of violence. Even if few aspects of the representative violence enjoy widespread support of the kind that could be established by opinion polls, it is only necessary for people to *understand* what is happening for it to create a generalised danger. Everyone might be a target for reprisal for something done in their name and without their approval.[4]

The operation of the criminal justice system is supposed to prevent such cycles of violence from coming into existence by outlawing violence on a universal basis that does not permit the plea that the action in question was provoked by violence of the other side. But its effectiveness in doing so depends on whether it enjoys a wide measure of legitimacy, a condition difficult to achieve in a deeply divided society.

Representative violence may have a variety of motives though revenge is likely to play some part in the motivation of all representative violence. However, deterrence of future acts may be as important a motive as retaliation for past acts of the other side. Where revenge is present as a motive, on its own or in combination with other motives, the relative restraint that is commonly a feature of violence carried out without revenge either as a motive or a justification, is likely to be absent. Consequently, representative violence tends to be associated with particularly lethal acts of violence where the intention of the perpetrator has often been to cause many deaths. There is nevertheless a constraint on the operation of representative violence that distinguishes such cases from the transnational terrorism practised by al-Qaeda and its affiliates and imitators. This is that representative violence is generally confined within the arena of the conflict. Thus, in the case of the Northern Ireland conflict, despite some high profile acts of violence, some of which did cause large loss of life, by the Provisional IRA in England and by Loyalist paramilitaries in the Republic of Ireland, there was relatively little spill-over of the conflict outside of Northern Ireland as measured by the overall level of casualties. The same is also true of the Israeli–Palestinian conflict unless actions by al-Qaeda are included as an extension of the conflict. However, not merely are too few Palestinians involved in the network to justify such a characterization of their actions, but it would constitute far too narrow a view of al-Qaeda's perspective on world events. The conflict in Sri Lanka, though extremely lethal, is another case that has given rise to relatively little violence outside the island itself, apart from the assassination of Rajiv Gandhi in May 1991.

Nevertheless, the dimension of revenge does suggest a connection between the lethal nature of representative violence in intercommunal conflicts and that of transnational terrorism of the kind practised by al-Qaeda. This is the immediacy of the pay-off for such violence. Justification, motive and purpose are tied together in the case of revenge. This is perhaps especially relevant in the case of suicide missions or martyrdom operations, to use the language of the perpetrators. In the case of revenge such perpetrators may die knowing they have accomplished their objective, since the usual gap that exists between means and ends in an act of violence does not exist. Thus, the Sikh bodyguards who assassinated Indira Gandhi on 31 October 1984 and the Tamil Tiger suicide bomber who killed Rajiv Gandhi on 21 May 1991 died knowing that they had achieved their purpose if that was limited to exacting vengeance for acts of the Indian government led respectively by Indira Gandhi and her son, Rajiv. In these particular cases, further explanation hardly seems necessary since the separatists in the two conflicts had developed in their own eyes at least ample grounds for extreme antagonism towards the two Prime Ministers. Of course, it may reasonably be argued that while the immediate perpetrators had little reason to consider the further consequences of their actions, the organizations behind such actions must necessarily consider the longer term impact of a particular act of violence.

Placing the events of 11 September, Bali, Madrid and London in the framework of revenge therefore may be helpful in understanding why they occurred but it by no means provides a complete answer. Lawrence Freedman in a book published in 2002 grapples with the issue of what al-Qaeda sought to achieve in attacking the United States, from an instrumental perspective. His puzzlement at al-Qaeda's failure to calculate more adequately the likely consequences of their actions is evident. He describes al-Qaeda's objective as 'working towards the creation of a series of mighty theocratic states'[5] and compares their attack on America to violence directed at American interventions in Lebanon and Somalia that achieved their objective of securing American withdrawal.

> The mistake made by al-Qaeda, therefore, was to go for a spectacular attack that turned a war of choice into a war of necessity, so that instead of being encouraged to leave the Middle East and Central Asia, as would have been hoped, the United States became drawn into those regions more deeply than before. This was the opposite of what had been intended.[6]

Freedman is probably right in inferring that al-Qaeda's calculations about the likely consequences of the organization's actions would have been derived from examining responses to previous acts of violence. It is certainly a safer basis for analysing the intentions of bin Laden and his co-conspirators than calculating these from the actual consequences of their actions.

Admittedly, Freedman's method may underestimate their capacity to have anticipated the likely reaction of the United States. Thus, it would be fully in keeping with calculations that sub-state groups engaged in clandestine violence have made in the past if the leaders of al-Qaeda banked on a strong reaction to the assault on the United States. Just as in the 1970s the theorists and practitioners of urban guerrilla warfare in Latin America and New Left militants such as the Baader-Meinhof Group believed that they could provoke the authorities to reveal their true repressive face by their violence, al-Qaeda may have considered that the jihadist cause would benefit from the American interventions in Muslim countries which their action was likely to bring about. In particular, al-Qaeda may have hoped that the reaction of public opinion to American interventions in countries in which Muslims constituted a majority of the population would be so strong as to make the position of secular regimes, or those perceived as allied to the United States, untenable. Certainly, such assumptions would not have required any special foresight on the part of the leaders of al-Qaeda.

A further line of argument is suggested by another of Freedman's insights: 'In this war with the United States, this strand of Islamic militancy may not see many other options than terrorism.'[7] This is in line with the argument that al-Qaeda's assault against America took place against the background of the waning of the momentum behind the Islamist resurgence across the Muslim world. Elements on the fringe of movements facing decline may resort to extreme violence simply in the hope that it will upset existing trends in unpredictable ways that may work to their benefit. When added to the motive of revenge, this may have provided sufficient reason for the leaders of al-Qaeda simply to have taken the gamble that their cause would be advanced through a spectacular attack on America or a series of such attacks. In this context, Jason Burke's analysis of the nature of al-Qaeda is suggestive. He argues that in the aftermath of 9/11 Americans in both government and the media vastly overestimated the scope and size of the conspiracy arrayed against them. In particular, he emphasizes the role that events in Afghanistan in the second half of the 1990s played in enabling bin Laden to provide a focus for the activities of radical Islamists.

> This period, from 1996 to 2001, is when 'al-Qaeda' matured. Yet it was still far from the structured terrorist group envisaged by many commentators. Al-Qaeda at the time consisted of three elements: a hardcore, a network of co-opted groups and an ideology.[8]

According to Burke, the responsibility for planning the major attack on the United States lay with the hardcore, which consisted at the time of 9/11 of bin Laden and a dozen or so close associates backed by 'around a hundred highly motivated individuals from throughout the Islamic world'.[9] In short, the strategy of attacking America was adopted only by a very tiny group within the much larger realm of associated jihadists, few of whom would have considered such a strategy as relevant to the objectives they were pursuing in the many regional conflicts in which they were involved.

Indeed, a number of radical Islamists were sharply critical of bin Laden and al-Zawahiri for adopting what they saw as a highly counterproductive strategy. Bonney quotes one such critic, Montasser al-Zayyat, as follows: 'Islamists across the globe were adversely affected by the September 11 attacks on the United States. Even Islamic movements that did not target the United States are paying the price of this folly'.[10] Al-Zayyat considers as being among the costs of 9/11 the overthrow of the Taliban in Afghanistan, which he describes as a regime that had protected Islamists. Like Freedman, he contends that the al-Qaeda leaders miscalculated the response expecting it to be 'similar to the one engendered by the bombing of the two American embassies in Nairobi and Dar-es-Salaam'.[11] However, Burke takes a very different view of what bin Laden set out to achieve through the assault on America. Burke contends that bin Laden's aim was 'to radicalize and mobilize those Muslims who had hitherto shunned his summons to action' and he argues that this had been 'the critical problem for radical Islamic activists for three decades'.[12] According to Burke, the objective of bin Laden has been to establish that there is 'a cosmic battle between good and evil underway, and that Islam, and thus all that is good and righteous and just, is in desperate peril'.[13] Writing after Madrid, he gloomily concludes:

> If bin Laden's aim is to radicalize and mobilize, then one would surmise that the aim of those running the war on terror would be to counter those efforts. A swift survey of popular newspapers in the Islamic world (and beyond) or of Friday sermons in the Middle East's mosques or a few hours spent in a bazaar or a shouk or a coffee shop in Damascus, Kabul, Karachi, Cairo or Casablanca, or indeed in London or New York, shows clearly whose efforts are meeting with greater success. Bin Laden is winning.
>
> The world is a far more radicalized place now than it was before 11 September. Helped by a powerful surge of anti-Americanism, by Washington's incredible failure to stem the haemorrhaging of support and sympathy, and by modern communications, the language of bin Laden and his concept of the cosmic struggle has now spread among tens of millions of people, particularly the young and the angry, around the world. It informs their views and, increasingly, their actions.[14]

However, in this context, a distinction needs to be made between agreeing with bin Laden's view of the world and supporting his strategy for promoting it. Thus, it cannot be assumed that bin Laden's political influence will necessarily translate into attempts to emulate his strategy of violence. Thus, the absence hitherto of further attacks on America, as well as the relatively small number of failed attempts to attack America, may reflect not just the difficulty of carrying out such attacks in the wake of the events of 11 September, but also that relatively few radical Islamists have been persuaded of the value of attacks on the American mainland, even for the purpose of exacting revenge for the actions of the American government since 11 September. Of course, that is not to rule out the possibility of further attacks, not least because others may seek to imitate the spectacular impact of the events of 11 September as a means of promoting altogether different ideologies from the one that currently is perceived as the main threat to America and other technologically advanced and affluent societies. The small numbers of people engaged in conspiracies of clandestine violence make it virtually impossible to predict the future course of terrorism, since their actions need not be reflective of broader trends and, indeed, may run counter to these. For the same reason, there is little justification for the claim that major terrorist atrocities in the leading capital cities of the world are inevitable or for treating singular attacks, such as the attack on Madrid in 2004, as evidence for this proposition. In fact, the pattern of jihadist attacks since 9/11 has been too episodic even for it to be clear whether attacks outside of major arenas of conflict, such as Iraq and Afghanistan, are likely to peter out or escalate.

Bonney, himself, like Burke, argues that the objective behind the assault on America was to provoke action by the United States that would prove counter-productive. Thus Bonney claims that the aim of 9/11 was 'to ensure that the United States would adopt an inappropriate policy, an overreaction, which would alienate Muslim opinion deeply and possibly permanently' and he adds 'The mistaken policies adopted in the Afghanistan War of 2001 and the Second Gulf War of 2003 have achieved that objective'.[15] However, the credibility of Bonney's position is somewhat undermined by his analysis of the Madrid bombings. His interpretation of this atrocity is that 'For the first time since the 1930s, a terrorist mass murder has immediately achieved its main political objective.'[16] By this Bonney means that the bombings led to the election of a new government committed to the withdrawal of Spanish troops from Iraq, on the assumption that this was the bombers' objective. However, it seems likely that the planning of the attack on Madrid had taken place long before the date of the Spanish general election was even known. Further, it also seems improbable that the radical Islamists who perpetrated the atrocity were much concerned with Spanish domestic politics.

In fact, had they been attuned to the likely impact of their actions on Spanish opinion, they would have been unlikely to have carried out the atrocity at such a time. The bombings themselves did not cause the Popular Party to lose the election. It was the attempt of the Popular Party to exploit the bombings for electoral purposes by blaming ETA that produced the backlash that ousted the Popular Party from power, when the evidence emerged before polling began that it had been perpetrated by jihadists. It would have been entirely impossible for anyone with even the most sophisticated appreciation of Spanish domestic politics to have anticipated this course of events. Thus, if the bombings had been handled differently by the Popular Party, it is a reasonable assumption that the government would have been re-elected as people rallied to the incumbents in the midst of a crisis. Arguing that the intention of the perpetrators was to bring about a change in the government in Spain and thus Spanish withdrawal from Iraq is to derive the motives of their actions from consequences they could never have predicted.

Understandably, after the event, radical Islamists were ready to lend credence to the arguments of conservative political commentators who described what had happened as a victory for terrorism, since it gave meaning and even a measure of legitimacy in some eyes to the bombings. Similarly, it cannot be inferred from the fact that bin Laden released a video message just ahead of the American Presidential election in 2004, that he intended to contribute to President Bush's subsequent narrow re-election. The opposite is just about conceivable, i.e. that bin Laden believed, wrongly, that his intervention would influence the outcome against the incumbent, on the basis of what happened in Spain and how that was interpreted in the media. It is also possible (and perhaps more likely) that bin Laden was indifferent to the outcome of the election, but aware that the timing of the statement just ahead of the election would maximize the coverage and attention his words received in the media.

While there have been a considerable number of lethal attacks by jihadists round the world since 11 September, none of these attacks has been on the same scale of lethality as the destruction of the twin towers in New York. Further, most of the attacks have taken place in countries where Muslims constitute a majority of the population. The most prominent cases of attacks outside the Muslim world since 11 September have been the train bombings in Madrid in March 2004 and the underground and bus bombings in London in July 2005. To these cases it is possible to add the attack on the Indian parliament in New Delhi in December 2001 and the simultaneous attacks on shoppers in the Indian capital in October 2005 that killed 61 people, as well as major atrocities in Russia. The worst of these was the school siege in Beslan, North Ossetia, in September 2004 in which 331 people died, over half of them schoolchildren. In the previous month two passenger jets on domestic routes within Russia were downed as a result of bombs smuggled on board the flights in which 89 passengers and crew were killed. One further case deserves to be mentioned, the placing of a bomb on a ferry in the Philippines which killed 116 people in February 2004. However, these attacks need to be seen in the context of ongoing conflicts within the boundaries of India, Russia and the Philippines. In short, they have more in common with the IRA bomb attacks in Birmingham and London during Northern Ireland's troubles than with the assault on America, even though the perpetrators in the case of the attacks in the three countries could be described as jihadists. However, it is unlikely that the perpetrators in these cases saw their actions as forming part of a global jihad, even if they saw similarities between their own struggles for self-determination and other situations of violent conflict involving Muslims.

Some attacks have also taken place in large countries where the majority of the population is not Muslim but in which Muslims form a majority of the population in the region affected. An example is the ongoing violence in the Indian state of Jammu and Kashmir. Admittedly, some of the most serious attacks within Muslim countries or regions have targeted foreigners, such as the attacks in Saudi Arabia on compounds housing foreigners in 2003, the attacks on the British embassy and a British bank in Istanbul in the same year, and an attack on the Australian embassy in Jakarta in September 2004, to mention just a few. The Bali bombing of October 2002 remains the deadliest example of such attacks. Different interpretations of such acts are possible. They may be viewed as part of al-Qaeda's global jihad to put alongside the events of 11 September. Alternatively, they may simply be seen as belonging among the most common form of spill-over, the tendency of combatants in a conflict zone to direct their violence against anyone they perceive as an enemy within the area in which they operate or even simply as allied directly or indirectly to the government they oppose. Such violence is by no means new and in a number of cases long pre-dates the formation of al-Qaeda.

Where tourism makes a significant contribution to a country's economy, the motivation for attacking tourists may be to damage the economy in the belief that the government's grip on the society will be loosened in such circumstances. Attacks on foreigners making some other contribution to the economy may be similarly motivated. That is, the objective may be to damage the economy by targeting the country's dependence on foreign expertise so as to undermine the government. While such acts may be as horrific as those committed as a part of a global jihad and just as ineffective in advancing the aims of their perpetrators, their basis is entirely independent of the strategy initiated by bin Laden and his close associates or what Burke calls the al-Qaeda hardcore. Because of the events of 11 September, many of the major acts of terrorist violence across the world that have occurred since then have tended to be attributed to al-Qaeda, though in fact they may have little to do with al-Qaeda, even in the loosest sense that Burke uses the term of an idea or ideology inspiring radical Islamists. In some cases, such as the attacks in Saudi Arabia, bin Laden's political influence probably does explain the upsurge in attacks on foreigners, but there is an obvious danger of overstating his influence and attributing all radical Islamist violence to a single source. At the same time, the highly lethal and indiscriminate nature of a number of the attacks may reflect the influence of al-Qaeda's example.

So far in this chapter's consideration of the issue of spill-over, the impact of regional wars or conflicts on terrorism outside the area in which the war or conflict has been taking place has been examined. Spill-over from a conflict zone most commonly occurs within the confines of large countries such as India and Russia. Next in frequency comes spill-over within particular regions, with spill-over to another continent very rarely occurring. For example, there has been virtually no spill-over outside of Africa of the conflicts in the Democratic Republic of the Congo, notwith-standing the fact that millions have died within the Congo itself. Thus, it is evident that fears which exist of spill-over from violent conflicts in other parts of the world have generally not been borne out in practice. Of course, it is possible to argue that in the absence of these violent conflicts, there would be virtually no terrorism at all in politically stable liberal-democracies. To that extent, a case can be made that conflicts, such as the Israeli–Palestinian conflict that has been a factor in support for al-Qaeda as a transnational terrorist network, belong among the causes of terrorism that need to be addressed.

Clearly, the much larger problem for the world is that of terrorism spilling over into regional conflicts and/or wars, with the worst case scenario of terrorism triggering a war with global significance. The obvious example in this context is the triggering of the First World War by the assassination of Archduke Francis Ferdinand in Sarajevo on 28 June 1914. The pretext for Israel's invasion of Lebanon in 1982, which Israeli critics of the inter-vention labelled Israel's first war of choice, was the attempted assassination of the Israeli ambassador in London on 3 June 1982.

However, it was simply a pretext rather the actual reason for Israel's invasion and in any event the intervention did not threaten to cause conflict between the superpowers. The closest an act of terrorism has come to triggering a major war in more recent times was the attack on the Indian parliament in December 2001, which came close to causing a war between India and Pakistan in 2002. This case merits examination in greater depth because of the wider consequences that a war between the two countries might have globally, in view of the fact that both India and Pakistan possess nuclear weapons. Another reason it merits attention is that the position of Kashmir, which was both the source of the crisis of 2002 and a cause of wars in the past between the two countries, remains unresolved, with Kashmir itself in the grip of violent conflict. What is more, jihadists, some of them connected to the al-Qaeda network, have played, and continue to play, a significant role in this conflict.

The roots of the present conflict in Kashmir lie in the complex political structure of British India and the circumstances of British withdrawal from empire. Britain did not govern India as a single political entity. Large parts of the sub-continent reflected the British preference for the co-option of indigenous rulers as a way both of extending its control and of enhancing the legitimacy of the empire when the area was annexed. Jammu and Kashmir was simply the largest of a very considerable number of princely states in British India, in which a local ruler had a free hand to rule as he pleased, subject to sufficient British supervision to ensure that the ruler did not act contrary to British interests across the sub-continent as a whole. The princely state of Jammu and Kashmir was the product of an alliance during the nineteenth century between a local strongman, who was rewarded by the British for his assistance during the First Afghan War of 1839–42 and for his neutrality during the First Anglo-Sikh War of 1845–6, though formally a vassal of the Sikhs. Both Gulab Singh and his son, Ranbir Singh, gave further support to the British during the Second Anglo-Sikh War of 1848, the Indian mutiny of 1857 and the Second Afghan War of 1878–80.

A consequence of the complex structure of British India was that the political reforms introduced by the British government in the first decade of the twentieth century under pressure from the Indian National Congress, which had been formed in 1885, did not apply to the princely states. Separately from both Congress and the Muslim League, formed in 1906, there was a campaign within Jammu and Kashmir by a locally based movement, known from 1939 as the National Conference, for democracy within the princely state and directed against the Maharaja of Jammu and Kashmir, Hari Singh. But while the National Conference was uniting Muslims, Hindus and Sikhs in its campaign within the princely state, the gulf between the Indian National Congress and the Muslim League over the question of the future of the sub-continent was growing wider. In 1940 the Muslim League adopted its Pakistan resolution calling for independence from the rest of the sub-continent for areas with Muslim majorities in the north-west and east of British India. The term, Pakistan, was a play on words, meaning land of the pure but also coined from the first letters of the areas targeted for inclusion in a new Muslim state. In this context, the K stood for Kashmir.

In 1946 the British government decided in principle that British India should be divided into two states. When Mountbatten became the Viceroy in March 1947, his brief was to move the sub-continent swiftly towards independence. A plan for the partition was published in June, with 15 August 1947 set as the date for the independence of the two states. The rulers of the princely states were given the option of deciding between joining India or Pakistan. However, the simple principle of contiguity dictated the choice of almost all of the princely states. Under the India Independence Act, none of the princely states was given the option of independence from either state. Jammu and Kashmir abutted both the proposed states of India and Pakistan. Its ruler was Hindu but the population of the state was predominantly Muslim. The Maharaja, Hari Singh, temporized and, it seems, he harboured hopes of sustaining the independence of his state contrary to British policy. At the moment when the two new states of India and Pakistan were proclaimed, Jammu and Kashmir's fate had still not been determined. It was, by default, independent, a situation that was to last for 73 days.

The events that followed are the subject of much dispute and controversy since they have a bearing on the legitimacy of current political structures in the area. The issue that sparked the conflict was unrest in the Poonch region of the princely state over taxes. It led to a rebellion by the predominantly Muslim population of the region and this in turn attracted support from Pashtuns in the North-West Frontier region of Pakistan, in part in reaction to violent events elsewhere, especially the inter-communal violence taking place in Punjab. The rebels were also joined by units of Pakistan's new army. Faced with the imminent fall of Srinagar, the state's summer capital, the Maharaja fled to his winter capital, Jammu, and appealed for support from India, on the basis that the state would accede to India. The fraught nature of these events was described by the Indian emissary, V.P. Menon, who secured the Maharaja's signature to a Treaty of Accession on 26 October 1947.

> The Maharaja had left instructions with his ADC that if I came back from Delhi, he was not to be disturbed as it would mean that the Government of India had decided to come to his rescue and he should therefore be allowed to sleep in peace; but if I failed to return, it meant everything was lost and, in that case, his ADC was to shoot him in his sleep.[17]

Indian intervention followed but, by prompting further intervention by Pakistan, failed to end the fighting. At the beginning of 1948 India took its dispute with Pakistan over the status of Jammu and Kashmir to the United Nations, which established a commission to investigate the situation on the ground. A resolution of the Security Council followed that called on Pakistan to withdraw its forces from the state. It also called on India to reduce its forces in the state to a minimum and declared that a plebiscite should be held on the question of the state's accession to either

India or Pakistan. However, the fighting continued, ending only in January 1949 with a ceasefire. The ceasefire line between the two sides partitioned the princely state. It placed the western third of the state under Pakistan's control. The northern part of this territory was absorbed into Pakistan while the southern part was constituted as Azad Kashmir (or Free Kashmir) with a measure of autonomy.

On the Indian side of the new border, Nehru had installed his old ally and leader of the National Conference, Sheikh Abdullah, as Prime Minister of what was now the Indian state of Jammu and Kashmir. It had not been India's intention by intervening to prop up the rule of the Maharaja and in 1949 Hari Singh was forced into exile. Initially, the strong support that existed within the Kashmir Valley for Abdullah helped to secure India's control of the only state in its union in which Muslims formed a large majority of the population. However, Nehru fell out with Abdullah over the issue of the state's autonomy. In 1953 Abdullah was arrested and accused of plotting independence. Internationally, Pakistan continued to contest the legitimacy of Indian rule in any part of Jammu and Kashmir on the basis that India had failed to fulfil its obligation to hold the plebiscite for which the Security Council had called. However, within the state of Jammu and Kashmir itself, Pakistan's stance appeared to have relatively little impact. Admittedly, the internationalized nature of the problem did mean that the Indian government had an interest in being able to present to the world locally elected leaders who enjoyed a measure of credibility. But in so far as such leaders sought to maintain their legitimacy by representing their constituents' desire for greater autonomy, they tended ultimately to clash with the centre. When that happened, the centre proved adept at exploiting local rivalries to reassert its control, but this manoeuvring over time was to erode the Indian government's legitimacy.

War between India and Pakistan in 1965 during which Pakistan infiltrated forces across the 1949 ceasefire line in Jammu and Kashmir failed to prompt a revolt against Indian rule within the state. Further war between India and Pakistan in 1971 also seemed to leave the population under Indian rule in Jammu and Kashmir largely unmoved. In negotiations between India and Pakistan in 1972 the two governments agreed to the designation of the old ceasefire line between them, slightly modified as a result of the 1971 war, as the line of control, a small step towards the recognition of the permanence of the division. A factor that had facilitated this acceptance from the outset had been that this border broadly coincided with pre-existing ethnic and linguistic divisions. However, Indian expectations that a final settlement of the dispute would follow were disappointed, though the source of the challenge to India's position was internal rather than external. The Indian government's manipulation of politics in the state finally rebounded on the centre in the late 1980s. The rigging of elections in 1987 prompted first protests and then a full-scale uprising in 1989 in the Kashmir Valley, the overwhelmingly Muslim heart of the state containing over half of Jammu and Kashmir's population of approximately 10 million. Since then more than 60,000 people have died in political violence in the state.

The insurgents comprised a wide variety of groups with diverse aims, though united in their hostility towards the Indian central government. In the first phase of the conflict to the mid-1990s, separatists in the Jammu and Kashmir Liberation Front (JKLF), whose aim was a state independent of both Pakistan and India within the boundaries of the old princely state, dominated the insurrection. The suppression of the separatists was followed by a new phase of Pakistani involvement in the conflict. In May 1999, India launched air-strikes against forces that had crossed the border with Pakistan and 'liberated' a remote mountainous area of Kargil in Ladakh, the most sparsely populated region of the Indian state of Jammu and Kashmir. India insisted that the incursion constituted straightforward aggression carried out under the direction of Pakistan's armed forces, while Pakistan claimed that the incursion had been carried out by freedom fighters. In fact, the invaders consisted of a mix of regular army units and jihadist volunteers. International concern centred on the fact that both India and Pakistan had conducted nuclear weapons tests in 1998. It was not coincidental that the incursion followed hard on the heels of Western intervention in Kosovo. The hope of the invaders was that their action would internationalize the conflict and prompt comparison between India's position in Kashmir and Serbian rule in Kosovo. Under enormous pressure from the Clinton Administration, the elected Prime Minister of Pakistan, Nawaz Sharif, ordered the withdrawal of the invading force. Sharif paid dearly for this retreat. In October 1999 his government was overthrown in a military coup led by General Pervez Musharraf, at least in part motivated by the army's humiliation over its Kargil adventure.

Nevertheless, by July 2001, there were the beginnings of a peace process between India and Pakistan with a summit between Musharraf and the Indian Prime Minister, Atal Behari Vajpayee, at Agra in India. However, the context changed rapidly, with first the events of 11 September in the United States and then much more seriously for India, an attack on the Indian parliament in New Delhi on 13 December 2001. A total of 14 people died in this episode, including the five jihadists who carried out the attack. The assailants themselves came from Pakistan but had received assistance from others from the Kashmir Valley, so the connection to the Kashmir conflict was evident. Increasingly jihadists belonging to a variety of different groups have come to dominate the conflict within the state of Jammu and Kashmir itself. The violence unquestionably has a cross-border dimension, though foreigners, including all Pakistanis in this category, constitute a minority of the insurgents. In response to the attack on the parliament, India mobilized for war, putting 700,000 troops on its border with Pakistan. Concerted diplomacy by the United States, restraining India on the one hand and putting pressure on Pakistan on the other to act against jihadists and to close down camps being used to train volunteers for the liberation of Kashmir staved off war. As the United Nations Secretary-General noted in September 2002, this was the closest the world had come to war between two nuclear weapons states for many years.

The first steps in a fresh peace process between India and Pakistan in 2005, underlined by the establishment of a bus service between Srinagar and Muzaffarabad in Azad Kashmir, has eased tensions between the two countries somewhat, but the threat that the continuing violence in the state of Jammu and Kashmir will spill over into wider conflict has by no means disappeared. If India's political initiatives, including both the efforts to improve relations with Pakistan and those to enhance the standing of the Jammu and Kashmir state government, fail, there is a danger that India will seek to justify a policy that relies on repression by connecting the conflict to America's war against terrorism. In the light of the role played by jihadists in the current phase of the insurgency, such a case would not be difficult to make. As it is, a premise of the current peace process, from the Indian perspective, is that General Musharraf himself has good reason to cooperate with India because of the threat that the jihadists pose to his government, especially in the light of his cooperation with the United States in the war against terrorism since 9/11. In short, recognition of the extent of alienation from Indian rule and the need to address that alienation, particularly but not solely in the Kashmir Valley, are not perhaps as central to the peace process as they should be. At the same time, a lessening of cross-border tensions may help to create a context in which the Indian government is more willing to recognize the role that its own security measures have played in fuelling the conflict. A major earthquake centred on the Pakistani part of Kashmir took place on 8 October 2005, adding to the region's misery. But the impact of this humanitarian emergency in which some 80,000 people died has had a limited effect on either transforming the conflict in the region or accelerating the peace process between India and Pakistan. However, the dialogue established between the two governments was instrumental in preventing the major bomb attacks on Delhi at the end of October 2005 from creating a fresh crisis in their relations.[18]

There are other conflicts besides the Kashmir problem that have the potential to spill over into inter-state war. The conflict in Colombia has caused tensions with that country's neighbours in Latin America that could conceivably result in war and in a number of the conflicts in Central Asia involving former republics of the Soviet Union, the possibility of spill-over is also strong. Further, it remains a danger in the Balkans. Of course, it may be objected that the level of violence in these conflicts exceeds or has exceeded that associated with terrorism and that the situation in a number of these cases is more aptly described as one of low intensity civil war. However, it is a moot point, as where such outrageous methods as suicide bombings and the taking of hostages are employed by insurgents, governments have some justification for using the label of terrorism to describe their actions. At the same time, these are, for the most part, conflicts that are not susceptible to resolution by the employment of security measures alone. Since the events of 11 September, the temptation for affected states has been to invoke the war against terrorism as a suitable template for combating violence that in fact has little or no relation to bin Laden's global jihad. The next chapter examines another dimension of the events of 11 September: the question of whether it represents part of a trend towards increasing lethality in acts of terrorism.

Notes

1 From Act III, Scene III of *Julius Caesar*. W.J. Craig, *The Complete Works of William Shakespeare*, Oxford University Press, London 1943, p. 836.
2 Patricia Gossman, 'India's secret armies' in Bruce B. Campbell and Arthur D. Brenner (eds), *Death Squads in Global Perspective: Murder with Deniability*, Palgrave Macmillan, Basingstoke 2000, p. 283.
3 Frank Wright, *Northern Ireland: A Comparative Analysis*, Gill and Macmillan, Dublin 1987, p. 11.
4 Ibid., pp. 11–2.
5 Lawrence Freedman, *Superterrorism: Policy Responses*, Blackwell, Oxford 2002, p. 42.
6 Ibid., p. 54.
7 Ibid., p. 53.
8 Jason Burke, *Al-Qaeda: The True Story of Radical Islam*, Penguin Books, London 2004, p. 8.

 9 Ibid., p. 9.
10 Quoted in Richard Bonney, *Jihad: From Qur'an to bin Laden*, Palgrave Macmillan, Basingstoke 2004, p. 361.
11 Ibid.
12 Burke, *Al-Qaeda*, p. 273.
13 Ibid.
14 Ibid., p. 274.
15 Bonney, *Jihad*, p. 378.
16 Ibid., p. 379.
17 Quoted in Victoria Schofield, *Kashmir in Conflict: India, Pakistan and the Unfinished War*, I.B. Tauris, London 2000, p. 54.
18 See Justin Huggler, 'India blames Delhi bombings on group linked to Kashmir', the *Independent*, 31 October 2005.

CHAPTER 8

A logic of escalation?

A common assumption in the literature on terrorism in the 1970s and 1980s was that the primary aim of terrorists, in so far as any generalizations could be made about the objectives of the diverse groups that resorted to such violence, was to achieve publicity for the cause they sought to advance and that the horrific nature of some of the atrocities they perpetrated were directed in the final analysis to securing maximum media coverage, not the maximum loss of life such groups could inflict. In particular, the deaths of innocent bystanders were seen as incidental to the purpose of the action rather like the collateral damage caused by conventional military action. While a readiness to take lives was regarded as a mark of the callousness of terrorist organizations, there was recognition that the taking of lives was, generally speaking, not the purpose of their actions. That was reflected in the fact that the annual number of deaths from all forms of international terrorism during this period remained below a thousand, even in years when terrorist organizations were at their most active. It was further reflected in the fact that the number of terrorist incidents usually outnumbered the number of deaths in any year. Appreciation of this reality was encapsulated in the widely quoted formulation that what terrorists wanted was few dead but millions watching.

This view started to be challenged long before the events of 11 September. A notable contribution to this debate was a chapter on 'Future Trends in International Terrorism' by Brian Jenkins in an edited collection on contemporary perspectives on terrorism published in 1988.[1] It was a significant piece not least because hitherto Brian Jenkins had been closely associated with the argument that causing mass casualties simply did not serve the interests of the sub-state groups engaged in terrorism. In that chapter Jenkins first reiterated that, generally, terrorists 'do not attempt to kill many, as long as killing a few suffices for their purpose' He continued:

> Arbitrarily taking 100 deaths as the criterion, only a handful of incidents on this scale have occurred since the beginning of the century. Lowering the criterion to fifty deaths produces a dozen or more additional incidents. This in itself suggests that it is either very difficult to kill large numbers of persons, or it is very rarely tried.[2]

He then changed tack:

> Unfortunately, as we have seen in recent years, things are changing. Terrorist activity over the past twenty years has escalated in volume *and* in bloodshed. At the beginning of the 1970s, terrorists concentrated their attacks on property. In the 1980s, terrorists increasingly directed their attacks against people – the soft target. The number of incidents with fatalities, and multiple fatalities, has increased. A more alarming trend in the 1980s has been the growing number of incidents of large-scale indiscriminate violence: huge car-bombs detonated on city streets, bombs planted aboard trains and airliners, in airline terminals, railroad stations, and hotel lobbies, all calculated to kill in quantity.[3]

Jenkins offered a number of explanations for the trend towards more lethal attacks. Brutalization as a result of long involvement in conflict was one explanation he gave on the basis that killing became progressively easier for the perpetrators. Another explanation was the public's gradual desensitization to terrorism as a result of which terrorists had to increase their level of violence to achieve the same measure of publicity. His next explanation was that terrorists were becoming technically more proficient and that was increasing their capacity to inflict higher casualties. He argued further that there was a tendency for more ruthless elements to displace those who had a more discriminating attitude to the use of violence. Jenkins also claimed that the increasingly religious dimension of terrorism was a factor in the escalation of killings as 'throughout history, the presumed approval of God for the killing of pagans, heathens, or infidels permits great acts of destruction and self-destruction'.[4] Last, he identified state sponsorship of terrorism as contributing to terrorist resources and know-how that also enhanced the terrorists' capacity for lethal violence.

However, Jenkins also identified a number of factors that he thought would tend to limit the escalation of terrorist violence. This included the likelihood that more stringent security measures would be introduced. Thus, he envisaged tighter security being introduced in airports if there were further episodes of bombs being placed on passenger airliners, as had happened in the case of Air India flight 182 in 1985. Jenkins also suggested that there were technical ceilings to the number of people terrorists could kill in a single incident unless they had recourse to more exotic weapons than they had hitherto had access to. Later in the chapter he considered this possibility in greater depth. However, on the basis of past experience he argued that the numbers killed in the deadliest terrorist atrocities would be likely to remain roughly on a par with the numbers killed in the worst accidents. He concluded: 'On balance, it appears that incidents involving large numbers of fatalities will probably become more common, with deaths in the hundreds remaining for the foreseeable future the outer limit of individual terrorist attacks'.[5]

With the single exception of the attack on the twin towers of the World Trade Centre on 11 September, all terrorist attacks since then have been within the parameters suggested by Jenkins and none has begun to approach the higher level of deaths associated with natural disasters such as major earthquakes and the like.

A method used by a number of terrorist groups to magnify the impact of attacks has been the carrying out of simultaneous attacks on a number of targets. But again with the sole exception of the events of 11 September, even the sum of such attacks has not raised the number of deaths above the level suggested by Jenkins. How far 9/11 deviated from the norm is worth emphasizing. More people died in that one day than had been killed in total in the previous decade of international terrorism. Admittedly, the statistics on international terrorism exclude those killed in domestic political violence of all kinds, including bomb attacks that would normally count as acts of terrorism. At the same time, the pattern of terrorism, both domestic and international, since 11 September has largely followed that foreseen by Jenkins of a substantial increase in the numbers killed in each episode, while the actual number of incidents has fallen rather than risen.

In considering the use of nuclear, chemical or biological weapons by terrorists, Jenkins argued that in the case of chemical and biological weapons, the most plausible scenarios were their deployment within a confined space such as a hotel, which might involve deaths in the hundreds. In other words, their use would not substantially enhance the number of casualties terrorists were capable of inflicting by using conventional explosive devices. In the case of nuclear weapons, he argued that it was unlikely that terrorists would succeed in deploying a nuclear bomb either to threaten to kill or actually to kill very large numbers of people. But he acknowledged that they might prove capable of what he called 'lesser terrorist acts in the nuclear domain' such as 'the seizure or attempted seizure of a nuclear reactor' or 'the dispersal of radioactive material'.[6] Jenkins contended that the obstacles to terrorists' using weapons of mass destruction were not simply technical, significant though these were for any small group seeking to operate clandestinely.

There are political considerations as well: terrorists fear alienating their perceived constituents. They fear provoking public revulsion. They fear unleashing government crackdowns that their groups might not survive. Certainly, in the face of a nuclear threat, any rules that now limit the police authorities in most democracies would change.

Terrorists must maintain group cohesion. Attitudes toward violence vary not just from group to group but also within a group. Inevitably there would be disagreement over mass murder, which could expose the operation and the group itself to betrayal.[7]

Jenkins ended his chapter by characterizing his stance on the future of terrorism as 'a depressing but conservative view of future trends'.[8]

However, events in the 1990s made it seem that Jenkins's view had been an overly optimistic one. Far more alarmist perspectives on the future of terrorism gained ground largely as a result of what was dubbed the new terrorism. The context in which a novel threat to the world was perceived as arising that warranted a new concept is well described by John Gearson.

In March 1995, six years before the terrible events of 11 September, another shocking event occurred. In an attack on the Tokyo underground using sarin gas, the Japanese cult Aum Shinrikyo killed 12 people and affected 5,000, and the way in which terrorism was understood changed for ever. For the first time, an independent substate group, acting without state patronage or protection, had managed to produce and deploy biochemical weapons on a significant scale. A crucial technological threshold appeared to have been crossed.[9]

Alarm at the nature of the attack that had been perpetrated by an obscure religious cult was compounded by a more general concern at the rise of religiously inspired terrorist groups. There was a tendency to assume that Aum Shinrikyo's actions were also an indication of what other religiously based groups might be capable of. For example, Rex Hudson wrote the following in a 1999 study for the Federal Research Department in the United States.

When the conventional terrorist groups and individuals of the early 1970s are compared with terrorists of the early 1990s, a trend can be seen: the emergence of religious fundamentalist and new religious groups espousing the rhetoric of mass-destruction terrorism. In the 1990s, groups motivated by religious imperatives, such as Aum Shinrikyo, Hizbullah, and al-Qaida, have grown and proliferated. These groups have a different attitude toward violence – one that is extranormative and seeks to maximize violence against the perceived enemy, essentially anyone who is not a fundamentalist Muslim or an Aum Shinrikyo member. Their outlook is one that divides the world simplistically into 'them' and 'us'. With its sarin attack on the Tokyo subway system on March 20, 1995, the doomsday cult Aum Shinrikyo turned the prediction of terrorists using WMD into reality.[10]

In fact, there was little reason to connect these three very different groups, apart from the significant role that religion played in each. However, the nature of the religious beliefs that provided the worldview of members of Aum Shinrikyo was entirely different from the fundamentalist versions of Islam espoused by Hezbollah and al-Qaeda. For that matter, Hezbollah, which was drawn from the Lebanese Shi'ite Muslim community and operated almost exclusively inside Lebanon, and al-Qaeda with its Sunni Muslim orientation, transnational membership and global ambitions were also dissimilar in many respects.

A brief description of Aum Shinrikyo will serve to underline the point that it owed little to the general trends in terrorism in the 1990s, so far as generalization is possible about the diverse universe of organizations engaging in terrorism in the last decade of the twentieth century. Aum Shinrikyo was an apocalyptic cult formed in 1987 by a charismatic former yoga teacher known to his followers as Shoko Asahara. He regarded himself as the Messiah and predicted that the world would soon be engulfed in a cataclysmic war. This provided the ideological context in which he advocated developing the cult's capacity for violence. In practice, the cult's use of violence arose from Asahara's paranoid attitude towards the outside world and his belief that the development of its capacity for violence would assist the cult to fend off intervention by the Japanese authorities. The cult attracted a mass transnational membership of perhaps as many as 40,000 at its peak, mostly in Russia and Japan. However, only the inner core of the organization played any part in the cult's violence.[11]

Asahara made a point of recruiting scientists and technicians for the purpose of acquiring biological and chemical weapons. To begin with, the focus was on the production of biological weapons. These efforts began in 1990 and were initially largely unsuccessful, but ultimately the cult produced quantities of both anthrax and botulinum toxin. In 1993 the cult turned its attention to the production of chemical agents. Its laboratories produced experimental quantities of sarin, tabun, soman and VX. According to the police, VX was used by the cult in a number of attempted assassinations, but the main effort of the cult was directed towards producing huge quantities of sarin. Prior to the attack on the Tokyo subway, members of the cult made repeated attempts to cause casualties using anthrax and botulinum toxin in Tokyo and its environs. None succeeded.

However, a chemical attack by the cult using sarin caused seven deaths and 144 injuries in the town of Matsumoto in June 1994. Among the injured were three judges the cult was targeting to disrupt a court case involving the cult. A VX attack in Osaka killed an office worker in December 1994. In part, the Tokyo subway attack was intended as a response to the police investigations into the cult that followed these earlier lethal attacks. The attack on the Tokyo subway received extensive worldwide publicity and prompted vigorous action by the authorities in a number of countries against the cult and its members. Members of the cult in Japan responded by attempting to cause further havoc in Tokyo by releasing hydrogen cyanide on the subway in May and July 1995. However, these attacks were largely ineffective. Fundamentally, the actions taken by the authorities in the wake of the sarin attack in Tokyo put an end to the violent activities of the cult as a result of the seizure of equipment to produce the dangerous chemical and biological agents, as well as of the cult's stockpiles of the agents themselves. Legal proceedings against the cult culminated in 2004 in the conviction of its leader on multiple charges of murder.

Writers on the new terrorism made much of the novelty of Aum Shinrikyo's use of chemical and biological weapons on the assumption that its actions created a precedent for the use of these methods by other terrorist groups. The further assumption was then made that because the chemical and biological agents manufactured by the cult were the same as those that states might use in weapons of mass destruction, this was tantamount to terrorists' acquiring weapons of mass destruction, with the frightening implication that a single terrorist attack might cause many thousands of casualties. Lending verisimilitude to this proposition was the fact that thousands of people received cursory medical attention as a result of the sarin attack on the Tokyo subway, though in fact the overwhelming majority of these commuters were physically unaffected by the attack.

The role of imitation in human affairs is such that it would be foolish to rule out the possibility that others will seek to emulate the methods employed by Aum Shinrikyo. Indeed, it is conceivable that the cult's actions provided the inspiration for whoever perpetrated the anthrax attacks in the United States in October 2001. Five people died as a result of these attacks. However, the limits of the precedent set by Aum Shinrikyo should be noted. The cult's attacks did not cause larger numbers of deaths than might have been achieved in the same circumstances by the use of conventional explosive devices. Thus, for any organization seeking to enhance the number of deaths it was able to inflict in a single attack, the cult's methods did not present a way of overcoming the limits on their lethality. Admittedly, the fear caused by the use of biological and chemical agents, the psychological impact of the attacks and the publicity the cult's attack on the Tokyo subway received could give others the incentive to copy what the cult did.

However, the influence of Aum Shinrikyo in the realm of terrorism should not be exaggerated. The cult was very far from being a conventional terrorist organization. In particular, it was not a sub-state group seeking to achieve political objectives through a campaign of violence. Indeed, its methods were singularly ill-suited to the pursuit of a sustained campaign of violence as the closing down of the cult's activities in the wake of the sarin attack in Tokyo underscored. Aum Shinrikyo is best compared not with other terrorist groups pursuing social and political objectives, but with other cults that have attracted members on the basis of predictions of the imminent coming of the apocalypse. The story of Aum Shinrikyo most closely resembles that of two other cults that met violent ends, the Branch Davidians and the People's Temple. The Branch Davidians were roughly contemporaneous with Aum Shinrikyo. Like Aum Shinrikyo, they were centred on a charismatic figure, in their case, David Koresh.

The cult's compound in Waco, Texas, was stormed by agents of the United States Bureau of Alcohol, Tobacco and Firearms after a 51-day siege on 19 April 1993. The authorities were concerned that the cult had acquired a substantial arsenal of weapons. Controversy surrounds the precise circumstances in which a fire was started in the compound during the assault and whether it was deliberately started by members of the cult or was set off inadvertently by the agents seeking to end the siege. However, there seems little doubt that the fire was responsible for the large number of deaths that occurred during the ending of the siege. A total of 74 people were killed in the ending of the siege. Exactly two years after these events a federal government complex in Oklahoma City was destroyed by a truck bomb. A total of 168 people died in the attack, which was carried out by Timothy McVeigh as revenge for the actions of federal agents at Waco.

Jim Jones was the charismatic leader of a religious cult known as the People's Temple based in San Francisco. Jones believed that the apocalypse would take the form of all-out nuclear war between the United States and the Soviet Union. He encouraged his followers to accompany him to Guyana as a safe haven from the coming conflict, though the timing of the move seems also have been motivated by the appearance of critical stories in the media about the cult's activities. Jones and his followers built a communal village, known as Jonestown, in the jungle in Guyana. The background to the cataclysmic end of the cult was the involvement of an American Congressman, Leo Ryan, in inquiries into its operations. Ryan's interest was first aroused by a newspaper story about the circumstances in which an individual seeking to leave the cult had met a violent death under the wheels of a train. As a result of the interest Ryan showed in the cult, he was contacted by a number of relatives of cult members who had gone to Jonestown. A common allegation of the relatives was that cult members had been forced to go to Jonestown against their will.

As a result of the concerns expressed by the relatives, Ryan decided to go to Jonestown himself. His party included a number of journalists as well as relatives. At Jonestown he met a number of cult members who told him that they wished to leave with him and a group of them accompanied him to the airstrip at Port Kaituma for the trip back to Georgetown. At this point, Ryan and a number of members of his party were ambushed by hostile cult members and shot and killed. But even more horrific events were taking place at the cult's settlement at more or less the same time as the ambush at the airstrip happened. On the instructions of their leader, cult members were drinking a punch laced with cyanide in an act of mass suicide. Five people, including Congressman Ryan, were killed at the Port Kaituma airstrip on 18 November 1978, while on the same day 913 people died in the mass suicide at Jonestown, including Jones himself. It is difficult to make rational sense of the sequence of events in Guyana, but Jones's extreme paranoia and fantasies about the outside world appear to have been at the root of the tragedy.

The violence of cults, regardless of whether directed at cult members or at the outside world, differs from political terrorism in being based on notions of reality disconnected from the beliefs of the rest of the world. While cults frequently do draw on the cosmologies of the major religions in their construction of reality, the views they espouse are not simply extreme versions of existing ideologies, as is generally the case in relation to the views espoused by conventional terrorist organizations. Thus, the opinions of Asahara, Koresh and Jones never achieved the same resonance outside the ranks of the closed world of their cults that, for example, the views of Osama bin Laden have clearly secured in parts of the Muslim world, even if confined to an extreme fringe of Islamism. Of course, understanding the broad political objectives of a sub-state group engaged in clandestine violence may go hand in hand with incomprehension at how such a group expects to advance its cause through a particular campaign of violence. Indeed, one reason why much terrorist violence appeared so grotesque to public opinion across the world in the 1970s and 1980s was the huge gulf that existed between the vast political pretensions of the groups that engaged in terrorism and the means at their disposal. This was particularly true of the groups on the extreme fringes of opinion such as New Left and Neo-Fascist groups that were active in Europe in this period.

By the 1990s many of these groups were defunct. By contrast, the separatist groups still engaged in terrorism tended to be credited with the pursuit of rational political strategies, even if their actions were seen as deplorable from a moral perspective. As peace processes unfolded in the course of the 1990s in which former terrorists entered into negotiations on the future of the societies in which they were based, the contrast became all the sharper between groups seen as relatively pragmatic and which could be accommodated in the political process and fundamentalists that made demands on which compromise was impossible and that could not be appeased. The fact that the end of the cold war rendered a number of regional conflicts more amenable to political settlements reinforced the perception that the new generation of terrorist organizations was more ruthless than the previous one.

As a number of the newer groups asserted a religious identity, there was also a tendency to draw a more general distinction between religious and secular terrorists and to make the assumption that the former had fewer inhibitions about killing than the latter. At the same time, the shock created by the sarin attack in Japan led to the focus being placed, as Gearson puts it, 'on the means and technology at the disposal of terror groups, rather than on the organisations themselves and their objectives' in 'a period of unprecedented interest in "superterrorism", as it came to be called, notably in the United States'.[12] Instead of considering how the use of weapons of mass destruction might serve the ends of any terrorist group, analysts of the new terrorism stressed the potential vulnerability of modern societies to such weapons. Given the demonic connotations of the very word, terrorism, the assumption that there was no limit to how many people terrorists would be ready to kill, if they could, hardly seemed to require special justification. A further justification for the concern that terrorists might use weapons of mass destruction was evidence that some groups, most notably al-Qaeda, were proclaiming their desire to acquire such weapons.

As Clarke records in his book, *Against all Enemies*, this threat was taken seriously by the American authorities before the events of 11 September and the anthrax attacks in October 2001 gave added impetus to the issue of what terrorists in general and al-Qaeda in particular might be capable of. Clarke notes:

> For years we had been receiving raw intelligence reports and finished CIA analyses saying that al Qaeda was seeking chemical or nuclear weapons. When we asked for further details, however, there were none. Frustrated, in early 2001 I called Charlie Allen, who had become the Assistant Director of Central Intelligence for Collection, a kind of overall coordinator of what all U.S. intelligence agencies were doing to get information. We agreed to assemble everyone from every intelligence agency who had any responsibility for collecting or analyzing information about al Qaeda and weapons of mass destruction. We met in a secret location in Virginia. There were a lot of people in attendance. Each agency briefed on what they knew. More rumors and shadows. Nothing specific, credible, or actionable.[13]

The absence of reliable information on both the intentions and capabilities of groups such as al-Qaeda provided a measure of justification for the emphasis on vulnerabilities. It also avoided too narrow a focus on terrorists, i.e. groups with social and political objectives as possible perpetrators of such attacks.

This was underlined by the case of Larry Harris. In 1995 Harris managed to obtain the bacterium that causes bubonic plague through pretending to be engaged in biomedical research that required the use of samples of the disease. Harris's actual intentions were obscure but he evidently toyed with plans to disseminate bubonic plague in the New York subway. Harris's motives were also unclear. He had extreme rightwing views, but his actions were unconnected to any group or political campaign. His case highlights a problem for modern society that is most evident in the cases of individuals who have created and then disseminated highly destructive computer viruses for motives that can only be described as nihilist or personal. The only safe procedure for protecting computers seems to be the assumption that hackers will breach the defences designed to frustrate their activities if they possibly can and not to ponder why anyone should want to disrupt the internet. Similarly, the Harris case underlined the need for the authorities to put in place procedures to make it difficult for male-factors of any kind to get hold of potentially extremely dangerous materials that might be used for the purpose of mass murder. An inadvertent by-product of the debate of whether terrorists might use chemical, biological or nuclear weapons in acts of clandestine violence may have been to stimulate the interest of individuals such as Harris in such possibilities. For his part, Harris claimed that his actions were in part motivated by a desire to alert Americans to the possibility that terrorists acting at the behest of a rogue state such as Iraq could carry out such attacks.

The debate that occurred prior to 9/11 on the possibility of terrorists' employing weapons of mass destruction needs to be seen in the context of the end of the cold war. While the end of the cold war removed the threat of nuclear war between the superpowers, it also gave rise to new threats. The availability of nuclear material for sale as a result of the dissolution of the Soviet Union was one reason why there was especial concern that terrorists might secure the material needed to develop a crude nuclear device. At the same time, overt conflicts in the Balkans and within the boundaries of the former Soviet Union tended to overshadow the issue of terrorism. The horrors of ethnic cleansing in the former Yugoslavia in the early 1990s and of genocide in Rwanda in 1994 meant that the combating of terrorism no longer appeared to be the priority it had once been. Even the simultaneous bombing of America's embassies in Kenya and Tanzania in 1998 failed to change this perception and that was reflected in the adverse reaction to the Clinton Administration's actions in response to the bombing.

Attitudes changed fundamentally only with the events of 11 September. While the attacks did not vindicate those who had warned of an attack by terrorists using weapons of mass destruction, they did demonstrate that sub-state, transnational organizations existed that had the will and possessed the means to cause death on a scale beyond anything that had previously been achieved by such groups. This outcome was achieved through employment of a relatively old technique, the hijacking of passenger airliners, but applying it in an entirely new way with devastating results. In retrospect, the simplicity of the conspiracy is what is striking, though that did not prevent a handful of commentators from arguing that the training of pilots to crash into specific buildings revealed a degree of sophistication that was beyond the capacity of a sub-state organization and to insist that there must have been state involvement in the plot. That would seem grossly to over-state the difficulty of acquiring sufficient skill to steer a large airliner. The financial outlays involved in the plot were extraordinarily modest and far below the level that might have alerted the authorities to the existence of suspicious transactions.

However, the scale of the attacks meant that the authorities everywhere had the strongest possible incentive to put in place measures to make any repetition of the seizure of passenger airliners for the purpose of turning them into flying bombs extremely difficult. Further, the assault amounted to little short of a declaration of war against the United States, far and away the most militarily powerful country in the world. It was evident in the immediate aftermath of 9/11 that America was likely to seek to destroy al-Qaeda in so far as that was militarily possible. This touched on a point commonly made before 9/11 by those who were sceptical that any terrorist organization would use weapons of mass destruction. This was the argument that it would be self-destructive for any sub-state group to embark on such a path, because of the size of the backlash such action would be likely to provoke. Al-Qaeda's apparent disregard of the likely consequences of 11 September strengthened the case of those who argued that terrorists might not be deterred by the consequences for themselves or their organization of carrying out a spectacular attack that caused massive loss of life.

Consequently, the question of whether terrorists were likely to develop the capacity to use weapons of mass destruction gained even added urgency after 9/11. Terrifying scenarios were set out of attacks that a terrorist organization might hypothetically be capable of perpetrating if it acquired the necessary materials. The United Nations High-level Panel on Threats, Challenges and Change identified terrorist detonation of a nuclear explosion as the most devastating of these possibilities.

> Experts suggest that if a simple nuclear device were detonated in a major city, the number of deaths would range from tens of thousands to more than a million. The shock to international commerce, employment and travel would amount to at least a trillion dollars. Such an attack could have further, far-reaching implications for international security, democratic governance and civil rights.[14]

The Panel explained why it considered such an eventuality not to be beyond the bounds of possibility.

> Today 1,300 kilograms of highly enriched uranium exist in research reactors in 27 countries. The total volume of HEU

stockpiles is far greater, and many HEU storage sites in the world are inadequately secured. States have publicly confirmed 20 cases of nuclear material diversion and more than 200 incidents involving the illicit trafficking in nuclear materials have been documented over the past decade. Scientists have repeatedly warned of the ease with which terrorists could, with parts from the open market, assemble a simple 'gun-type' nuclear device that simply collides two quantities of HEU.[15]

The context of the Panel's analysis was the need for the international regime on the non-proliferation of nuclear weapons to be strengthened. In practice, the obstacles to the scenario presented by the Panel remain very formidable, not least the difficulties that any clandestine organization would encounter in handling the necessary materials and in escaping prior detection of the plot to use such a weapon.

As a consequence, more attention has tended to be given to another scenario. This is that terrorists will use radioactive materials to create a so-called dirty bomb, a bomb not designed to produce a nuclear explosion but which uses conventional explosives to contaminate an area with radioactivity. In the aftermath of the bombs in London on 7 July 2005, the *Independent* published a hypothetical scenario involving the use of such a weapon in the British capital. The scenario assumes that the perpetrators employ a conventional explosion, which kills five people directly in Kensington High Street, as their radiological dispersal device. It suggests the terrorists use caesium 137 rather than plutonium or highly enriched uranium since it would be much easier for a clandestine group to obtain the caesium since it is 'commonly used in medicine, industry and agriculture, and rarely stored with proper security'.[16] The devastation that such an attack could conceivably cause is spelt out.

A health physics team from the National Radiological Protection Board at Didcot in Berkshire discovers that a cigar-shaped area stretching 15 miles downwind and five miles across at its widest point is contaminated with radioactivity. This stretches from Kensington to Dagenham, and covers the entire centre of London from Islington to Brixton, taking in Westminster, the City and Canary Wharf.

Meanwhile Londoners – particularly in the area where the bomb went off – pick up radioactivity on their clothes and bodies and carry it home, contaminating public transport on their way. Vehicles also pick it up and spread it far and wide.

The authorities decide that most of the affected area will have to be evacuated and decontaminated, at a cost of hundreds of millions of pounds, but the radiation is extremely hard to remove from buildings. In the end the only solution is to demolish them. Much of the centre of London and its greatest landmarks, including Buckingham Palace, the Houses of Parliament, St Paul's Cathedral, the Swiss Re 'gherkin' and Canary Wharf, are reduced to rubble.[17]

It is also possible to construct similarly catastrophic scenarios in relation to the use of biological and chemical weapons. Thus, the UN High-level Panel asserts that 'under worst-case assumptions, an attack using only one gram of weaponized smallpox could produce between 100,000 and 1,000,000 fatalities'.[18]

As in the case of both nuclear and radiological weapons, however, securing and handling the material required, as well as deploying it to maximum effect, constitute formidable difficulties for any small clandestine organization, as would ensuring that no word of their plans reached the authorities or anyone else who would want to frustrate such an attack. It is commonly argued that these difficulties make it highly improbable that any terrorist group could mount an attack that caused fatalities in the tens of thousands or higher. The principal circumstance in which a terrorist group might be able to overcome the obstacles to the mounting of such an attack would be if it received assistance from a state. The fear that rogue states either possessing or capable of producing weapons of mass destruction might assist terrorists to carry out such an attack provides one of the arguments that have been advanced for intervention in such states so as to prevent that possibility.

However, all scenarios involving terrorists' employing weapons of mass destruction to cause fatalities on a scale suggested in the nightmare scenarios described above, whether with or without the assistance of a state, force us to ask the question: what could conceivably motivate any group to carry out such an attack? This is one of the issues examined in the debate that took place between Kenneth Waltz and Scott Sagan on whether the spread of nuclear weapons constitutes a threat to world peace or extends deterrence, thus preventing war. Waltz makes out the case that it would not make sense for rational terrorists to use such weapons:

> Fear of nuclear terror arises from the assumption that if terrorists *can* get nuclear weapons they *will* get them, and then all hell will break loose. This is comparable to assuming that if weak states get nuclear weapons, they will use them for aggression. Both assumptions are false. Would the courses of action, we fear, if followed promise more gains than losses or more pains than profits? The answers are obvious. Terrorists have some hope of reaching their long-term goals through patient pressure and constant harassment. They cannot hope to do so by issuing unsustainable threats to wreak great destruction, threats they would not want to execute anyway.[19]

In his response to Waltz, Sagan argues that it is possible to identify the types of terrorists who are interested in acquiring nuclear and/or radiological weapons. He identifies three general kinds:

> millenarian groups, who think the end of the world is just over the horizon; neo-Nazi and other racist hate groups, who seek to kill people because of their religious or racial identity; and Islamic Jihadi groups who believe that mass murder is both morally justified and effective in pursuing their political objective of creating radical Islamic governments in the Middle East.[20]

Sagan and Waltz are in broad agreement on the danger that millenarian groups might pose. They differ on the likelihood of jihadists' seeking to use weapons of mass destruction. Waltz argues that the perpetrators of the assault on America on 9/11 were motivated by the desire to punish America for policies such as support for Israel. He contends that the continued pursuit of this objective would be put in jeopardy by the use of weapons of mass destruction. He·calls this a question of logistics.

> Terrorists live precarious lives. Nobody trusts them, not even those who finance, train, and hide them. If apprehended, they cannot count on the help of others. They have learned how to use conventional weapons to some effect, but nuclear weapons would thrust them into a world fraught with new dangers. Terrorists work in small groups. Secrecy is safety, yet to obtain and maintain nuclear weapons would require enlarging the terrorist band to include suppliers, transporters, technicians, and guardians. Inspiring devotion, instilling discipline, and ensuring secrecy become harder tasks to accomplish as numbers grow. Those who want to punish others have to preserve their organizations in order to continue to administer their perverted justice.[21]

Waltz does not consider the third case Sagan raises, the use of weapons of mass destruction as a very extreme case of hate crime. However, the use of weapons of mass destruction for this purpose is open to the obvious objection that such weapons are indiscriminate in their impact and therefore ill-suited to targeting particular communities.

While Waltz's arguments are reasonable, they are open to the objection that it is not sufficient that they hold in virtually every case, they have to hold in all, if a potential catastrophe is to be prevented. It is therefore understandable that governments should approach this issue on the basis of protecting their societies against worst-case scenarios. However, the issue of whether terrorists would ever seek to use weapons of mass destruction with the purpose of causing huge numbers of fatalities has to be put in a much wider political context than simply an examination of the motivations of potential perpetrators. A distinction fundamental to the analysis of terrorism, though underemphasized, is that between domestic and international terrorism. It is not merely that these describe acts of political violence at different levels. As will be explained below, there is a normative difference between the two levels. The term, terrorism, carries a connotation of absolutely illegitimate violence. That is one reason why concepts such as superterrorism or hyperterrorism have not become part of general usage. Rather than prompting the use of new terms, 9/11 has altered the public's understanding of what terrorism entails to include attacks causing a huge number of fatalities, reinforcing the association of terrorism with what is most evil, most unacceptable and absolutely illegitimate.

It is common for definitions of terrorism to emphasize that the term encompasses categories of violence widely viewed as outrageous in any circumstances, such as hostage-taking and the deliberate killing of innocent bystanders or non-combatants. Such a simple approach to the issue of definition attracts many adherents, some of whom have expressed intense irritation with the tortuous debates that continue to take place on the definition of terrorism, because they make the simple assumption that the targeting of non-combatants provides an obvious answer to the problem of what constitutes terrorism. What this approach overlooks is that the term, terrorism, is very commonly used in relation to the assassination of political leaders or attacks on security forces of all kinds that fall outside this simple definition. It also overlooks the importance of context in how an act of violence is viewed and whether the term, terrorism, is universally employed to describe it.

In particular, however outrageous, political violence that takes place within a zone of conflict tends to be seen in a different light to violence against a backdrop of peace. Three main kinds of violence tend to take place against a backdrop of peace, the violence of a fringe that does not accept the status quo in the society in question as legitimate, violence spilling over from a conflict zone and the violence of transnational networks ready to carry out attacks in any part of the world. All three of these categories of violence tend to be viewed as illegitimate and are commonly labelled as terrorism. The first of these helps to make up what is generally seen as a peripheral category, domestic terrorism. However, the main focus of the study of terrorism tends to be on the second two categories, with the further addition of fringe groups that target foreign targets in their own societies. Together these make up the category of international terrorism that forms the basis of most data collection, chronologies and statistics in the field. In fact, when the term, terrorism, is used, it is commonly taken for granted that what is actually meant is international terrorism. This is why estimates of the numbers killed in terrorism in the last decade are in the thousands and not the millions that have died in political violence of all kinds in that period. This is because the statistics on terrorism typically exclude the victims of violence in conflict zones.

Of course, within conflict zones, the term terrorism does continue to be used by the protagonists, especially governments, though with a limited capacity to persuade the rest of the world that the violence of anti-state forces should be seen in that light, except sometimes in relation to particularly outrageous atrocities. Massacres of civilians that take place against the background of violent conflict are more commonly referred to as war crimes than as terrorism, whether perpetrated by the forces of the state or by those who have taken up arms against the state. The importance of context is also reflected in a general reluctance to use the term, 'terrorists', in the setting of a violent conflict. Other terms tend to be used. Examples are the use of the term, 'paramilitaries', in Northern Ireland; 'militants' in Kashmir; 'militias' in Lebanon; 'insurgents' in Iraq and 'guerrillas' in Sri Lanka, Nepal and Colombia. But when groups involved in such conflicts extend their violence beyond the boundaries of the conflict itself, they are likely to be labelled as terrorists. Operating outside a conflict zone constitutes a violation of an important norm roughly equivalent to, though not with quite the same emotive power as, deliberately killing innocent bystanders.

Insurgents often do recognize this norm and do not attempt to extend their violence beyond the region in which they seek to rule in the case of separatists and beyond the confines of the polity in the case of revolutionaries. A good example of an organization that demonstrated such restraint in its struggle for power was the African National Congress (ANC). The ANC's limited armed struggle was confined to South Africa.[22] In particular it did not seek to attack representatives of the apartheid state abroad, to attack South African commercial interests in foreign countries, or to hijack planes of South African Airways. Part of the explanation for the ANC's restraint was the existence of a worldwide anti-apartheid movement that supported the ANC's broad political objectives, which would have been put in jeopardy if the ANC had extended the theatre of its violent operations outside of Southern Africa. By contrast, the apartheid government did not exercise similar restraint and its agents carried out acts of violence in countries thousands of miles from South Africa.

However, there are grounds for concern that this norm is being eroded. The reason is the erosion of the more general norm of which insurgents' not extending their violence beyond the combat zone is simply an instance. This is the norm of non-intervention. The readiness of the major Western powers to intervene coercively in the affairs of other states has increased exponentially since the end of the cold war. The disappearance of the restraining force of bipolarity has blinded political leaders to the dangers of aggressive interventionism, the primary proponents of which have been the British Prime Minister, Tony Blair, theorists of a new ethical imperialism, such as Robert Cooper, and the American neo-conservatives. The disregard of the norm of non-intervention, reflected in the frequency with which the leading Western powers have taken military action without securing authorization by the Security Council, has its counterpart in the emergence of terrorism with a global reach. Factors such as increased mobility and the ready availability of destructive materials are part of the explanation of the increased lethality of international terrorism, but the emergence of networks such as al-Qaeda also needs to be seen in a political context, a point that will be developed further below.

Notes

1 Brian Jenkins, 'Future Trends in International Terrorism' in Robert O. Slater and Michael Stohl (eds), *Current Perspectives on International Terrorism*, Macmillan, Basingstoke 1988.
2 Ibid., p. 253.
3 Ibid.
4 Ibid., p. 255.
5 Ibid.
6 Ibid., p. 261.
7 Ibid., p. 262.
8 Ibid., p. 265.
9 John Gearson, 'The Nature of Modern Terrorism' in Lawrence Freedman (ed.), *Superterrorism: Policy Responses*, Blackwell, Oxford 2002, p. 7.
10 Rex A. Hudson, *The Sociology and Psychology of Terrorism: Who Becomes a Terrorist and Why?*, Federal Research Division, Library of Congress, Washington DC 1999, p. 1.
11 A useful account of the cult is given by David E. Kaplan, 'Aum Shinrikyo' in Jonathan B. Tucker (ed.), *Toxic Terror: Assessing Terrorist Use of Chemical and Biological Weapons*, MIT Press, Cambridge, MA 2000, pp. 207–26.
12 Gearson, 'The Nature of Modern Terrorism', p. 7.
13 Richard A. Clarke, *Against All Enemies: Inside America's War on Terror*, Free Press, New York 2004, pp. 177–8.
14 High-level Panel on Threats, Challenges and Change, *A More Secure World: Our Shared Responsibility*, United Nations, New York 2004, p. 40.
15 Ibid.
16 'What if . . . there was a "dirty bomb" attack on London', *Independent on Sunday*, 10 July 2005.
17 Ibid.
18 High Level Panel on Threats, Challenges and Change, *A More Secure World*, p. 41.

19 Scott D. Sagan and Kenneth N. Waltz, *The Spread of Nuclear Weapons: A Debate Renewed*, W.W. Norton and Company, New York 2003, p. 130.
20 Ibid., p. 160.
21 Ibid., p. 129.
22 The nature of the ANC's campaign is explored further in Chapter 10.

CHAPTER 9

Counter-terrorism

When President George W. Bush declared a war against terrorism
in the aftermath of the events of 11 September, the framing
of America's response to the attacks was criticized on a number of
grounds. Thus, some commentators argued that it was a mistake
to declare war on an abstraction. They argued that terrorism was
not a concrete concept but rather constituted a judgement on
violent actions without clear boundaries. A similar point was made
by others who argued that it was a mistake to declare war on a
tactic, reflecting a common approach to the definition of terrorism as encompassing the use of particular methods of violence.
According to such critics, it might have been wiser for President
Bush simply to have committed the United States to uprooting al-
Qaeda as the network responsible for the attacks. Indeed the
Administration's initial narrow formulation of its task as the defeat
of terrorism with a global reach, if it had been held to, might have
largely satisfied these critics. Other critics focused on the issue of
whether it was sensible to couch the struggle against al-Qaeda as
a war at all. Lawrence Freedman summarizes their objections
as follows:

> First, redefining obnoxious criminal acts as warlike dignifies
> them and gives the perpetrators an unnecessarily heroic
> status. Second, instead of objectives being framed in terms
> of law enforcement and the successful prosecution of the

perpetrators, they are framed in terms of military victory. Third, in a war the gloves are off and governments can do things they cannot do when the problems are described in more civilian terms, for example in finding ways to bypass the civil rights of anyone, including foreign nationals, suspected of being implicated in terrorism. This leads in exactly the opposite direction to a judicial approach. Fourth and finally, power within governments shifts to the military and the Pentagon civilians, leading to a harsh foreign policy with scant hope for diplomatic initiatives, let alone attention to the conditions which breed terrorism.[1]

Freedman accepts that there is 'something to all these arguments', but contends that the scale of 9/11 attacks made war 'not a matter of choice but a strategic imperative'.[2] At the same time, he acknowledges that among the consequences of war is that it 'sharpens divisions and ensures that multilateralism is only partial in the form of an alliance'.[3]

A justification for the initiation of a war against terrorism is that it put the Bush Administration's response in a larger normative framework than simply focusing on the elimination of a particular organization would have done. To put these arguments into a wider context, a brief history of terrorism and counter-terrorism is provided, so the implications of the framework adopted by the Bush Administration can be explored in greater depth. That is followed by a typology of state strategies for the handling of political violence, before the question of how terrorism was addressed as an international problem prior to 9/11 is considered. Then the actual conduct of President Bush's war against terrorism will be examined. It begs a number of questions which the chapter will seek to address. Why, despite an unprecedented level of support for the United States in the immediate aftermath of 9/11, did the Bush Administration choose to follow a path that was bound to alienate much of world opinion? Has the Bush Administration's unilateralism enhanced the prospect of further terrorism on the scale of 9/11? What was the background to the disgrace of conditions at Guantánamo Bay and the shame of Abu Ghraib? Finally, what influence has American conduct of the war against terrorism had on the behaviour of other countries in their approach to the issue of terrorism?

The term, 'terrorism' dates back to the French revolution when it was applied to the reign of terror under Robespierre. In short, it was used to describe what some writers today would refer to as state terrorism, though this term is by no means unproblematic as the scale on which governments accused of state terrorism kill has no equivalent in the realm of sub-state groups, even in networks as lethal as al-Qaeda. Briefly in the early nineteenth century the term acquired another meaning that has fallen out of use. This was the meaning of terrorist as an alarmist and reflected the use made of the horror evoked by the violent events of the French revolution to damn proponents of radical reform. Gradually, through the course of the nineteenth century there was a shift in the primary meaning of the term to refer to violence from below rather than above. In particular, it came to be associated with rural agitation in Ireland, especially the violent actions of tenants against landowners and their agents. A feature of this agitation was the mutilation of farm animals, conduct that aroused strong emotions in England, and provided one of the justifications for the use of the term 'terrorism' in this context. But even more important was the development of the association of the term with the wave of anarchist violence in a number of European countries in the second half of the nineteenth century.

Indeed, the association of terrorism and anarchist violence underscored two elements that have been central to the term's usage ever since. The first was that terrorism is absolutely illegitimate violence. In the nineteenth century anarchists were seen not just as the enemies of particular governments, but as the enemies of all governments. This prompted the view that anarchism lay outside the scope of the norm of non-interference in the internal conflicts of other societies that existed within Europe. It was reflected in a readiness of British courts, for example, to permit the extradition of anarchists in circumstances where they refused to extradite persons whose crimes, including that of murder, arose out of internal political conflict. The second was the association of terrorism with the anarchist slogan, 'propaganda by the deed', which underlined that the purpose of their actions was to convey a message to a much larger audience than the immediate target of their violence. In addition, two forms of violence closely associated with anarchism, the placing of bombs in public places and political assassinations, remain commonly identified with terrorism. Admittedly, the question of whether political assassination should be characterized as a type of terrorism is open to argument since both the aspects of seeking to convey a message through such a deed and of seeking to instil fear in society at large may be entirely absent from its motivation.

Nevertheless, global international cooperation over the issue of terrorism was first prompted by such violence. Following the assassination by Croatian nationalists of the King of Yugoslavia and of the French foreign minister in Marseilles in 1934, the League of Nations referred the matter to a committee of experts. As a result of the committee's work, an international conference was held in 1937. It approved the texts of two conventions – one on the prevention and punishment of acts of terrorism (with the emphasis on attacks on heads of state) and another proposing the establishment of an international criminal court to try such crimes. This effort was overtaken by larger events. Only one country, India, ratified the two conventions. After the Second World War, the term terrorism was applied by the colonial powers to some of the violent movements they faced in the era of decolonization. However, given the doubts that existed over the legitimacy of colonial rule, there was some reluctance to describe the members of such movements as terrorists in an unqualified manner. There was somewhat less reluctance to describe particular atrocities as acts of terrorism.

The problem of how to describe people seen as pursuing legitimate ends by illegitimate means posed an enduring problem for commentators. It gave rise to what has become a cliché, that one person's terrorist is another person's freedom fighter. Of course, the governments affected had no difficulty in seeing both the ends and means as illegitimate. Yet even among colonial governments in the 1950s there were reservations about using the term 'terrorism'. Thus, in Malaya, largely ethnically Chinese insurgents were colloquially referred to as CTs, which was short for Communist Terrorists. However, the official designation of the person heading counter-insurgency operations in Malaya was Director of Anti-Bandit Operations. The insurgents targeted soldiers and one objection to the use of the term 'terrorism' was the British army's dislike of any implication that its soldiers could be put in fear by the insurgents. The completion of the process of decolonization by the mid-1960s in most parts of Africa and Asia led to a hardening of attitudes towards violence by nationalist groups who disputed the boundaries of the new states or who wished to apply the principle of self-determination to metropolitan heartlands.

The motive of drawing the line against such violence combined with reaction to a number of other developments in the 1960s led to the labelling of a number of different strands of political violence that emerged in the 1960s as terrorism. The perceived illegitimacy of much of this violence provided a strong justification for the consensus that developed to describe it as terrorism. In the case of New Left and Neo-Fascist groups that appeared across the industrialized world, the perception of their illegitimacy stemmed from both realistic appreciation of their miniscule public support and the massive gulf between the means at their disposal and the ends being sought. In the case of Middle-Eastern and Latin American movements, condemnation of their violence as terrorism stemmed from the nature of the means they employed, such as hijacking for the purpose of hostage-taking or attacks on diplomats, and from their propensity for operating outside the arena of conflict and for attacking the nationals of other countries. By copying such methods, a fifth category, separatist nationalist movements with some claim to a local following, alienated potential support externally and also found themselves categorized as part of the new terrorist phenomenon. All these different elements combined to produce the view that the late 1960s had witnessed the onset of an age of terrorism.

The widespread use of the term, as well as the collecting of statistics on international terrorism and the academic analysis of the phenomenon, gave further credibility to this perspective. Chronologies on international terrorism often took one particular event in the late 1960s as their starting point. This was the hijacking by the Popular Front for the Liberation of Palestine of an El Al airliner en route from Rome to Lod on 23 July 1968. In the late 1960s and through the 1970s, the focus of international concern was on small groups which operated clandestinely across national boundaries, while seeking publicity for their causes by claims of responsibility and elaborate manifestos. The term 'transnational terrorism'was widely used in the academic literature of the time to describe the phenomenon and to separate it from previous usage of the term 'terrorism' in relation to earlier colonial conflicts. The response of the international community was the outlawing of particular methods of violence.

It was reflected in the adoption of a series of conventions, most notably the 1970 Hague Convention for the Suppression of the Unlawful Seizure of Aircraft, the 1971 Montreal Convention for the Suppression of Unlawful Acts against the Safety of Civil Aviation, the 1973 Convention on the Prevention and Punishment of Crimes against Internationally Protected Persons, i.e. diplomats, and the 1979 International Convention against the Taking of Hostages. However, attempts to outlaw terrorism as such ran into difficulties. In 1972 following Black September's attack on Israeli athletes at the Munich Olympics, the then UN Secretary-General, Kurt Waldheim, asked the General Assembly to examine the issue. The United States put forward a draft convention, but it encountered opposition from Third World states concerned that it would undercut the legitimacy of groups fighting for self-determination against colonial or minority rule.

The absence of a convention outlawing terrorism in general is one of the issues recently addressed by the Secretary-General's High-level Panel. Its report contends:

The United Nations' ability to develop a comprehensive strategy has been constrained by the inability of Member States to agree on an anti-terrorism convention including a definition of terrorism. This prevents the United Nations from exerting its moral authority and from sending an unequivocal message that terrorism is never an acceptable tactic, even for the most defensible of causes.[4]

The assumption of the Panel seems to be that the targeting of civilians by sub-state groups provides a straightforward and unproblematic definition of terrorism. In response to the criticism that the exclusion of states from the definition is unjustifiable, the Panel argues that state behaviour of targeting civilians is covered in existing international law by the concept of a war crime, while the Panel maintains that those resisting foreign occupation, for example, are never justified in targeting civilians. Further, the Panel makes no distinction between domestic and international jurisdiction. It is a short step to saying that killing anywhere for any purpose should be universally recognized as a crime. Under the Panel's approach, those who attempted to assassinate Hitler or members of the French resistance during the Second World War would count as terrorists. While the intention may be to prevent groups today from undeservedly claiming the mantle of such famous predecessors, it is simplistic and naïve to imagine that circumstances will never arise in the course of the twenty-first century to justify resort to the extreme means such groups employed or that the context in which violence is used does not matter hugely. However, in the current climate of opinion, states may well be prevailed upon to sign up to what the Panel is proposing, much as states in the 1920s were prevailed upon to commit themselves to forswear the waging of war.[5]

In the 1980s, there was increasing interest in the role played by particular states in supporting and sponsoring the violence of small groups. It was encapsulated in a notion promoted by the Reagan Administration, the terrorist state. It should be noted that this did not mean states terrorizing their own citizens but states which harboured small groups which carried out hijackings, attacks on diplomats, bombings and the like in other countries. Thus, Iraq was labelled a terrorist state by the State Department not because of its conduct towards its own Kurdish population but, ironically, for supporting the PKK (Kurdish Workers' Party) in Turkey. In the 1990s, the term terrorism lost some of its force with the development of peace processes in societies previously strongly associated in the public mind with terrorism, such as Israel/Palestine and Northern Ireland. In addition, the outbreak of ethnic conflicts in a number of countries, especially in the former Yugoslavia, led to a focus on the larger horrors of overt conflict.

Nevertheless, the issue of international terrorism remained of sufficient concern to prompt the adoption of further conventions, such as the 1980 Convention on the Physical Protection of Nuclear Materials, the 1988 Convention for the Suppression of Unlawful Acts against the Safety of Maritime Navigation, the 1997 United Nations Convention for the Suppression of Terrorist Bombing and the 1999 United Nations Convention for the Suppression of Financing Terrorism. In the last of these, reference is made to the previous conventions to provide a working basis for establishing what acts terrorism encompasses, in the absence of the general convention setting out a definition of terrorism. A sensible recommendation of the Secretary-General's High-level Panel is to urge member states to sign and ratify the existing conventions on terrorism. But as with all international conventions, their effectiveness in practice depends on the readiness of individual states to enforce their provisions.

A controversial step towards transnational enforcement of the law was taken in July 1998 by the UN Diplomatic Conference of Plenipotentiaries on the Establishment of an International Criminal Court. This conference in Rome adopted a treaty for such a Court and the Statutes of the Court. To come into force the treaty required to be ratified by 60 states which it achieved in 2002, despite strong opposition from the United States. The court's remit is confined to the most serious crimes of international concern, defined as genocide, crimes against humanity and war crimes. International terrorism as such does not fall within the scope of the court. It was excluded because of a lack of consensus on a definition, because the perception at the time of the Rome conference was that the problem of international terrorism was a lower priority than responding to events in the former Yugoslavia and the genocide in Rwanda, and because of the relatively small number of victims of international terrorism by comparison with the ethnic conflicts that had flared up since the end of the cold war. There has been some discussion since the events of 11 September of extending the remit of the court in due course to international terrorism and some commentators have pointed out that it might be possible to prosecute actions of the scale of 9/11 under the rubric of a crime against humanity.

Even were the International Criminal Court to develop in this direction, primary responsibility for the combating of political violence would lie with individual states. Their approaches vary very widely and, indeed, the strategies of particular states themselves vary very considerably over time and in relation to different challenges. However, it is possible to categorize state strategies in this area in terms of a simple typology. The principle of the typology is this: how does the state treat politically motivated suspects and violent offenders in comparison with suspects and violent offenders who do not have a political motivation for their actions (or alleged actions)? There are three possible answers. First, the state can treat politically motivated suspects and violent offenders more leniently than ordinary decent criminals, a useful colloquialism from Northern Ireland for violent offenders who are not politically motivated. This approach may be called accommodation. Second, the state can insist on treating politically motivated suspects and violent offenders in exactly the same way as it does the equivalent ordinary decent criminals. This approach may be called criminalization. Third, the state may treat politically motivated suspects and violent offenders more harshly than it does non-politically motivated equivalents. This may be called suppression.

A brief example will serve to illustrate the spirit of the three categories. Shortly after the Provisional IRA (Irish Republican Army) ceasefire in Northern Ireland in 1994, the following graffiti appeared on the wall of a toilet at Queen's University of Belfast. On the wall someone had written 'Free all political prisoners' – accommodation. Underneath somebody else had written 'There are no political prisoners' – criminalization, while a third person contributed the sentiment, 'Hang the bastards' – suppression. A weakness of the approach of accommodation is that it may simply come to constitute or be seen to constitute a policy of appeasement that rewards violent political groups. Criminalization has the limitation that it is a policy of containment rather than the elimination of the threat posed by violent groups. It also tends to entail a denial of the political problem underpinning political violence. Its assumption of individual responsibility makes it particularly questionable as a means of addressing inter-communal or ethnic conflicts. Suppression does acknowledge the political nature of terrorism but usually denies any legitimacy to the cause for which it is employed. Suppression carries the danger of encouraging a disproportionate response from the state. It also can greatly exacerbate an inter-communal or ethnic conflict. It may reasonably be argued that different levels, different contexts call for different approaches. However, in practice, it may be difficult to separate responses in a neat manner. And following different approaches may give rise to charges of inconsistency and hypocrisy. The prevailing climate of opinion is also likely to militate against nuanced responses to different threats.

However, instances do exist of governments' pursuing the three approaches simultaneously by distinguishing among different challenges. Britain currently provides the most clear-cut example. In the case of Northern Ireland, the approach of the British government in the context of a peace process that it is extremely keen to sustain has been one of accommodation. The Republican movement has secured a stream of concessions, including the release of IRA prisoners serving sentences for murder, in return for maintaining a ceasefire. By contrast, the government's approach to the problem of violence by animal liberation groups is best characterized as one of criminalization. In this case the government is very mindful of the extent of public support for the causes espoused by animal liberation groups as opposed to the methods used by their most extreme elements. Even before the events of 11 September suppression characterized the approach taken by the British government to the issue of international terrorism. It was reflected in the passage of the extraordinarily wide-ranging Terrorism Act of 2000, described by Helen Fenwick as 'an immensely controversial and draconian piece of legislation'.[6]

After 9/11 the government went even further by introducing provision for detention of suspects without trial in the Anti-Terrorism Crime and Security Act of 2001. So as not to fall foul of the European Court of Human Rights over this provision, the government was forced to derogate from the fundamental right of the person to liberty under the European Convention on Human Rights, action that was tantamount to a declaration of a state of emergency. The bomb attacks in London in July 2005 prompted the government to put forward proposals for even more authoritarian laws targeting not merely the indirect encouragement of violence, but extremism, as that was conceived by an increasingly narrow-minded and intolerant government. The government's approach was strongly criticized in an editorial in the *Independent*, which conveyed well the frenetic nature of the government's response. The editorial was headed 'Anti-terror measures: Another day, another half-baked proposal'.[7]

In domestic legislation terrorism is commonly equated with any form of violence with some social or political purpose that causes serious damage, injury or death. In a few cases, of which Holland is an example, its use is confined to lethal actions. Of course, it is not surprising that governments tend to view violent challenges to their authority as absolutely illegitimate, whether or not it puts the lives of civilians in danger. External opinion may be more reluctant to describe such violence as terrorism, especially in any situation where the government's legitimacy is in question. However, a different attitude tends to be taken towards international or transnational terrorism. Political violence across national boundaries outside the zone of conflict often attracts the label of terrorism because virtually regardless of the form or context of such violence, it tends to be regarded as generally illegitimate to perpetrate acts of violence beyond the boundaries of one state and outside the arena in which the conflict is taking place. Much as piracy has attracted especial condemnation for seeking to use the international realm for carrying out crime, so too the use of the international realm to further political causes through violence tends to be seen as wholly unacceptable.

There is no precise equivalent at the international level for the different strategies that states may adopt to deal with political violence. However, a rough equivalent to accommodation at the international level is the oft-expressed insistence that the root causes behind terrorism need to be addressed in any programme for combating international terrorism. A rough equivalent to suppression is resort to a unilateral military response, while the multilateral approach of reliance on international cooperation in the context of the adoption of international conventions most closely resembles the approach of criminalization. Prior to 9/11, the multilateral approach tended to hold sway among states. After 9/11 the United States adopted a unilateral military approach. Indeed, the Bush Administration seemed almost embarrassed by the extent of international solidarity for America in the wake of these attacks and made little effort to harness this goodwill, seeing it not as an asset but as a constraint on American actions. By extending the war against terrorism to Iraq in 2003, the Administration successfully isolated itself from much of world opinion. A few governments, most notably those in Israel, Colombia and Spain (prior to March 2004) sought to place the violent conflicts inside their societies within the scope of the Bush Administration's war against terrorism.

The Constitution of the United States places constraints on what measures any American government can adopt within the boundaries of the country. The approach of the Bush Administration has been to seek to extend the powers of the Executive internally under such measures as the Patriot Act, as far as the constitution will allow, while adopting extremely aggressive policies externally where it is subject to far fewer constraints. By creating a facility for the detention of suspects at the country's naval base on the island of Cuba, the Bush Administration has sought to evade the jurisdiction of the American courts over its actions, while it has simultaneously interpreted its obligations under international law to the civilized treatment of detainees in such narrow terms as to render them worthless and meaningless. The consequences of these policies in terms of the actual treatment of prisoners at Guantánamo Bay have been described in detail by Amnesty International. Tony Judt summarizes the findings of the Amnesty International report on the situation as follows:

> The Amnesty report lists sixty alleged incarceration and interrogation practices routinely employed at U.S. detention centers, Guantánamo in particular. These include immersion in cold water to simulate drowning, forced shaving of facial and body hair, electric shocks to body parts, humiliation (e.g., being urinated upon), sexual taunting, the mocking of religious belief, suspension from shackles, physical exertion to the point of exhaustion (e.g., rock-carrying), and mock execution.[8]

Judt notes that such practices would be known to anyone familiar with Eastern Europe in the 1950s or Latin America in 1970s and 1980s.

> But American interrogators have also innovated. One technique has been forcibly to wrap suspects – and their Korans – in Israeli flags: a generous gesture to our only unconditional ally, but calculated to ensure that a new generation of Muslims worldwide will identify the two countries as one and hate them equally.
>
> All of these practices – and many others routinely employed at Guantánamo, at Kandahar and Bagram in Afghanistan, at al-Qaim, Abu Ghraib, and elsewhere in Iraq – are in breach of

the Geneva Conventions and the UN Convention against Torture, to both of which the U.S. is a signatory.[9]

The Amnesty International report also referred to other measures taken by the Bush Administration outside of the United States, including extrajudicial executions or, in other words, targeted assassinations of suspects and the outsourcing of the interrogation of detainees to regimes notorious for their use of torture and identified as such in American government reports that monitor the observance of human rights.[10] At the same time, even after the scandal at Abu Ghraib forced some modification in the official stance on how prisoners should be treated, the Attorney-General of the United States, Alberto Gonzales, continued to rely on the distinction between torture very narrowly defined and cruel, inhuman and degrading treatment to justify rough treatment of prisoners. The harm the Bush Administration has been inflicting on America's reputation in the world stems not just from the nature of its conduct of the war against terrorism, but its scale, as the Amnesty International report pointed out.

Guantánamo is just the tip of the iceberg, however. Around the world, there are believed to be thousands of detainees held in secret, incommunicado or indefinite detention without trial in the 'war on terror'. Many of these detainees are in direct US custody – in Iraq, Afghanistan and in secret locations. In Iraq alone, for example, in early May 2005 there were more than 11,350 detainees held in US custody in Abu Ghraib, Camp Bucca, Camp Cropper and in holding centres elsewhere. They are held in incommunicado or virtual incommunicado detention. At least 500 detainees are believed to be held in the US air bases in Bagram and Kandahar in Afghanistan. An unknown number are held in other US holding facilities elsewhere in the country. Several dozen 'high-value' detainees are believed to be held in secret CIA facilities in these countries or elsewhere. In addition, there are hundreds if not thousands of 'war on terror' detainees held in other countries, allegedly at the behest of the USA, or with its knowledge and access for its agents. In Yemen, for example, there are believed to be some 200 detainees so held, in Pakistan some 400 and hundreds in Saudi Arabia.[11]

This and other revelations in the media about CIA practices, including what was called the extraordinary rendition of prisoners, finally forced a change in the stance of the Administration over these practices in December 2005, but it remains to be seen whether the Administration has finally abandoned authorizing ill-treating suspects altogether.[12]

Danger signs that America's response to 9/11 would include widespread violation of human rights were evident in the initial reactions in the United States to the enormous trauma such an attack represented for a society that had been insulated from political violence on this scale on its own mainland for generations. Seymour Hersh gives the following summary of the mood within America's intelligence community in the aftermath of the attacks.

> In late September 2001, after two weeks of around-the-clock investigation into the terrorist attacks on the World Trade Center and the Pentagon, the intelligence community was confused, divided and unsure about how the terrorists operated, how many there were, and what they might do next. There was consensus on two issues, however: the attacks were brilliantly planned and executed, and the intelligence community was in no way prepared to stop them.[13]

Fear that the events of 11 September would be followed by further spectacular attacks of a similar character or scale encouraged the reaction that the country could not afford to put any constraints on efforts to secure the necessary information to protect the United States from the possibility of further horrors. Ominously, a feature of commentary in the aftermath of 9/11 was discussion as to whether in such extreme circumstances permitting the torture of suspects might be justified.

A second important element in explaining the American response to 9/11 was a profound misconception of the nature of the enemy America faced. Thus, there was a strong tendency among Americans both inside and outside the Administration to regard what was the strategy of a relatively very small number of jihadists centred on one leader among many in the world of radical, violent Islamism as representative of politicized Islam as a whole. Only slowly did the picture of al-Qaeda in Jason Burke's book on the subject gain currency. The view that the Americans had of Osama bin Laden was not unlike that of one of the villains in the Bond novels of Ian Fleming heading an organization conspiring to achieve global domination, with al-Qaeda itself rather like SMERSH. It was only after the defeat of the Taliban in Afghanistan and their failure to uncover an extensive infrastructure for the conduct of international terrorism in the Tora Bora caves that this impression started to be modified. Self-interest on the part of governments facing radical Islamist opposition was partially responsible for misleading the Bush Administration as to the nature of al-Qaeda. As Burke explains,

> During the autumn of 2001 al-Qaeda cells, previously undetected, were 'discovered' in scores of countries. Tashkent suddenly branded the Islamic Movement of Uzbekistan, a group whose links to bin Laden are tenuous, as 'al-Qaeda'. For Beijing it was the Uighur Muslims who are designated as the local branch of bin Laden's network, despite the fact that, though some individuals in some of the various Muslim groups resisting Chinese rule in the southeast of China may, at one time or another, have spent time in Afghan training camps, unrest in the region dates back to the first moments of Chinese domination. In Macedonia in March 2002 eight young Pakistani men were shot dead by the police. The minister of the interior was swift to proclaim a victory for his, fairly unsavoury, government in the war against bin Laden. The men were merely illegal economic migrants.[14]

Another example given by Burke is the Abu Sayyaf group in the Philippines with roots in a longstanding Islamic movement struggling against Christian domination in the Southern part of the archipelago. The Philippines government's attachment of the label of al-Qaeda to the group has persuaded the Bush Administration to deploy hundreds of troops in the Philippines to assist in its eradication. In short, America has been drawn into a number of conflicts with radical Islamism that have little to do with those responsible for 9/11. In particular, it is a reasonable assumption that extremely few of those currently detained by the United States or on its behalf ever had the slightest intention to attack the mainland of the United States or, for that matter, any plans to target Americans as such, with the exception perhaps of American forces in Iraq. Even experience of detention may not alter their wish to focus on local struggles.

A third element that helped to explain America's response to 9/11 was the hostility of the American right and the neo-conservatives to international institutions, especially the United Nations, despite America's dominant position of influence in the organization since the end of the cold war. International obligations seem to the American radical right to be designed to contain the military power of the United States. On this point, John Guelke quotes from an article that appeared in the *Financial Times* on 6 May 2004 on the neo-conservative outlook on international standards and norms.

> A recent article by David Scheffer, former US ambassador at large for war crimes issues, in the *Financial Times*, highlights the neo-conservative argument that 'Europeans and human rights organisations are waging "lawfare" against the US' in relation to complaint at the revelations concerning the activities in Abu Ghraib prison, maintaining that they seek to 'constrain the use of US military power worldwide through the "soft" weapon of international law and its "sovereignty-bashing" treaties, as well as anti-US interpretations of principle of customary international law'.[15]

Finally, American conduct in the war against terrorism has also been a product of the Bush Administration's decision to exploit the crisis over 9/11 for the pursuit of a pre-existing foreign policy agenda aimed at ensuring America's continuing position of predominance in the world. While the Administration justified the invasion of Iraq on the basis of its relevance to the larger war against terrorism, within the Administration there were few illusions about the adversarial relationship between Saddam Hussein and Osama bin Laden. Most other countries understand that the intervention had a very different motivation from the basis on which it was promoted among the American people and in the media.

The international unpopularity of the war has been reflected in the difficulty the United States has encountered in securing much more than token contributions from other countries to the Coalition of the Willing. To buttress its position in Iraq, America has made extensive use of private military companies that have drawn on the veterans of past conflicts in recruitment for their operations. Notable in this context has been the high number of former members of the apartheid-era South African security forces recruited to Iraq, including individuals amnestied for their crimes by the South African Truth and Reconciliation Commission, former members of the Vlakplaas death squad, and former members of Namibia's notorious counter-insurgency unit, Koevoet. Links between former members of South African Intelligence, now running private security firms, and former members of the British Special Air Services (SAS) who have gone into private business have facilitated their employment. In 2004 the South African Department of Foreign Affairs estimated the number of South Africans in Iraq at more than 4,000. The present South African government, which was strongly opposed to the war in Iraq, is in the process of strengthening the provisions of the Foreign Military Assistance Act to facilitate their prosecution as mercenaries.[16]

America's descent into barbarism to combat terrorism needs to be put into context. Terrorism tends to bring out the very worst in any society. The unprecedented scale of the events of 9/11 led to a justifiable anxiety in the United States that further attacks of a similarly lethal nature in future were possible. Such fears were compounded by the anthrax attacks in October 2001. It is understandable in such circumstances that public safety is seen as having priority over any other considerations. Also the desperation of the authorities to obtain intelligence by all means at their disposal is also comprehensible. Even though in practice the suppressive measures which states introduce at the onset of terrorist campaigns frequently prove counterproductive, some allowance needs to be made for mistakes by those in power in dealing with the onset of a new phase of terrorism, especially when the full extent of the dangers to the society are largely unquantifiable. However, other factors were in play besides legitimate concern to protect the country from further attacks in the Bush Administration's response to 9/11.

In many affluent liberal-democracies, ever since the electoral success achieved by Ronald Reagan in the United States and Margaret Thatcher in Britain, radical authoritarian populists have tended to displace traditional conservatives as standard bearers of major rightwing political parties. Examples of such figures are George W. Bush, John Howard in Australia, Silvio Berlusconi in Italy, and José Maria Aznar in power in Spain between 1996 and 2004. Their success has been due to the exploitation of public fears, commonly centred on issues such as crime, immigration and terrorism. This security agenda has also played an important role in Ariel Sharon's victories in successive Israeli elections and in the consolidation of Vladimir Putin's position of political dominance in Russia.[17] Of course, what measures should be put in place to meet the threat of terrorism, whether this comes from forces inside or outside the country, is a legitimate subject of political contention and debate. However, the manner in which this issue has been exploited for purposes of partisan political advantage has had little to do with rational debate or deliberation. A striking example is the manner in which the Bush Administration, leading members of the Republican Party and their supporters in the media in the United States persistently linked the events of

11 September and the regime of Saddam Hussein in Iraq, despite the absence of any evidence of such a connection and even after the Administration had grudgingly acknowledged as much. A further disturbing implication of the success of the politics of fear and hatred is that it may lead (or perhaps has already led) to putting politicians in power who see their own interests as best being served by the continuation of a particular terrorist emergency.

Britain provides a particularly interesting case study of these themes, not least because of the strong contrast between the policies of suppression the government has adopted towards international terrorism and its accommodationist policies in Northern Ireland. Further, the accommodationist policies the government is currently pursuing in Northern Ireland themselves need to be seen in the context of previous phases of suppression and criminalization. The troubles in Northern Ireland began as a result of street disturbances in the late 1960s. In fact, British troops were dispatched to aid the civil power even before the formation of the main paramilitary organizations, the Provisional Irish Republican Army (IRA) and the Ulster Defence Association. But it was IRA violence that prompted the adoption of policies of suppression. The most important of these was the introduction of internment without trial in August 1971. The release of the Cabinet papers from 1971 in January 2002 has cast an interesting light on how this policy came to be adopted.[18] The primary motive for the policy was political – to bolster the position of Northern Ireland's Unionist Prime Minister, Brian Faulkner. At the time the Unionists were allied to the British Conservative Party. The security forces for the most part advised against the adoption of the policy. In the event, the introduction of internment led to a massive deterioration in the security situation in the province, a huge upsurge in political violence and increased support among Catholics for the IRA. Following adverse international reaction to the events of Bloody Sunday in which 14 civil rights demonstrators were killed by British paratroopers in January 1972, direct rule was introduced from London, negating the original political motive behind the introduction of internment.

A criminalization phase followed in the mid-1970s, marked by the ending of detention without trial in 1975 and the transfer of the primary responsibility for the maintenance of law and order from the army to the police in 1976. However, there was a reversion to much harsher policies during Thatcher's premiership. In particular, there were allegations that the security forces had adopted a 'shoot to kill' policy in which they stalked or ambushed and then killed terrorist suspects in circumstances in which there appear to have been no reasonable legal justification for the use of lethal force. In short, the government was being accused of authorizing extrajudicial executions under the guise of conducting counter-insurgency operations. The cases that inevitably caused most difficulty for the authorities were ambushes set up at the location of hidden arms caches that led to the deaths of ordinary civilians mistaken for terrorists. After the Anglo-Irish Agreement of November 1985, efforts were made by the government to tackle Catholic alienation resulting from the earlier phases of security policy, ultimately paving the way to the policies of accommodation that accompanied the peace process initiated in 1993. But the past policies were not forgotten by the Catholic community and the significant political legacy of policies of suppression was the enduring electoral boost they gave to Sinn Féin, the IRA's political wing.

The British government has entirely ignored this history in its responses to the threat posed by al-Qaeda and its imitators since 9/11. Indeed, Blair has proved as relentlessly populist as Bush in his exploitation of the issue, despite his leadership of a left of centre political party. In particular, he has constantly pandered on these issues to the radical rightwing agenda of the Murdoch press. The measures the government has authorized have included extending detention without trial and, following the suicide bomb attacks and attempted attacks in London in July 2005, the noisy announcement of the adoption of a 'shoot to kill' policy in relation to suicide bombers. The fruits of the policy were quickly seen with the shooting dead of an individual at a tube station in London. He had been under constant surveillance by the police after he had left a block of flats. He turned out to be a Brazilian electrician, Jean

Charles de Menezes, with no connection whatever with terrorism. Since under any circumstances in any country the use of lethal force is permitted to protect members of the public where there is an imminent threat to life, either the 'shoot to kill' policy is meaningless posturing or, more disturbingly, as the circumstances in which the Brazilian was shot, on the face of it, might suggest, constitutes the entirely illegal adoption of a policy of extrajudicial execution under the guise of protecting the public. While a number of the proposals the government has put forward since the July 2005 bombings seem likely to fall foul of its international legal obligations and may be abandoned, that may not matter to the government that recognizes the political payoff to be gained from association with tough and controversial proposals that wrong-foot the opposition parties.

In Northern Ireland an important determinant of political attitudes was whose violence one feared most. Thus, a factor in lessening revulsion against terrorist violence of the IRA among Catholics was fear of the random attacks of Loyalists and resentment at the heavy-handed behaviour of the army during the early years of the IRA's campaign. While the utterly indiscriminate violence of global jihadists has little capacity to elicit significant support in any community in Britain, the combination of a very marked increase in racial attacks since 7 July and reaction to the shooting of the Brazilian has already created a situation in London where some travellers on the underground have stated that they fear being the victim of a racial attack or being shot at by the police more than they fear being caught up in a suicide bomb attack, because of the possibility of their being mistaken for suicide bombers due to their age and appearance. The panic created by the July attacks was reflected in thoughtless reactions from even the most august opinion-makers. For example, the *Financial Times*, noting the use of racial profiling by the police in the stopping and searching of passengers using public transport in London after the attacks, commented: 'While race should certainly not be the only criterion for such searches – not least because it thereby opens up a loophole – it is absurd, and possibly irresponsible, to ignore it'.[19]

What price Britain and the United States will end up paying for the ill-considered policies adopted by Blair and Bush and their unsavoury political exploitation of the issue of terrorism is very difficult to predict. Their conduct of the war against terrorism may have little bearing on the calculations of those committed to using violence on behalf of the global jihadist project, particularly as a continuing campaign of violence in non-Muslim countries outside of zones of conflict has little to recommend it on instrumental grounds. If it is continued at all, it is likely to be perpetrated by a tiny fringe of opinion, far narrower than the range of opinion targeted by the British government as extremists. Further, some of the more sensible and politically non-controversial measures that have been adopted since 9/11, such as improvements in airport security, may also help to limit attacks by groups seeking to imitate or emulate al-Qaeda. What is more likely than any repeat of 9/11 is that, ironically, radical Islamists pursuing their objectives by political means will prove to be the principal bene- ficiaries of current Western policies, as they benefit from the backlash in Muslim countries against the nature of the American war against terrorism, just as in the long run the Provisional Republican movement in Ireland made political headway on the back of British mistakes and misconduct during the early years of Northern Ireland's troubles, even if the movement's aim of a united Ireland remains unrealized. But as will be illustrated towards the end of the next chapter, Bush's war against terrorism has already had some surprising consequences for conflicts in other parts of the world.

Notes

1 Lawrence Freedman, 'The Coming War on Terrorism' in Lawrence Freedman (ed.), *Superterrorism: Policy Responses*, Blackwell, Oxford 2002, pp. 44–5.
2 Ibid., p. 45.
3 Ibid., p. 44.

4 High-level Panel on Threats, Challenges and Change, *A More Secure World: Our Shared Responsibility*, United Nations, New York 2004, p. 51.

5 As many historians have noted, the Kellogg–Briand Pact of August 1928 outlawing war did not advance the cause of peace in practice.

6 Helen Fenwick, 'Responding to 11 September: Detention without Trial under the Anti-Terrorism, Crime and Security Act 2001' in Lawrence Freedman, *Superterrorism: Policy Responses*, Blackwell, Oxford 2002, p. 80.

7 *Independent*, 10 August 2005.

8 Tony Judt, 'The New World Order', *New York Review of Books*, Vol. LII, No. 12, 14 July 2005, p. 17.

9 Ibid.

10 *Guantánamo and beyond: The continuing pursuit of unchecked executive power*, Amnesty International, May 2005, p. 11.

11 Ibid., pp. 62–3.

12 See Holly Yeager, 'Principled McCain prevails over White House', *Financial Times*, 17 December 2005 and Denis Staunton, 'Bush backs down and agrees to ban torture', *Irish Times*, 16 December 2005.

13 Seymour M. Hersh, *Chain of Command: The Road from 9/11 to Abu Ghraib*, Allen Lane, London 2004, p. 73.

14 Jason Burke, *Al-Qaeda: The True Story of Radical Islam*, Penguin, Harmonsworth 2004, p. 15.

15 John Guelke, 'The Political Morality of the Neo-Conservatives: An Analysis', *International Politics*, Vol. 42, No. 1, March 2005, p. 111.

16 See 'Law to prosecute mercenaries soon', *Mail & Guardian online* (www.mg.co.za), 29 June 2005 and 'More South Africans expected to die in Iraq', *Mail & Guardian online* (www.mg.co.za), 13 October 2004.

17 See, for example, the analysis of the Russian case in Sarah Oates, 'Selling Fear? The Framing of Terrorist Threat in Elections' in *Security, Terrorism and the UK: ISP/NSC Briefing Paper 05/01*, Chatham House, London, July 2005.

18 See the analysis of the state papers of 1971 in 'The British army commander repeatedly advised Edward Heath against introducing internment', *Irish Times*, 2 January 1972.

19 'Western democracies wrestle with terror', *Financial Times*, 9 August 2005.

CHAPTER 10

Peace processes and terrorism

Peace processes and terrorism are very nearly opposites. Peace processes are associated with the strategy of accommodation towards political violence, including a readiness to enter into negotiations on the issues giving rise to the violence, while terrorism is commonly met by a strategy of suppression that affirms the absolute illegitimacy of those engaged in violence. Thus, the very use of the term 'terrorists' by the authorities is commonly an indication that the government has no intention of entering into negotiations with the political representatives of the insurgents in question. Indeed, it is usually an indication that they hope to be able to suppress the insurgents by force and therefore avoid the political claims that lie behind the campaign of violence. Admittedly, unwillingness to address the political demands of those using violence is only one dimension of why the term 'terrorism' may be applied to a particular campaign of violence. The nature of the violence is also an important factor in whether or not it is widely labelled as terrorism, not merely by the government affected but more widely. In this context, significant criteria are whether those using violence adhere to norms such as confining acts of violence to the conflict area, eschewing outrageous methods such as the taking of hostages and exercising restraint over targeting so as to minimize the dangers to innocent bystanders.

Of course, everywhere governments tend to represent anyone challenging their legitimacy by violence as fully deserving of the description of terrorists, at least while the violence is continuing and before any prospects of ceasefires and negotiations exist. However, arriving at objective judgements about the conduct of campaigns of violence are by no means easy, since the consequences of an act of violence is not necessarily an indication of the intentions behind it. The difficulty with the approach of the High-level Panel referred to Chapter 9 is that the simple rule that no-one should target civilians or non-combatants is an inadequate basis for reaching sensible conclusions about the legitimacy of the actions either of governments or insurgents. Context and circumstance inevitably do matter. The use of lethal violence of any kind, regardless of its targets, would not be legitimate in the pursuit of frivolous causes, while some degree of collateral damage (i.e. causing the deaths of civilians) might be justifiable if the stakes were high enough. Of course, it is to be expected that people of different religions and cultures might differ on the interpretation of these issues in practice. It is unlikely in any event that people outside a society affected by conflict would have the knowledge needed to make such judgements. Furthermore, outsiders are generally little affected by the decisions that a particular society makes in this area, whereas the inhabitants have to live with the consequences. That makes the emphasis commonly placed on 'no immunity' and 'no impunity' especially foolish, both in its prescribing how different societies should seek to deal with violent conflict and its aftermath and in its failure to recognize the importance that amnesties play and have always played in enabling societies to overcome conflicts and move on.

An obvious problem is that the term 'terrorism' lends itself to the making of absolutist judgements, such as 'once a terrorist always a terrorist', 'there should be no negotiations with terrorists', and 'putting former terrorists in government is unacceptable in any democracy', to give some frequently quoted examples. In his monthly press conference on 26 July 2005, the British Prime Minister, Tony Blair, grappled uneasily with these issues when he was challenged on the contrast between his approach to the violence of al-Qaeda and his attitude to the IRA.

And one of the reasons why . . . my entire thinking changed post-September 11 is that belief that you have a different form of terrorism, it is not to say that you justify any sort of terrorism, but it is different, I think it is different in its political demands and most essentially it is different in the way that it operates and in the numbers of people it is prepared to kill.[1]

Earlier in the same reply, Blair declared: 'I don't think the IRA would ever have set about trying to kill 3,000 people'.[2] But while it is perfectly rational to distinguish the character of different campaigns of political violence, the term terrorism is poorly suited for drawing such distinctions. The worst that terrorists do is what tends to form the yardstick of what terrorism is. That is one reason why terms such as superterrorism or hyperterrorism have not caught on. Blair was pressed further on the difference between the demands al-Qaeda was putting forward and those of the IRA during its campaign of violence. He responded as follows:

No, I think what I said . . . is that they do indeed have demands, but they are not demands any sensible person can negotiate on, I think that is what I said. And the reason for negotiating with the IRA is nothing to do with terrorism, the reason for being prepared to enter into dialogue with Republicanism is because you do have a demand that is, I may agree or disagree with it, but you can hardly say it is a demand that no sensible person can negotiate on, it is a demand shared by many of our citizens in the north.[3]

Unsurprisingly, Blair's comments prompted a furious reaction from Unionists in Northern Ireland, who viewed his comments as according a measure of legitimacy to the IRA. The *Belfast Telegraph* gave over a full page of its large-format paper to a stinging denunciation of Blair's comments to the press conference by the leader of the United Kingdom Unionist Party, Robert McCartney.

Of course, the nature of the demands is of no relevance if the murderous methodology is entirely similar, and, as such, wholly comparable. The incredible nonsense of Blair's response ignores entirely the total similarity of human suffering and the terrorists' contempt for democratic principles.[4]

McCartney opposed the Good Friday Agreement and remains opposed in principle to a political settlement that includes Sinn Féin, the political wing of the IRA. His viewpoint that former terrorists cannot be trusted is commonly to be found in societies that have experienced a prolonged period of violent conflict. Indeed, this sentiment may be sufficiently widespread that it impedes negotiations even when the violence stops. For example, there remains strong opposition in Spain to the notion that even in the event of a permanent ceasefire, the government should initiate negotiations with the Basque separatist group, ETA (Basque Homeland and Freedom), despite the sharp fall-off in the level of ETA violence that has taken place in recent years.

The demonization of violent organizations as intending not merely the very worst consequences of their most lethal acts of terrorism, but ten times worse than that, as Blair has stated of al-Qaeda, may make the transition to the politics of negotiation particularly difficult. However, in this context, the onus is not simply on government to ensure that violent organizations have an incentive to pursue their aims by other means, as British governments were careful to do in Northern Ireland. There is also a very large responsibility on violent organizations themselves to conduct their campaigns in a way that does not make future co-existence impossible. Indeed, it can be argued that groups seeking fundamental political change ought to eschew violence altogether if the non-violent alternative of civil disobedience is a feasible strategy in the circumstances. These themes are very well illustrated by the case of South Africa and this is explored in some depth in what follows. The South African example also illustrates another important theme, which is both how campaigns of violence begin and how they come to an end.

On 6 August 1990, the African National Congress (ANC) and the South African government signed the Pretoria Minute. Under it 'the ANC announced that it was now suspending all armed actions with immediate effect'.[5] This marked the end of a campaign of violence that had formally been launched by Umkhonto we Sizwe (Spear of the Nation or MK) on 16 December 1961. But it did not put an end to other forms of political violence. Indeed, more people died in political violence in South Africa in the next three-and-a-half years than in the 30 years of the armed struggle. Nevertheless, the Pretoria Minute was widely seen as paving the way towards negotiations on a new political dispensation, though the shape of the final settlement between the parties was far from apparent at this stage. In fact, some saw President de Klerk's bold initiative to liberalize the South African political system in February 1990 as an indication of MK's failure. As it turned out, the ANC leadership was more realistic in its assessment of the strength of the movement's bargaining position at the outset of the country's transition to democracy. However, principle, as well as political judgement of the balance of forces, played a part in the decision to suspend the armed struggle just as it had in the decision to embark on a campaign of violence in 1961. Indeed, the role that principle played in the campaign from beginning to end is most visibly reflected in the ANC's willingness to subject its actions throughout the period to public scrutiny and for its conduct to be judged according to established international norms.

Notwithstanding some pertinent criticism of omissions in its lengthy justification of its campaign of violence in its submission to the Truth and Reconciliation Commission (TRC), the ANC's claim to have acted largely in accordance with international norms does have a measure of substance. However, it received relatively little credit for doing so. In particular, conservatives in the West characterized MK's armed struggle as terrorism and disregarded the constraints that were placed on the campaign for normative as well as political reasons. In fact, the most significant factor in how they viewed the ANC was its links with the South African Communist Party (SACP) and this coloured their view of the legitimacy of its actions. By contrast, it is arguable that among liberals and the left in the West, the illegitimacy of apartheid tended to be regarded as providing a sufficient basis for support for the ANC and its violent struggle against apartheid. However, for the ANC itself, throughout the course of the armed struggle, it remained important that the methods MK employed (and not simply the ends to which they were directed) could be distinguished in moral terms from those employed by the South African state and be defensible, so as not to put at risk support it received internationally for its cause. Ironically, in view of the characterization of the ANC as a terrorist organization, most notably by Margaret Thatcher, the ANC itself used the term terrorism to distinguish between forms of political violence.

Arguments over the morality of the ANC's armed struggle are inevitably intertwined with conflicting interpretations of the transition itself. However, some relatively straightforward propositions about why its campaign ended can be made. First, there is little basis for doubting that the overwhelming majority of African South Africans (constituting three-quarters of the electorate in 1994) regarded MK's campaign as legitimate, at least in retrospect. The outcome of the 1994 elections, the first opportunity that the African electorate had to express its opinions freely, provided a massive endorsement for the ANC. The very poor showing of the Pan-Africanist Congress (PAC), which had been a substantial competitor of the ANC at the time that both organizations were banned in 1960, appears to have been at least in part attributable to the fact that the PAC could not point to a record of resistance in any way comparable to its rival. A second relatively uncontroversial proposition is that government repression in the late 1980s was incapable of ending the crisis of governability that had been in evidence inside South Africa since 1976. Third, the ANC and its allies in the Congress Alliance, while encompassing a wide range of opinions, constituted a cohesive political force under the towering leadership of Nelson Mandela, following his release from prison.

The simplest explanation of why the ANC suspended MK's armed struggle is that the government satisfied the ANC's demands for the ending of its campaign, as a brief history of the organization will underline. The ANC was formed in 1912, but it did not become a mass movement until the 1950s. The impetus for the organization's transformation came from the ANC Youth League formed in 1944. The Youth League persuaded the ANC to adopt a Programme of Action in December 1949 that envisaged civil disobedience, a change from its previous tactics of petitioning and lobbying. This was put into effect in the 1952 Defiance Campaign. Following the Sharpeville massacre on 21 March 1960, when police opened fire on a crowd defying the pass laws, killing 69 of the demonstrators, the government banned the main African nationalist movements, the ANC and the Pan-Africanist Congress (PAC). The PAC had been formed in 1959 by Africanists who rejected the non-racial approach of the Freedom Charter and objected to the extent of influence of white Communists over the Congress Alliance.

After its prohibition the ANC went underground attempting to sustain mass passive resistance and a commitment to non-violent methods, despite being an illegal organization. Following the failure of the ANC's call for a stayaway from work in May 1961, discussion began among ANC members on the adoption of a campaign of violence. The context was described by Nelson Mandela at his trial in 1964:

> At the beginning of June 1961, after long and anxious assessment of the South African situation, I and some colleagues came to the conclusion that as violence in this country was inevitable, it would be wrong and unrealistic for African leaders to continue preaching peace and non-violence at a time when the government met our peaceful demands with force.[6]

Mandela emphasized that one of the purposes of the campaign was 'to canalize and control the feelings of our people'[7] in order to avoid greater bloodshed as a consequence of spontaneous outbursts of anger. He also stressed that the form of violence that MK chose was not terrorism:

> Four forms of violence were possible. There is sabotage, there is guerrilla warfare, there is terrorism, and there is open revolution. We chose to adopt the first method and to exhaust it before taking any other decision. In the light of our political background the choice was a logical one. Sabotage did not involve loss of life, and it offered the best hope for future race relations. Bitterness would be kept to a minimum and, if the policy bore fruit, democratic government could become a reality.[8]

This choice reflected the MK's insistence that the object of its campaign was to persuade the government to enter into negotiations with leaders of African nationalist opinion. The demand for negotiations was to be a constant factor in the ANC's approach to the conflict.

MK's campaign of violence went through a number of phases. The leadership rapidly concluded that sabotage had failed in its aim of inducing a change in the direction of government policy. Analysing the move towards violence from the perspective of the 1990s, the SACP leader, Joe Slovo, argued that 'no-one believed that the tactic of sabotage could, on its own, lead to the collapse of the racist state'.[9] He presented sabotage as marking a decisive break with the previous policy of non-violence and as intended as a form of armed propaganda aimed at encouraging young militants to join the underground. Slovo also made clear that the setting up of MK was a joint decision of the Central Committee of the SACP and 'the Johannesburg Working Group of the ANC'.[10] By the time of the arrest of the principal leaders of the campaign following a police raid on Liliesleaf farm in Rivonia north of Johannesburg on 11 July 1963, preparations were already being made for the start of rural guerrilla warfare. However, the objective circumstances for the waging of any kind of campaign were to prove extremely unfavourable in this period.

During the 1960s it was widely believed that majority rule was inevitable in South Africa, the Portuguese colonies of Angola and Mozambique, and Southern Rhodesia as part of the continent-wide process of decolonization. This led to the prospects for change in

South Africa being overestimated. However, once South Africa had got through this period, internal conditions became the focus of attention and in this context, the survival of white rule seemed assured precisely because of the successful repression of opposition during the 1960s. Consequently, the prospects for change came to be underestimated. In particular, there was a failure to recognize the vulnerability of white rule to a crisis of governability. To force the government into negotiations on the opposition's terms did not require the overthrow of the regime's formidable security apparatus. The existence of apparently endemic instability was sufficient to engender doubts as to the regime's durability, not least among the foreign investors whose confidence was required to sustain economic growth. In fact, white rule proved surprisingly brittle. Pushed along the path of reform by a crisis of governability after the Soweto uprising of June 1976, the government discovered that each concession it made empowered its opponents further, necessitating more concessions.

Trials of the leading figures in the ANC and in MK and a general security clampdown had effectively destroyed the African nationalist movement inside South Africa by the mid-1960s. At the same time, the buffer of white-ruled or colonial states that surrounded the country through the 1960s presented a formidable obstacle to the infiltration into South Africa of members of MK from exile, where the ANC had established camps for the purpose of providing military training to recruits. When the ANC met in conference in 1969 in Morogogo in Tanzania, conditions for the advancement of its cause through rural guerrilla warfare either in South Africa or in neighbouring states seemed most inauspicious. This was reflected in a document prepared for the conference, entitled 'Strategy and Tactics of the ANC', which emphasized the need for political mobilization as a precondition for the success of the campaign of violence.[11] However, the prospect of the ANC's being able to mobilize the masses in South Africa in accordance with this rhetoric seemed extremely remote.

The situation changed with the Portuguese revolution of 1974, which led to independence for Angola and Mozambique in 1975, and even more with the Soweto uprising of 1976. Although the ANC played little part in the events that led up to the Soweto uprising, it was the major beneficiary of the crisis. The flight into exile of many of the militants involved in the uprising and the subsequent unrest across the country provided the ANC in exile with a fresh generation of recruits. After a gap of a decade, MK resumed operations inside South Africa in October 1976 with the sabotage of a railway line. Of particular importance in raising the profile of the MK during the late 1970s and early 1980s were a series of spectacular attacks on prestige targets, such as the destruction in 1980 of a plant that produced oil from coal, an important symbol of the country's self-sufficiency and capacity to overcome an oil embargo.

The South African government responded to the challenge presented by the resumption of the MK's campaign by adopting a total strategy including a policy of the destabilization of neighbouring states designed to punish them for harbouring MK units. However, the total strategy was undermined by increasing instability inside South Africa itself as the government lost control of the townships. In September 1984 the Vaal and East Rand townships erupted in protest against rent increases, a revolt that coincided with a failed attempt by the government to widen its support by coopting the Coloured and Indian minorities through the adoption of a new constitution. By this time the ANC was able to characterize its struggle against apartheid as resting on four pillars: mass mobilization, armed operations, underground organization and international solidarity work. ANC rhetoric that it was making the preparations to conduct a people's war no longer seemed incredible, even if in reality the ANC had little control over the militants acting in its name in the townships.

The following year, 1985, saw the first attempts by the government to explore the possibilities for negotiations with leaders of the ANC, including the imprisoned Nelson Mandela. A meeting between Mandela and the Minister of Justice, Kobie Coetzee, in November 1985, initiated four years of secret talks between Mandela and the government. Two concerns dominated Mandela's discussions with government ministers. The first was the urgency of negotiations between the government and the ANC, given the turmoil in the country. The second was that his talks with the government should not in any way undercut the position of the ANC. In preparation for a meeting with President Botha in July 1989, Mandela drew up a memorandum on the terms of his discussions with the government that was designed to allay any fears that his ANC colleagues had about them. In particular, Mandela was adamant in his rejection of each of what he described as the 'three main demands set by the government as a precondition for negotiations, namely that the ANC must first renounce violence, break with the SACP and abandon its demand for majority rule'. His memorandum concluded by suggesting parameters for the negotiations:

> Two political issues will have to be addressed: firstly, the demand for majority rule in a unitary state; secondly, the concern of white South Africa over this demand, as well as the insistence of whites on structural guarantees that majority rule will not mean domination of the white minority by blacks. The most crucial tasks which will face the government and the ANC will be to reconcile these two positions.[12]

The official position of the ANC on negotiations at this time was set out in the Harare Declaration, endorsed by the Organization of African Unity in a meeting in Zimbabwe in August 1989. This placed the onus on the South African government to create the climate for negotiations by releasing political prisoners, lifting the bans on African nationalist organizations, removing troops from the townships, ending the state of emergency and ceasing political executions.

The release of Mandela from prison was not immediately followed by negotiations between the government and the ANC. When the two sides finally met in May 1990, the government agreed to lift the state of emergency, while both sides agreed to establish a joint working group to deal with such matters as the release of political prisoners and the return of exiles. The report of the joint working group established the definition of a political offence and dealt with the question of the release of prisoners, thereby providing the basis for the Pretoria Minute under which the ANC suspended all armed actions on 6 August 1990. The mechanism for the release of prisoners required them to apply for indemnity individually, as provided for in legislation that parliament had enacted. Mandela records that some of the prisoners on Robben Island he visited after his release objected to this procedure as falling short of the unconditional blanket amnesty the ANC had demanded in the Harare Declaration. Mandela told them they were being unrealistic in view of the fact that the government had not been defeated on the battlefield.[13]

According to Mandela's autobiography, the actual decision to suspend the armed struggle was taken by the ANC National Executive Committee at the initiative of Joe Slovo, in advance of its August meeting with the government. Mandela puts the decision partly in the context of the government's discovery in July 1990 of Operation Vula, under which the ANC was continuing to build underground structures and the capacity to sustain a campaign of violence against the state, should the government attempt to reverse its liberalization of the political system. The discovery of Operation Vula had deeply shocked the government, which presented it as a SACP plot to overthrow the government by force and demanded the SACP's exclusion from the negotiations. Slovo's proposal to suspend the armed struggle, which Mandela supported, led to a lengthy debate within the National Executive Committee before being adopted. The proponents argued that the armed struggle had achieved its aim of bringing the government to the negotiating table. Mandela explains why, nevertheless, the issue proved so controversial as follows:

> Although MK was not active the aura of the armed struggle had great meaning for many people. Even when cited merely as a rhetorical device, the armed struggle was a sign that we were actively fighting the enemy. As a result, it had a popu-

larity that was out of all proportion to what it had achieved on the ground.[14]

At the level of policy and of rhetoric, MK's armed struggle through all its various phases was remarkably principled. The objective of the campaign to achieve inclusive negotiations was clearly a moderate one, from an international perspective. However, it is understandable that this appeared a huge step from the perspective of the South African government since the extension of the franchise to the African majority was unavoidable in any negotiated settlement as nothing less was likely to be regarded as legitimate by international opinion. This put the ANC in a very strong position given the likely outcome of democratic elections in South Africa. The means employed by the ANC were also by and large principled, by the standards of modern warfare. When the Geneva Conventions of 1949 were supplemented by the addition of two Protocols in 1977 with the purpose of extending the concept of international armed conflict so as to cover cases of guerrilla warfare, the ANC undertook to adhere to the Convention and its Protocols and took part in a special ceremony at the headquarters of the International Committee of the Red Cross in November 1980 to underline its commitment to the observance of international humanitarian law.

However, the intensification of the conflict inside South Africa in the 1980s put pressure on the stance of avoiding civilian casualties and that was reflected in one of the decisions made by the Kabwe conference in 1985, which came close to condoning attacks on soft targets. Further, in practice, the actions of MK members did not always conform to the standards demanded of them by their leaders. This was acknowledged by the ANC in its submission to the TRC. It discussed examples of breaches of its code of conduct. In particular, it gave a detailed account of the 1980 Silverton Bank siege, 'the only incident in which MK cadres, in contravention of ANC policy, seized hostages for political ends'.[15] However, the submission glossed over the reaction in the townships to the siege and the debate the episode gave rise to within the ANC itself. Thus, according to Howard Barrell, to the ANC's amazement, an estimated 10,000 Sowetans attended the funeral of the three MK combatants, and an opinion poll commissioned by a newspaper revealed that three out of four Sowetans felt some degree of sympathy with the three MK men.[16]

This reaction strengthened the case being made by some leading members of MK for the placing of fewer restraints on the conduct of its operations.

The ANC submission discussed a number of other instances in which MK operations led to the deaths of civilians, such as the car bomb attack on the headquarters of the South African Air Force (SAAF) in Pretoria in May 1983, in which 19 people were killed (of whom 11 were SAAF officers). Mandela commented on this episode that it was 'the inevitable consequence of the decision to embark on a military struggle'.[17] The ANC submission also sought to justify the use by MK, from late 1985, of landmines in the border areas. The context of their use was the promulgation of border areas as military zones by the government in an effort to stem infiltration across the country's borders by MK units. It was a sensitive issue for the ANC because, although military patrols were the intended targets of the landmines, a considerable number of civilians were killed or injured by them in practice.

Tom Lodge, in general a sympathetic observer of the ANC, strongly criticized the ANC submission to the TRC. His main complaint is that it is 'too much of a lawyer's defence rather than what it should be: a moral acknowledgment of the extent to which the organization transgressed human rights'.[18] Lodge, noting that between 1977 and 1989 at least 1,426 attacks were attributed to the ANC, pointed to numerous omissions in the report, such as its failure to comment on a car bomb placed outside the Ellis Park sports stadium in 1988. Lodge was also critical of the report's treatment of the conduct of ANC-aligned self-defence units (SDUs). These sprung up in townships across the country with the growth of unrest in the mid-1980s. The ANC submission made great play of the instances, such as the case of the Phola Park

SDU, where the SDU's misbehaviour can be attributed to its subversion by the state, and of the fact that the SDUs were not formally a part of the ANC or MK. What the submission underplayed was the readiness of prominent ANC leaders inside and outside the country to defend atrocities carried out by SDUs in support of the objective of making the country ungovernable, including the use of the 'necklace' against those the SDUs accused of being informers or collaborators. The 'necklace' was a tyre filled with petrol that was placed over the suspect and ignited.

The ANC submission was more candid about the ill-treatment of MK recruits in camps in Angola during the 1980s, including the execution of a number of recruits for mutiny when they revolted against the leadership over the issue of helping the Angolan government in its civil war. Lodge's criticisms of the ANC's submission to the TRC proved to be an accurate barometer of the TRC's attitude and foreshadowed its findings. The TRC criticized poorly planned and unplanned operations of MK which resulted in civilian casualties; MK's landmine campaign in rural areas of the Transvaal between 1985 and 1987; extra-judicial killings of suspected informers; and widespread atrocities by ANC-aligned groups.[19] The TRC's criticisms of the ANC need to be placed in context of much harsher criticism of other parties to the conflict. In fact, the lack of restraint in the conduct of the total strategy and the complete indifference of the South African security forces to international norms in the conduct of warfare present a striking contrast to the policy of the ANC and help to explain the ANC's readiness to subject its own conduct of the conflict to public scrutiny. Thus, the ANC approached the question of truth-telling about the atrocities of the past in the strong expectation that its political adversaries would come off very much worse in any such reckoning.

A factor that contributed to the comparatively principled nature of the MK campaign was its small scale. Its impact derived from the symbolic effect rather than from any actual damage that it was able to inflict on the South African state, which was very slight. Thus, it was only one of a considerable number of factors that led to President de Klerk's decision to liberalize the South African political system. Indeed, it is possible to argue that the ANC's campaign of violence was unnecessary and counter-productive. John Kane-Berman has been the most forthright advocate of the proposition that structural factors, particularly developments in the economy, made the demise of apartheid inevitable. He also maintains that the strategy pursued by the ANC during the 1980s of making the country ungovernable left a legacy of disorder at the root of many of the country's post-apartheid social ills, including its very high rates of crime.[20] Even very sympathetic accounts of MK, such as Howard Barrell's short book on the subject, recognize the claims that can be made for the effectiveness of the armed struggle are limited. However, while it can be argued that MK played a minor role in the demise of apartheid, its role in what followed apartheid was arguably much more crucial. In particular, from the perspective of the townships, the sacrifices suffered by members of MK, among which must be numbered the long years of imprisonment of its first commander-in-chief, Nelson Mandela, and of other leading figures in the movement, imbued the ANC with immense moral and political authority, enabling it to secure the votes of an overwhelming proportion of those who had been previously disenfranchised. But while it is arguable that apartheid would have disappeared without MK, the far more significant point is that circumstances would have been very much worse if the ANC's violent campaign against apartheid had been conducted with fewer constraints.

The end of the cold war was a significant factor in the decision of President de Klerk to initiate South Africa's transition to a new political dispensation. He believed, wrongly as it transpired, that the coming down of the Berlin Wall would weaken the position of the ANC because of its alliance with the SACP. The South African case was far from unique and the end of the cold war played a significant role in unfreezing a number of other conflicts as well. Consequently, the 1990s became an era of peace processes.[21] Admittedly, in some cases the necessity for peace processes arose out of conflicts begun in the vacuum created by the collapse of Communism in Eastern Europe and the former Soviet Union. But during the course of the 1990s peace processes were also initiated in a number of long-running conflicts commonly associated with terrorism, notably the conflicts in Israel/Palestine, Northern Ireland, the Basque Country and Corsica. However, none of these peace processes was completely successful, though with the exception of Israel/Palestine there was a decline in lethal political violence in all these societies.

The events of 11 September cast a long shadow over efforts to achieve negotiated political settlements in situations of violent conflict. Shimon Peres had famously declared at the height of optimism in the Oslo peace process that the end of the cold war had facilitated the move from a world of enemies to a world of problems. The obvious implication was that whereas enemies necessitated a military response, problems could be resolved through discussion and dialogue. With the assault on America, it appeared as if the clock had been turned back to a world of enemies once again. In particular, governments could claim to be enlisting in the war against terrorism in their military suppression of anyone engaged in political violence within their realm, especially if elements among the insurgents were, or could plausibly be represented as being, jihadists. However, even where those engaged in violence were not Muslims, there were governments which sought to portray the conflict in which they were engaged as connected to a global war against terrorism.

The Aznar government in Spain before the defeat of the Popular Party in the elections of March 2004 provides a case in point in its attempts to mobilize international opinion against violent Basque separatists. But while the Aznar government's stance contributed to the polarization of opinion in the Basque country between nationalists of all kinds and their opponents, it did not reignite the conflict. Violence has remained at a low level, despite the political impasse over the future of the Basque country. Another example is that of the government of President Uribe in Colombia. In particular, Uribe has used a case against Irish Republicans who had entered the country on false passports and had established links with the insurgents to make the case that Colombia's multifaceted and extremely lethal conflicts belonged within the scope of the war against terrorism, a stance supported for a variety of reasons by the Bush Administration. However, while there is considerable sympathy for the people of Colombia afflicted as they are on all sides by the most outrageous forms of violence, such as hostage-taking, there is little disposition outside the country to view the violence as a global issue, though there is some measure of concern over the potential for conflict between Colombia and neighbouring countries arising out of Colombia's internal problems.

Somewhat surprisingly, in the case of two long-running and extremely lethal conflicts, the impact of 9/11 instead of undermining the prospects for the initiation of peace processes has had the opposite effect, though the chronology of events leading to negotiations in the two cases is not by any means a straightforward one. Further, in both cases, the peace process is at an early stage and success in reaching a political settlement is far from assured. The two cases are Kashmir and Sri Lanka. The Kashmir case was discussed extensively in Chapter 7, so the focus in this chapter will be on the Sri Lankan case. The Sinhalese constitute approximately three-quarters of the population of Sri Lanka. After being ruled successively by the Portuguese, the Dutch and the British, the island became an independent state in 1948. The main feature of the country's post-independence politics has been competition between two large Sinhala-dominated political parties. The consequence was the increasing ethnization of the political system with Sinhala becoming the sole official language and Buddhism, the principal religion among the Sinhalese, receiving state support. In the process the largely Hindu Tamil minority became increasingly alienated. A further factor in their alienation was anti-Tamil violence.

The result was the formation of the LTTE or Tamil Tigers committed to the establishment of independent Tamil homeland. Further anti-Tamil violence followed. After 13 soldiers were killed in a LTTE ambush in 1983, there were widespread riots in which several hundred Tamils were killed. This effectively marked the start of a civil war on the island and in the course of the next

20 years, over 60,000 people died in the violence. There were attempts by the government to initiate negotiations in the mid-1980s and the mid-1990s, but each of these failed and prompted a further escalation of the violence. There was also an attempt by India to mediate in the conflict, which led to the dispatch of an Indian peace-keeping force to the island, but this was withdrawn in 1990 after the breakdown of a ceasefire and attacks on the force by the LTTE. In the course of the civil war the LTTE acquired a reputation as one of the world's most ruthless terrorist organizations, in part, because of its association with the tactic of suicide bombings. In fact, the Tigers were responsible for more such attacks in the last two decades of the twentieth century than any other group in the world, a problem for those who proposed that suicide missions were the mark of a new terrorism based on religion since the Tamil Tigers were a secular group with a separatist agenda. The manner in which the Tigers conducted their campaign of violence led to Amnesty International taking the unusual step of highlighting the organization's violations of human rights, marking a break with Amnesty's previously exclusive focus on the transgressions of states.

Against this unpromising background, Norway announced its readiness to act as a mediator in the conflict in February 2000, amid considerable doubts that negotiations were possible given the nature and leadership of the LTTE. In July 2001 a suicide attack by the Tigers on the country's international airport killed 14 people. Nevertheless, neither this attack nor the impact of 9/11 undermined popular support for Norway's efforts and that was reflected in the election of a new government in the country in December 2001. In February 2002 the government and the Tamil Tigers agreed to a permanent ceasefire and the initiation of talks on a political settlement. While the negotiations on a political settlement broke down after five rounds of talks in 2003, the ceasefire has held, though not without some significant violations, which have led to uncertainty about the continuance of the peace process. Further uncertainty over the future of the peace process has been created by Sri Lanka's Presidential elections in 2005, which resulted in the victory of the candidate most opposed to any further concessions to the LTTE. Nevertheless, the readiness of the LTTE to contemplate a solution based on the autonomy but not the full independence of the north-east of the island suggests that a political settlement may be achievable, despite the difficulties. An important factor in persuading the LTTE to agree to a ceasefire was the organization's recognition that there was a danger in the post-9/11 context that the conflict would be seen as part of the war against terrorism, with the dismissal of the very notion of a negotiated settlement.

Peace processes constitute one of the ways in which terrorist campaigns may come to an end. They are essential in the case of long-running and seemingly intractable conflicts. However, they are far from the only way that terrorist campaigns end. The isolation of the terrorists and their lack of any support in the society may make it impossible for those who have resorted to violence to sustain their campaign. While individuals, including individuals within terrorist groups, may enjoy killing for its own sake, for terrorist groups, killing is only ever a means to an end. Consequently, if it is evident that a campaign is not advancing the cause for which it is being employed, the group itself is likely to abandon violence. For this reason, many campaigns of violence are short-lived. A heavy-handed response by the state may appear to succeed, when in fact the negative political response to the violence would in any event have led to its abandonment. An example is the rapid disappearance of violent Quebeçois separatism in the early 1970s. Attempts to promote violent Scottish or Welsh separatism have proved equally unsuccessful. A common mistake by governments is to equate terrorism and political extremism, though as the cases of Scottish, Welsh and Quebeçois separatism underscore, supporting what some might consider to be the extreme objective of independence does not by any means translate into support for the use of violent methods to bring it about.

Admittedly, suppression may also at great cost bring a campaign of terrorism that attracts a measure of support to an end. However, if fundamental political grievances lie at the root of the violence, the respite from violent conflict is unlikely to prove long-lasting. Further, suppression is frequently counter-productive. Indeed, it may infuse terrorist acts without any clear purpose with meaning that they would otherwise not have. Indiscriminate attacks on public transport systems used by people of every class and background form an obvious example of terrorism that has little or no possibility of generating any level of support in any society without the assistance of very ill-considered reaction from the authorities. However, poor judgement and political posturing in such circumstances can increase the likelihood of copycat attacks and enhance the fears of commuters, greatly magnifying the impact of an almost meaningless act of terrorism. Of course, a strong public reaction is to be expected to atrocities in which large numbers of people lose their lives, but ensuring that is constructively channelled into support for the victims, rather than exploiting the atrocity for partisan political purposes, is the course that any responsible government should follow. Suppression also tends to be indiscriminate in its impact and often succeeds in alienating people previously neutral in their political sympathies or even supportive of the state in question. The manner in which the Bush Administration has managed to antagonize much of world opinion since 9/11 is a striking example of such an outcome.

It may be objected that not all terrorism is of an instrumental nature and that is why the possibility of the terrorist use of weapons of mass destruction, for example, is to be feared. As discussed in Chapter 8, religious cults with anti-scientific cosmologies have episodically given rise to extremely destructive as well as self-destructive acts of violence. But in so far as their beliefs led them to make assumptions about the world, such as the prediction of the imminence of cataclysmic events, that are susceptible to falsification, they tend to have a limited capacity for survival in the long run. It is, of course, also the case that religious fundamentalists tend to propound anti-scientific cosmologies, but generally these are usually of a sufficiently transcendental kind as not to be subject to falsification in the ordinary course of events. Admittedly, it is troubling not merely that there are people in the United States who apparently believe that the dinosaurs and human beings inhabited the earth at the same time, but also that there are politicians willing to indulge such beliefs. However, while the prevalence of such anti-scientific cosmologies has extremely alarming implications for a number of areas of policy, such as the environment, they have less obvious relevance for terrorism or counter-terrorism. The other source of non-instrumental violence is nihilism. But in practice adherents of nihilism are extremely rare and nihilist groups, as opposed to individuals, rarer still. In the immediate aftermath of 9/11, al-Qaeda was widely portrayed in these terms, but this is not an accurate representation of a group with a clear set of political aims, even if they are, as Blair put it, 'not demands any sensible person can negotiate on'.[22] But that is not to under-estimate the threat that global jihadists pose by virtue of their readiness to extend their struggle to the whole world. This issue is taken up in the next chapter.

Notes

1 Transcript of PM's Press Conference on 26 July 2005, www.number-10.gov.uk.
2 Ibid.
3 Ibid.
4 Robert McCartney, 'Blair's shame . . .', *Belfast Telegraph*, 3 August 2005.
5 From the text of the Pretoria Minute, quoted in Carole Cooper, Robin Hamilton, Harry Mashabela, Shaun Mackay, Joe Kelly, Elizabeth Sidiropolous, Claire Gordon-Brown and John Gary Moonsamy, *Race Relations Survey 1991/92*, South African Institute of Race Relations, Johannesburg 1992, pp. 513.
6 From 'Statement during the Rivonia Trial, by Nelson R. Mandela, 20 April 1964' quoted in Thomas Karis and Gail M. Gerhart (eds), *Challenge and Protest: Volume 3 of From Protest to Challenge*, University, Stanford CA: Hoover Institution Press, (Stanford) 1977, p. 777.
7 Ibid., p. 772.

8 Ibid., p. 778.

9 Joe Slovo, *The Unfinished Autobiography*, Ravan Press, Johannesburg 1995, p. 152.

10 Ibid., p. 151.

11 The text of 'Strategy and Tactics of the ANC (document adopted by the Morogogo Conference of the ANC, meeting at Morogogo, Tanzania, 1969)' is available under the heading of ANC historical documents at the ANC's web-site, http://www.anc.org.za.

12 From the text of 'The Mandela Document: a document presented by Nelson Mandela to P.W. Botha in July 1989', available at the ANC web-site (see note 11).

13 Nelson Mandela, *Long Walk to Freedom: The Autobiography of Nelson Mandela*, Macdonald Purnell, Randburg 1994, p. 573.

14 Ibid., p. 578.

15 African National Congress, 'Statement to the Truth and Reconciliation Commission', August 1996, especially Chapter 6, headed 'Did the ANC perpetrate any gross violations of human rights?' available on line from the ANC's web-site (note 11).

16 Howard Barrell, *MK: the ANC's armed struggle*, Penguin, Johannesburg 1990, pp. 45–6.

17 Mandela (as at note 13), p. 506.

18 Tom Lodge, 'Taking great pains to justify a "clean war"', *Mail and Guardian* (Johannesburg), 23–29 August 1996.

19 *Truth and Reconciliation Commission of South Africa Report: Volume 2*, Macmillan Reference Limited, Basingstoke and Oxford 1999, pp. 326–66.

20 John Kane-Berman, *Political Violence in South Africa*, South African Institute of Race Relations, Johannesburg 1993, pp. 79–88.

21 See, for example, Elizabeth Craig and Christine Bell, 'Appendix: A Decade of Peace Agreements' in Christine Bell, *Peace Agreements and Human Rights*, Oxford University Press, Oxford 2000, pp. 323–74.

22 See note 1 above.

CHAPTER 11

Injustice and inequality

While terrorism itself is generally regarded, virtually to the point of definition, as absolutely illegitimate violence, it is widely, through by no means universally, acknowledged that legitimate grievances underpin resort to terrorism. For example, the Secretary-General's High-level Panel refers to 'the imperative to develop a global strategy of fighting terrorism that addresses root causes' and includes among the facilitators of terrorism, occupations and poverty and unemployment.[1] While in particular cases, the root causes of terrorism may be regarded as residing in very specific circumstances, more commonly root causes tend to be conceived under the broad headings of injustice and inequality and their relationship to terrorism is what is examined in this chapter. It is frequently contended that root causes tend to be neglected in the analysis of terrorism. For example, writing shortly after 9/11, the journalist, Jonathan Freedland complained about their absence in American coverage of the aftermath of the events of 11 September, observing : 'You will find more opinion pieces on airport X-ray machines and new check-in procedures than about global injustice'.[2] However, part of the reason for this absence was not simply that Americans disregarded the causes of terrorism, but the prevalence in the United States of another narrative, frequently articulated in the speeches of President Bush, that terrorism was the product of an evil ideology, the mainspring of which was hatred of the values for which America stood.[3]

All of these explanations beg a lot of questions about the connections between their discrete elements. From a political perspective President Bush's formulation had the obvious advantage that it implicitly rejected the contention that the policies pursued by American governments had played a part in creating the condition for terrorism, an assumption commonly made by commentators outside of the United States. However, the conflicting political attitudes underlying these formulations tend to disguise what they have in common, which is their treatment of terrorism as a single, large and important phenomenon of the times. All are open to the criticism of failure to conceive of different terrorisms with a variety of root causes. Also crucially, they fail to distinguish between terrorism at different levels. In particular, they do not address the importance of the distinction between violence that is largely confined within the framework of a particular state and violence that is global in both its manifestations and the ambitions of the perpetrators. Before any other questions about the motivations of terrorists are examined, the issue of context needs to be addressed. Indeed, it is argued that context matters hugely and looms much larger in the justification of violence than might appear at first sight.

In a book first published in the late 1960s, the French sociologist, Raymond Aron famously wrote that there was no such entity as a planetary society, i.e. a human society encompassing the whole world. Even then the argument was becoming fashionable that economic interdependence, or globalization in current parlance, was fundamentally altering the nature of the international political system. Aron did not deny the significance of technological developments in increasing the scope for transnational relations, but he argued forcefully that these did not change the fundamental role of the state within the international political system or the intrinsically asocial nature of the system.

A sovereign collectivity is one which makes its own laws and whose leaders acknowledge obedience to no one else in certain matters – those affecting so-called vital interests, which in certain circumstances involve the choice between war and peace. The state is not solely, but it is at the very least and in any case, that agency which possesses the monopoly of legitimate violence. Now this monopoly must be effective and not merely legal. What army would be capable of fulfilling for the whole of mankind the function entrusted to the police force in nation-states? All civilizations (or societies, in Toynbee's use of the term) have known a violent history whose mainspring has been the relations between states. Modern civilization, while planetary in its technico-economic dynamism, has not eliminated or even morally modified interstate relations, which, despite our individual condemnations of their cruelty and our desire to shake off their yoke, continue mercilessly in their unreasonable rationality to forge our common destiny.[4]

The picture Aron paints of power residing at the level of the state and the centrality of the state in most people's lives still holds and remains little modified by the most significant change in world affairs since he wrote his book, which is not (*pace* Blair) 9/11, but the end of the cold war.

Individuals or groups seeking to challenge the status quo in any part of the world are likely to do so through the state or else to come up against the power of the state. In all but extremely exceptional cases, it is the state that punishes those who use violent means in the pursuit of political power. Further, in most cases, the task of maintaining order against the challenge of insurgents is carried out by security forces of the country in question and the involvement of the security forces of other countries is relatively unusual. Admittedly, the exceptions, such as Iraq, Kosovo and Bosnia, tend to receive a disproportionate amount of attention. In large countries, power may be devolved from the centre so that the insurgents may initially come into conflict with local rather than national security forces, but what does not exist is a global police force of any kind. Even peace-keeping operations of the United Nations are carried out on the basis of ad hoc arrangements involving contributions by individual states, though there has long been debate on the issue of whether a permanent force should be established, to be at the disposal of the United Nations Secretary-General, subject to authorization of its deployment by the Security Council.

Some constraints do exist on the behaviour of sovereign states and these have become slightly more extensive since Aron's day. The establishment of the International Criminal Court (ICC) has created a form of transnational justice in respect of war crimes, crimes against humanity and genocide and, on an ad hoc basis, international tribunals exist in relation to the past conflicts in the Balkans and the genocide in Rwanda. However, the ICC remains highly controversial. It faces the active opposition of the United States government. Admittedly, American fears that the ICC would restrict their country's freedom of action seem overstated. However, there are more substantial grounds for questioning the wisdom of the creation of the ICC than America's concerns for its own citizens. The much greater danger than the prosecution of any American is that the court will apply the law selectively and politically against weak and unpopular figures in the poorest countries of the world.[5] The application of the criminal law outside the private realm is in any case highly problematic. In the context of private crimes, the law can be applied more or less universally and equally, even if rich defendants may be at an advantage in most systems of criminal justice.

However, crime that is not committed for private advantage is much more difficult to deal with in the context of any criminal justice system, whether it involves a soldier transgressing the law in the context of counter-insurgency operations, political parties violating laws on fund-raising, riots provoked by perceived miscarriages of justice or other widely felt grievances. In such cases, both public opinion and political expediency may dictate the application of some flexibility in the enforcement of the letter of the law. How this is managed is best considered at the level of the state or locally, but certainly not at a global level. As emphasized earlier, amnesties have an important role to play in the resolution of conflicts and there is a danger that developments such as that of the ICC will constitute an obstacle to political settlements in the most lethal conflicts. In particular, to regard the events in the Balkans in the 1990s or in Rwanda in 1994 as the product of individual criminal behaviour is clearly a very superficial, and indeed dangerously shallow, way of viewing and handling these tragedies, even if public opinion in states outside the zone of conflict may be satisfied by this approach as relieving their own societies of any sense of responsibility for what happened.

Another constraint on the sovereignty of states has been the pooling of sovereignty by states in Europe in the European Union (EU). The EU has provided a framework that has been able to transcend national divisions. For example, British and Irish membership of the European Community since 1973 has been a factor in cooperation between the two governments over the issue of Northern Ireland, since involvement in the process of European integration has given the two states a strong incentive not to allow the conflict in Northern Ireland to affect their relations in other areas. At the same time, the conceptualization of Northern Ireland as a region in the EU has lent credibility to the notion that it is possible to accommodate different national identities within the same polity and that Northern Ireland does not have to be either 100 per cent British or 100 per cent Irish. European integration has made it possible to consider the question of sovereignty in other than zero-sum terms, in which a gain for one community automatically constitutes a loss for the other. That is reflected in the Good Friday Agreement's promotion of both closer ties within the British Isles (or Britain and Ireland, in nationalist language) and between the two parts of Ireland. Scottish, Welsh, Basque and Corsican nationalists have also been attracted by the idea that regionalization within the EU might provide a context in which their grievances against overcentralization may be addressed.

The impact of the EU on ethnic conflicts, however, has been even greater in the context of countries wishing to become members of the EU, since the insistence by the EU that candidate countries should measure up to contemporary standards of democratic government, including those for the treatment of minorities, has had an impact both on the behaviour and in the confidence of minorities. Most dramatically, the prospect of EU membership practically reversed attitudes towards the political reunification of the island of Cyprus, with the Turkish Cypriot minority voting in favour of a United Nations plan in April 2004 that would have ended the partition of the island, albeit on the formula of the creation of a bicommunal, bizonal federation, but with Greek Cypriots voting against the plan. The context was Cyprus's imminent membership of the EU, with the attraction of being included within the EU overcoming Turkish Cypriot fears of how they might be treated as a minority within the polity of Cyprus. In the Balkans, too, the prospect of membership of the EU at some future date has had a pronounced impact on the approach of the governments in the region. Slovenia has already achieved membership of the EU and the other states hope to follow.

However, the rejection by the French and the Dutch of the European constitutional treaty, which was designed to streamline the functioning of the EU in the context of the expansion of membership, has cast a shadow over the Balkan states' hopes for early entry into the EU. The crisis within the EU reflects disillusionment over both the functioning and policies of the EU within a number of countries. In particular, fears that social security guarantees will be weakened under the guise of harmonization within the EU have prompted a powerful backlash against the further progress of European integration. Other factors contributing to disillusionment with the EU were economic stagnation and high unemployment following the adoption of the Euro as a currency in a number of countries in the EU, the differing attitudes of member states towards the war against Iraq and the irrelevance of the EU to the behaviour of the large states within the EU on the issue.

In spite of the current difficulties, the European example has considerable resonance for other parts of the world, most particularly South Asia. The growth of cooperation among the states of the region found institutional expression in the creation of the South Asian Association for Regional Cooperation (SAARC) in

1985. The same seven countries, India, Pakistan, Bangladesh, Sri Lanka, Nepal, Bhutan and the Maldives established the South Asian Free Trade Association (SAFTA), coming into effect in January 2006. On the analogy of European integration, it is envisaged that these steps will facilitate the evolution of a South Asian identity that might help to provide a context for the solution to problems in the region that revolve round the issue of national identity, such as the conflict in Kashmir. Underpinning these expectations is the perception that many of the conflicts in the region have been exacerbated by inter-state rivalry, reflected in the assistance that insurgents have secured from time to time from neighbouring states. It is arguable that in some cases, at least, there is a danger that the local roots of the conflict and the sources of alienation within the society may be underplayed and under-estimated. In particular, friendly relations between India and Pakistan, as well as extensive cooperation between the two states economically, will not of themselves resolve the complex problems of the state of Jammu and Kashmir.

The legal equality of sovereign states does not of course mean that all states are anything like equal in practice in their capacity to exercise their sovereignty. Indeed, what characterizes Third World states in general, with the exceptions of such giants as India and China, is precisely their vulnerability to external pressures. The bipolarity that characterized the era of the cold war placed significant constraints on the behaviour of the most powerful states within the international political system. In particular, both superpowers feared that military intervention in internal conflicts in other states would both provoke and legitimize similar action by the other superpower, while alienating opinion in countries where the two superpowers were competing for political influence. Consequently, both superpowers stressed their commitment to the maintenance of such international norms as self-determination, territorial integrity and non-intervention. Admittedly, in practice, within their own spheres of influence, neither superpower showed much respect for these norms, so that in the case of Latin America the United States intervened to overthrow a number of left-leaning governments, while the Soviet Union intervened in Eastern Europe to put down revolts against Communist rule or to prevent the unauthorized liberalization of the system.

Outside of these regions, however, the fear that intervention might lead to conflict with the other superpower and escalate into an unwinnable war between the superpowers themselves was an obstacle to naked imperialism. Even so, one of the factors behind the onset of an age of terrorism in the late 1960s was the belief in the case of the New Left in the ubiquity of American imperialism. However, these groups were unsuccessful in securing any significant measure of support for their strategy of violence directed at American targets, not least because in Europe, the potential threat that the Soviet Union presented had sufficient resonance to secure widespread support across the political spectrum for an alliance with the United States, premised on the defence of democratic government. More credibly, both anti-government political parties and violent movements in Latin America accused the American government of propping up authoritarian military regimes for strategic reasons and this provided the justification for attacks on American targets by so-called urban guerrillas. However, the period when such a case could be made was comparatively short-lived since after the American defeat in Vietnam, American governments were no longer willing to give unconditional support to authoritarian regimes in Latin America simply because they were reliably anti-Communist.

Those engaged in campaigns of violence on behalf of separatist causes were commonly in conflict with the existing international order with its anathema against secession. Despite this, it was only relatively rarely considered by separatists to be in their interests to extend their campaigns beyond the area for which they hoped to achieve independence. But for some groups the guarantee of much wider coverage of the conflict in which they were engaged did provide an incentive to internationalize the issue by attacking foreigners in their midst, particularly diplomatic representatives of major powers, since that ensured their actions would be noticed. To small groups especially, notoriety was preferable to being

241

disregarded. To these cases must be added the much more sub-stantial case of the Palestinians. In their case there was a very conscious strategy of launching attacks at an international level as a protest at the world's ignoring of their plight. For Palestinians, the impulse to secure international recognition of their exis-tence by any available means overrode the calculation that their actions would be widely condemned because of their extension of the conflict outside of the Middle East. However, it is worth underlining that some of the outrageous actions which helped to establish the almost automatic association of the Palestinian cause with terrorism were carried out by small factions within the wider Palestinian movement rather than by groups linked to the mainstream of Palestinian opinion.

In so far as any single theme could be said to link the different terrorist groups of the 1970s and 1980s, it was the theme of anti-imperialism. However, it should also be underlined that Third World leaders, who saw themselves as the true champions of the cause of anti-imperialism, were by and large hostile to these groups, their violence and their claims to be advancing the anti-imperialist cause through their actions. The same is largely true in the case of the Soviet embrace of anti-imperialism, an ideological posture complicated by criticism of Soviet imperialism, not just by China but much more widely. A persistent theme of some of the writing on terrorism during the cold war was of Soviet involve-ment in terrorism as part of a covert war by the Soviet Union against the West. Little substantive evidence of such a Soviet conspiracy emerged, however, when the collapse of Communism gave researchers access to fresh information about links between the Soviet Union and such groups.

Of course, the claim to be engaged in a struggle against imperi-alism implied not merely the existence of a global order dominated by imperialist powers but the possibility of the existence of an alternative global order. For Marxists the notion of an interna-tional proletariat encapsulated in slogans referring to workers of the world tended to form the basis of this vision. The end of the cold war has for practical purposes undermined the expectation of any such transformation of the global order in the foreseeable future. At the same time, the end of the cold war also removed a major constraint on intervention by the major Western powers in other conflicts. Further, the belief in the universality of Western values and political practices, even their appropriateness to culturally different societies and to societies with standards of living a fraction of those of technologically advanced states, has created an ideological basis for interventionism.

What is more, the advocates of intervention have also been able to latch on to movements with fundamentally altruistic or idealistic objectives. Thus, those seeking to promote respect for human rights across the world now find that they run the risk of their work being used by the proponents of a fresh *mission civilisatrice* for purposes that are, practically speaking, the opposite of those they intended. Whether the frequency of Western interventions since the end of the cold war can yet be described in terms of a new age of imperialism is a moot point, but what is evident is that there has been a much greater propensity for Western states to intervene in other parts of the world since 1990 for a variety of motives and increasingly in defiance of international law, that is to say, without legal authorization from the United Nations Security Council or the alternative legal justification of self-defence. However, in large part because of the absence of a credible alternative to a world order based on capitalism and globalization, the backlash against Western interventionism has not been articulated in terms of the anti-imperialism of the past. It has taken more particularistic forms. From the perspective of this book, the most significant of these forms has been the global jihad launched by Osama bin Laden. The primary objective of bin Laden and his followers is the restoration of Muslim political power so that in the first instance Muslims are able to conduct their affairs free of external interference. By comparison with that of revolutionary Marxism, this is a limited aim. Admittedly, Osama bin Laden and his followers also harbour the much more problematic aim of the recovery of previously Muslim lands from their current occupiers. But it is not the hypothetical return of land where Muslims once lived to the

Muslim nation conceptualized by the jihadists that has provided most of the impetus behind such movements. Rather, the impetus has come from the number of violent political conflicts involving Muslim populations, several of which have erupted since the end of the cold war.

Of course, this is to put a label on the participants in such conflicts which they might not seek themselves. Thus, the conflicts from which the jihadists derived their inspiration were often formulated in other terms by most of those directly engaged in these struggles. The more conventional formulations were that the people concerned were engaged in a struggle for self-determination or were resisting foreign occupation. The obvious advantage of these formulations was that these justifications enjoyed a measure of legitimacy in the wider international community, particularly since many governments in the Third World still honoured founders who had engaged in somewhat similar struggles. In the post-cold war context, insurgents had another reason for couching their demands in nationalist terms. This was the erosion of the anathema against secession. At the conclusion of the era of decolonization that followed the Second World War, the United Nations gave retrospective legitimacy to anti-colonial movements by declaring self-determination to be a right in pursuit of which the people of the territory in question were entitled to seek and to receive support. However, the United Nations simultaneously underwrote existing territorial divisions to undercut the justification of secession from any sovereign and independent state. This was in 1970.

An exception to these principles soon arose, with the creation of Bangladesh in 1971. It was possible to cite special factors in this case in order to legitimize the secession without destroying the credibility of the norm. These included the fact that Pakistan itself had been the product of a partition, the fact of the territorial separation of the two wings of Pakistan, and the fact that the people of East Pakistan constituted a majority of the population of the country. However, the demise of Communism in Eastern Europe and the disintegration of the Soviet Union presented a much greater challenge to the norm. Aspects of the changes could be accommodated within the existing norm. The independence of the Baltic states could be viewed as the restoration of their sovereignty, since they had once been members of the League of Nations. Similarly, the division of Czechoslovakia could be justified on the basis that it had been the product of the mutual consent of the leaders of both parts of the country. But the break-up of Yugoslavia could not be presented as anything other than the shattering of the norm of self-determination as it was formulated in the United Nations Declaration of 1970.[6] At the same time, a number of the affluent countries that face challenges to their existence in their present form from secessionist movements, such as Spain, Canada and France, have continued to insist that the anathema against secession remains in place. This is despite the role that these countries played in the break-up of Yugoslavia. The way in which this inconsistency was defended was the contention that the state's violation of the basic human rights of the inhabitants in contested regions justified secession.

The dangers of this doctrine soon became evident in the Balkans in the case of Kosovo. The easiest way for any disaffected group of people to ensure violations of human rights by the authorities was to engage in terrorism designed to provoke strong action by the state in question. The non-violent approach hitherto taken by Kosovan nationalists was abandoned after the Dayton agreement on Bosnia. By resorting to violence radical Kosovan nationalists were successful not merely in provoking a violent reaction from the Serbian authorities but also in persuading the Western powers that the population of the Kosovo was being ruthlessly suppressed and that large-scale atrocities were taking place. However, after the war, the mass graves that were supposed to have resulted from the actions of the Serbs proved almost as elusive as Saddam Hussein's weapons of mass destruction.[7] Of course, it may reasonably be concluded in this case as in others that it is not difficult to manipulate those who have other reasons for wishing to intervene and are themselves seeking cover for their actions. Sudan presents another case where the objective of secessionists in the region of Darfur has been to set in motion a similar sequence of events. Reaching sensible judgements about such cases depends on the existence of disinterested and reliable witnesses. Unfortunately the aid agencies that have a presence in conflict zones and might be expected to act in this role frequently interpret conflict in terms of a highly simplistic duality of victims and perpetrators, since identifying blameless victims is often central to their fund-raising efforts.[8] Consequently, in practice, the notion of humanitarian intervention has proved far more valuable to major powers seeking pretexts for advancing their own strategic interests than it has been to the generality of victims of gross violations of human rights.

At the same time, the post-cold war spirit of interventionism has given encouragement to those engaged in terrorism whether within states or globally to expand their activities in the hope that they will in the end be the beneficiaries of the wider conflicts their actions might engender. Further, those seeking to secede from an existing state have the additional incentive of the uncertainty that exists over the current interpretation of the principle of self-determination, a situation that has facilitated the emergence of a large number of new states since the end of the cold war. The considerable number of cases of regions with Muslim majorities seeking secession from existing states has also given impetus to violence at the global level by furnishing the proponents of global jihad with emotive and contemporary material of violence against Muslims and of Muslim suffering for attracting fresh recruits. The muddle that exists over the legitimacy of the existing borders between states and the circumstances and context in which it might be admissible to pursue their revision by violence have contributed to the sense of a world in flux in which those who seize the moment are able to shape the future.[9]

Wherever large numbers of people are dying in political violence, examples of extreme injustice are common and very rarely simply on one side of the conflict. However, beyond the obvious, if nevertheless important, conclusions that violence tends to breed further violence and that violence tends to have a brutalizing effect on victims and perpetrators alike, the existence of injustice *per se* does not provide an answer to how the issues of the creation of new states ought to be decided. Indeed, it can reasonably be argued that the absence of clear rules and procedures on this question has itself been a contributing factor to great injustice by providing encouragement to the pursuit of violent solutions to resolve such disputes. In practice, the identification of people as the victims of injustice may simply be a roundabout way of saying that the speaker or writer considers their cause (commonly a nationalist one) both to be legitimate and a justification for resort to violence by the people in that region, whether the grounds used for arriving at such a judgement are based on history, their current plight, the interpretation of some political principle or a combination of these.

Commonly bracketed with the issue of injustice is that of inequality. The latter is often interpreted in economic terms, though it should be noted from the outset that other forms of inequality may be as significant in alienating a community from the state. Thus, in many conflicts, the ethnic composition of the security forces looms large as an issue for opponents of the existing order. However, the focus in what follows will primarily be on economic disparities since it is these that adherents of the view that inequality is a cause of terrorism generally have in mind. Not merely is the world more unequal in terms of the living standards of its inhabitants than it has ever been in any period of human history, but there is little evidence the political will exists among the richest and most powerful states of the world to halt this trend of increasing inequality, let alone to attempt to reverse it. Gestures have been made in the form of forgiving the debts of some of the most impoverished countries in sub-Saharan Africa, but little is actually being done to address the structural basis of poverty, such as unfair trade. The sorry story of efforts in the last decade to tackle global economic inequality is clearly outlined in a report, *The Inequality Predicament*, issued by the United Nations in August 2005, which notes that the commitment to redress global imbalance between rich and poor which had been made at the 1995

World Summit for Social Development in Copenhagen and endorsed in the United Nations Millennium Declaration is not being sustained, notwithstanding the fact that '[80] per cent of the world's gross domestic product belongs to the 1 billion people living in the developed world', while 'the remaining 20 per cent is shared by the 5 billion people living in developing countries'.[10]

Of course, this inequality is not new. The origins of global inequality can be traced back to the impact of the industrial revolution and is clearly reflected in the reversal that took place in the location of world manufacturing industry between 1750 and 1900, so that what would currently be considered Third World countries accounted for almost three-quarters of world manufacturing output in 1750, but barely more than 10 per cent by 1900. Technological change during the twentieth century increased rather than diminished the gulf, though prior to the end of the cold war, the political influence of ideologies espousing the achievement of greater equality through redistribution of wealth was sufficiently strong that at least within countries, a relatively small ratio between the incomes of the rich and poor was seen as a mark of a country's social development. Even before the collapse of Communism, the impact of the oil crises of the 1970s had eroded support for egalitarian objectives within the affluent countries of North America and Western Europe, with priority being given to the restoration of economic growth over social justice. The failure of the Communist economic model further discredited egalitarianism. Its demise was mirrored by the rise of rightwing populism seeking to roll back state involvement in the economy and to reduce direct taxation, with the consequence that in many industrial countries the richest 20 per cent of the population no longer pay a higher proportion of their incomes in tax of all kinds than do the poorest segment of the population.

Within rich countries socialists have adapted to the new climate of opinion and assumptions about the superiority of the market as an engine for economic growth by identifying themselves with a range of other causes, including feminism, multi-culturalism, regionalism and environmentalism, that have taken the place of previous commitments to the general redistribution of wealth. However, within the Third World, secular political elites that were at least nominally committed to socialism in the past have generally had much greater difficulty in adapting to the political climate of the post-cold war world. In particular, the authoritarianism and the corruption of such elites have been important factors in the rise of Islamist political parties and movements within the Muslim world. As the poor have lost faith in either the capacity or will of the elites to deliver improvements in their lives, they have been drawn to other ideologies, including Islamism. However, in so far as Islamists have commonly championed the interests of the poor, they have done so in terms of the moral and religious responsibility of Muslims towards other members of their community rather than in terms of any doctrine of equality. A further indication of the decline of economic egalitarianism is the prevalence of claims for reparations of past injustices, including those being made on behalf of descendants of the Atlantic slave trade. The assumption is in the current climate that such specific claims for redress have a much more realistic chance of success than has a general plea for social justice couched in universalistic terms.

The extent to which the world is becoming more unequal in economic terms both within and between states is worth underlining. Further, despite the supposedly flattening impact of globalization, the world viewed from a global perspective is far more unequal than even the most unequal state in terms of the distribution of income and wealth. Thus, according to figures from the World Bank for 2003, average per capita incomes in high income economies encompassing 15.5 per cent of the world's population were 60 times those in the low income economies encompassing 36.8 per cent of the world's population.[11] Admittedly, the disparity appears slightly less stark if the figures are adjusted for the purchasing power of money in the different countries, in which case the incomes of high income countries are merely 13 times those of low income countries. But an even more startling illustration of economic inequality was provided in 1999 by a publication of the United Nations Development Programme. This noted the following:

> The world's 200 richest people more than doubled their net worth in the four years to 1998, to more than $1 trillion. The assets of the top three billionaires are more than the combined GNP of all least developed countries and their 600 million people.[12]

However, connecting global inequality to terrorism is far from straightforward. The summary of *The Inequality Predicament* makes out the case that there is a connection in both directions, i.e. that the impact of terrorism is to increase inequality while the social situations resulting from inequality provide a breeding ground for terrorism. Ocampo puts the argument as follows:

> Global insecurity resulting from the rise in international terrorism has contributed to increased national security spending in many countries, leading to a further diversion of resources from social development. The violence associated with national and international acts of terrorism should be viewed in the context of social inequality and disintegration. In situations in which inequalities are extreme and there is competition over scarce resources, the likelihood of social disintegration and violence increases. Violence is more common where inequalities are greater, and trends suggest that growing up in poverty often leads to social exclusion, which can contribute to crime. Countries with high rates of poverty and inequality generally have poorer social support and safety nets, more unequal access to education, and fewer opportunities for young people. The likelihood of armed conflict is also greater under such adverse social conditions.[13]

Ocampo wisely places terrorism in the much wider context of violence in general, since otherwise he would be faced with the impossible task of seeking to connect pervasive conditions of inequality to terrorism, which, if interpreted as the clandestine violence of small groups in an international context, remains by comparison an extremely rare phenomenon.

This is the approach taken by Karin von Hippel, but then her purpose is to suggest that it is a myth that poverty is a root cause of terrorism. She points out:

> The nineteen hijackers who committed the 11 September atrocities, and their spiritual father bin Laden were neither poor nor uneducated. Others noted that a large proportion of the Egyptians who belonged to one of the groups affiliated to al-Qaeda came from 'stable middle-class homes and were university educated'. If poverty really were the root cause of terrorism, more terrorists would come from the poorest part of the world, sub-Saharan Africa, and this, so far, is not the case.[14]

However, all that von Kippel's argument demonstrates is that being poor does not make someone become a terrorist, a highly unsurprising conclusion since even on the broadest possible definition of terrorism that encompassed practically all forms of political violence within states, as well as violence at an international level, the poor (however defined) would massively outnumber the perpetrators of political violence. In fact, for quite obvious reasons the absolutely poor tend not to be politically active anywhere since their lives are taken up with securing enough on a day-to-day basis simply to survive. Thus, activists in socialist movements are also typically drawn from those who are not poor. However, that is not a good reason for doubting the seriousness of their commitment to the redistribution of wealth and the creation of a more equal society. Of course, the mere existence of inequality in human living conditions does not explain the existence of socialist movements. They are a product of a set of beliefs that surely include the proposition that inequality is wrong but also, crucially, other beliefs, including how to transform the existing society in a way that embodies socialist values.

A further point about level needs to be made in this context. The commitment of most socialists was to the achievement of greater equality within the society in which they worked. At best, the achievement of a larger measure of global equality was secondary to this objective. Applying these arguments to the relationship between contemporary terrorism with a global reach and current international economic inequality suggests that the connections are even more attenuated in this case. In the first place, the ideology of global jihadists is not egalitarian. Their objective is not to create a more equal world but rather to establish Islamist governments in Muslim lands, while also extending the influence, power and size of the Muslim community or nation. Admittedly, a by-product of the achievement of such an aim might well be that the world became a more equal place in terms of economic living standards, but that is not central to the values they espouse. In the second place, the highlighting of considerations of social and economic inequality has played a comparatively small role in efforts to recruit Muslims to the global jihad. The same is also true of the recruitment of Muslims to the jihadist cause within states. What tends to be emphasized in such recruitment efforts is injustice, often in the form of acts of lethal violence, as well as the effectiveness of jihadist violence as a means for righting such wrongs. It is worth underlining that it is much easier to convince potential recruits of the effectiveness of violence within an existing conflict zone than it is in a peaceful society. In addition, it is also generally easier to convince potential recruits of both the legitimacy and utility of violence within states than transnationally. If this were not the case, attacks by al-Qaeda and its imitators would be frequent rather than the episodic events they are.

Nevertheless, this does not entirely exhaust the issue of a relationship between inequality and terrorism, though admittedly it is important to acknowledge that these connections are far more indirect and open to argument than, say, the link between global warming and Hurricane Katrina.[15] The argument that there is an indirect link between inequality and terrorism commonly takes the form that inequality creates the social, economic and ultimately political conditions that provide breeding grounds for the emergence of terrorist movements. This is basically the thrust of Ocampo's case quoted above. Yet the relative stability of a number of the poorest countries in the world such as Tanzania, as well as of a number of the most unequal in terms of wealth and income distribution such as Brazil underscores the fact that there is no automatic correlation between poverty and/or inequality and political upheaval. The causes of violent political conflict are primarily to be found in the political realm. In cases where the authorities are widely seen to be politically legitimate, economic conditions are unlikely by themselves to give rise to violent conflict. By contrast, where there is already a question mark over the legitimacy of political authority, deteriorating economic conditions can provide a further impetus towards conflict. And the converse is also true. Economic effectiveness in terms of the delivery of higher standards of living for the many and not just the few may have an ameliorating effect on a regime's lack of political legitimacy.

Perhaps the most significant instance where deteriorating economic and political conditions tends to be mutually reinforcing is that of the failed state. The failed state also has an especial importance to transnational terrorism, since the existence of areas of the world where the writ of the state effectively does not run, has long provided havens for terrorist networks. However, Karin von Hippel, who prefers the terms collapsed or imploded states to failed states, questions the link on the basis that 'if cases of state collapse or partial collapse were considered serious breeding grounds for terrorism, then numerous other parts of Africa [in addition to Somalia and Sudan] should be on the list, such as Congo'.[16] Nevertheless, von Hippel treats the attraction of collapsed states to global terrorist networks as of sufficient importance to advocate action by the international community to address the issue.

Holistic reconstruction plans that encompass reform of government, security sector and economy would certainly go some way to prevent these places from becoming potential breeding grounds for terrorism. While it may not be realistic to assume that Western donors will embark on an enormous programme of state-building in these states throughout the developing world, more serious effort, attention and financial assistance would make an enormous difference.[17]

Somewhat similarly, Bruno Frey contends that deterrence can be an ineffective and even counter-productive approach to preventing terrorism. By contrast, he argues that the adoption of positive economic measures can provide the basis for an effective anti-terrorist strategy.[18]

Yet even such well-meaning and enlightened approaches to tackling terrorism tend to miss a rather fundamental point. This is that by comparison with other threats to human life, such as disease, natural disaster or accidents, terrorism does not deserve the attention it receives, when taking into account the numbers of people who have died in terrorist atrocities. This applies particularly to terrorism with a global reach, which hitherto has remained episodic if spectacular. Admittedly, there is a danger that such occurrences could become more frequent, especially if the policies adopted by the major powers continue to alienate Muslim opinion and enlarge the constituency to which global jihadists can appeal. But even then such violence would need to have an instrumental rationale for it to be sustained on a long-term basis and it is difficult to imagine how such a rationale could be constructed. At the same time, it also cannot be ruled out that groups without any connection to Islamic fundamentalism or Muslim societies might start to imitate the methods of al-Qaeda for reasons that are not presently evident.

The fervour with which the radical right denies that injustice and inequality have any bearing on the question of terrorism may be self-serving in so far as it indicates an unwillingness to address questions of global equity, but it does remain the case that the connections between these at a global level are far more tenuous than they are within particular societies. However, the explanation of al-Qaeda's emergence in terms of the spread of an evil ideology is scarcely more illuminating. It begs the obvious question as to whether what is being described as evil is radical Islamism itself or, more narrowly, justifying the use of violence across national boundaries in such a cause. In short, are global jihadists the enemy or should the whole phenomenon of Islamic fundamentalism be viewed as a threat to world peace? If the former, then on the basis of all that has happened since al-Qaeda became active in the 1990s, the wide scope of the war against terrorism has very little justification. If the latter, then why should Islam be singled out? Should not that judgement also be applied to all the other religious fundamentalisms that have flourished in the last decades of the twentieth century?

Notes

1   High-level Panel on Threats, Challenges and Change, *A More Secure World: Our Shared Responsibility*, United Nations, New York 2004, p. 48.

2   *Guardian* (London), 14 November 2001, quoted in Dilip Hiro, *War without End: The Rise of Islamist Terrorism and Global Response*, Routledge, London 2002, p. 409.

3   See, for example, the report on President Bush's speech in Utah to the Veterans of Foreign Wars. 'Bush defiant on Iraq as criticism of war escalates', *Irish Times* (Dublin), 23 August 2005.

4   Raymond Aron, *Progress and Disillusion: The Dialectics of Modern Society*, Penguin, Harmondsworth 1972, p. 206.

5   The point is underlined by the fact that the first arrest warrants issued by the ICC were for leaders of the Lord's Resistance Army of Uganda. See Meera Selva, 'Head of "Lord's Army" faces war crimes trial', *Independent*, 8 October 2005.

6   Its full title was the *Declaration of Principles of International Law concerning Friendly Relations and Cooperation among States in accordance with the Charter of the United Nations*.

7   For a comparison of the two cases, see Lawrence Martin, 'Another case of mass deception?', *Globe and Mail* (Toronto), 2 September 2004. The number of people killed in the conflict in Kosovo was in the low

thousands. After the war, forensic investigators uncovered some evidence of atrocities against *both* Albanians and Serbs in Kosovo, though not on a scale that might have justified the pre-war rhetoric of Western leaders, including Blair's claim that 'racial genocide' was being perpetrated by the Yugoslav authorities in Kosovo.

8 In this context, the poor response to appeals on behalf of the victims of the earthquake in Kashmir is noteworthy. See 'Abandoned: a second disaster hits Kashmir – why didn't the world prevent it?', *Independent*, 30 December 2005.

9 A case can reasonably be made that the international community's approach both to the question of intervention and that of secession was too absolutist in the 1960s and 1970s, but that is a separate issue from the current confusion over the interpretation of these norms.

10 *The Inequality Predicament: Report on the World Social Situation*, United Nations, New York 2005. From the opening paragraph of the Executive summary by José Antonio Ocampo, published online.

11 Calculated from tables in the World Bank's *World Development Report for 2005*, Oxford University Press, New York 2004.

12 *Human Development Report 1999*, Oxford University Press, New York 1999, p. 3. Published for the United Nations Development Programme.

13 From the Executive summary of *The Inequality Predicament* as cited in note 10 above.

14 Karin von Hippel, 'The Roots of Terrorism: Probing the Myths' in Lawrence Freedman (ed.), *Superterrorism: Policy Responses*, Blackwell, Oxford 2002, p. 26.

15 See, for example, Bill McKibben, 'The Coming Meltdown', *New York Review of Books*, 12 January 2006, p. 16.

16 Karin von Hippel, 'The Roots of Terrorism', p. 33.

17 Ibid., p. 34.

18 Bruno S. Frey, *Dealing with Terrorism – Stick or Carrot?*, Edgar Elgar, Northampton, MA 2004.

CHAPTER 12

Conclusion

Terrorism and global disorder

The question posed at the outset of this book was: did the world change fundamentally on 11 September 2001? The view of this author is that such a proposition both overstates and misconceives the significance of 9/11. The central claim of this book is that 9/11 was a symptom of trends in the international political system, which primarily resulted from what was undoubtedly a watershed in world affairs, the end of the cold war and dissolution of the Soviet Union. These trends had both structural and ideological dimensions, which are summed up further below. But what should also be evident is that if one leaves aside moral considerations, the strategy of attacking America, though explicable in terms of the trajectory of violent Islamism, always constituted a dead end. Admittedly, the inept manner in which President Bush responded to the assault during his first term of office has almost succeeded in giving meaning to a grotesque atrocity incapable in itself of advancing the cause of its perpetrators. That is not to say that the project of establishing Islamist regimes in predominantly Muslim countries was in any event an attractive one. However, from the perspective of jihadists intent on establishing such regimes, attacking America was a singularly misguided way of pursuing this objective and that was underlined by the fall of the Taliban regime within months of 9/11.

Instead of focusing on the narrow task of finding, identifying and capturing the global jihadists at the core of al-Qaeda, the Bush

Administration broadened its war on terrorism to attacks on enemies not remotely connected to the events of 11 September. Egged on by the British Prime Minister, Tony Blair, President Bush diverted resources to a war against Saddam Hussein. In the process, the Administration failed even to uproot al-Qaeda, permitting bin Laden and others round him to enhance their popularity among the millions of people that American policies had alienated and to continue to threaten further violence against politically stable societies. Perhaps even more seriously, it allowed al-Qaeda to project its actions as a model for others to follow. The Bush Administration also alienated much of world opinion by its actions. This was remarkable, given the political and economic means at America's disposal to secure influence round the world and the widespread support for America from the rest of the world in the immediate aftermath of 9/11. Even more extraordinary was the Bush Administration's apparent indifference to this outcome, which is primarily explicable in terms of the grip on the Administration of the radical rightwing ideology of neo-conservatism. But it should also be noted that while Bush's handling of the crisis was lamentable from the perspective of any objective consideration of American interests, his performance on the issue not merely did not prevent his re-election, but was the principal basis on which he was able to secure re-election.

Predicting the future course of terrorism is practically speaking an impossible task. Unlike earthquakes over which human beings have little or no control, terrorism involves a multitude of human choices, not just directly by the perpetrators themselves or by those tasked with prevention, but by political actors whose actions help to shape the world in which we live. In this context, of vital importance is the distinction between violence, including actions widely and even reasonably characterized as terrorism, which takes place within a conflict zone and terrorism that disregards this distinction and treats the whole world as a legitimate arena for acts of violence. It is worth underlining that the second sort of terrorism has been exceptionally rare and that the surviving victims of such violence have good reason to regard themselves as extremely unfortunate. The obvious comparison is that approximately a hundred times as many people died in the Asian tsunami of December 2004 as in the events of 11 September. While the tsunami was an altogether exceptional event, in general, natural disasters have proved to be far more lethal than terrorism.

This leads to the asking of a number of questions. Why do governments devote so much attention and resources to a problem that has such negligible consequences in terms of fatalities compared to other sources of violent death? And, for that matter, what is the justification for all the books on the subject, including this one? A variety of answers to these questions is possible. One line of argument that could be made in response to the first question is that if governments disregarded the problem or even gave it a lower priority, then such terrorism would cause many more deaths. This is certainly the impression that governments seek to convey to the general public. However, it is not borne out by the record that emerges from court cases. Arrests within politically stable countries in connection with terrorism are far commoner than convictions.[1] Terrifying scenarios that appear in newspaper print have a habit of dissolving when subject to the test of evidence. Indeed, feasible plots on the point of implementation foiled by the security forces scarcely outnumber actual atrocities, testament not to the incompetence of the authorities but rather to the difficulty of preventing attacks in which only a very small number of people is directly involved.[2] Another line of argument is that the moral affront represented by terrorism obliges government to give it a high priority. An analogy here can be drawn with serial murderers who like terrorists also attract a disproportionate amount of attention in the media by comparison with far commoner sources of violent death. Partly, this may be due to the fact that, like terrorists, serial murderers cause widespread fear across a society that bears no relation to the actual threat they represent. But it is also partly due to the fact that members of most societies attach higher importance to protecting society from the ravages of serial murderers or terrorism than they do to protecting it from other dangers.

While a case can be made that society is right to give a higher priority to deaths that are the product of human intentions, it is almost certainly true that much of the public is ignorant of the primary sources of violent death in a society and, if better informed, might demand different priorities from both politicians and the media. The consequences of the neglect of other more serious threats to society has been powerfully underlined by the widespread carnage caused in New Orleans by Hurricane Katrina, in considerable part because of the diversion of resources from the mundane matter of flood defences and fixing the levees, to the war against terrorism and/or tax cuts. In the midst of Northern Ireland's recent troubles, Kevin Boyle and Tom Hadden pointed out that not merely did more people die annually in Northern Ireland in road accidents than in political violence, but that proportionately to population fewer people died in Northern Ireland in both road accidents and political violence than died in road accidents alone in France.[3] Their simple calculation caused widespread surprise. Of course, Northern Ireland as a society in the midst of a violent conflict can hardly be regarded as typical. Within politically stable societies, terrorism would scarcely register at all in the most detailed breakdown of the causes of violent death. The record of the media and of politicians of seeking to allay people's fears about terrorism is a poor one. Journalists have long been aware that alarmism sells newspapers; just as broadcasters know it attracts viewers, while political leaders who seek to educate and inform rather than mirror the public response to events are relatively uncommon. However, since 9/11 the record has got a lot worse. The explanation is to be found in the political and ideological exploitation of the issue of terrorism and the successes it has achieved.

The response of the British government to the attacks on London in July 2005 provides an interesting case study in this respect. Far from seeking to allay public fears about the dangers of further attacks, the British Prime Minister sought to use the attacks to vindicate his contention that the world changed on 11 September 2001. He promised to meet the challenge of terrorism head-on. At the same time, he strongly denied that the events in London were connected in any way with the occupation of Iraq. In support of this denial, he pointed out that there had been other terrorist attacks by Islamic fundamentalists before the invasion of Iraq. In response to the attacks, a raft of controversial anti-terrorist measures and proposals was announced. Whereas many of the controversial measures introduced by the Bush Administration after 9/11 derived their inspiration from the worst aspects of Israeli practices,[4] the model for the British government's proposals seems to have been apartheid South Africa. In particular, there was a similar emphasis on the criminalization of activities of an entirely non-violent character but which in the government's eyes bore some relationship to the ideology of those who has resorted to violence. But by far the most striking similarity with the security measures of apartheid South Africa was the proposal in the government's 2005 terror bill for yet another extension of the period in which a suspect could be held without trial, to 90 days. The South African government introduced its notorious provision for the detention without trial for 90 days in 1963. The consequence according to South Africa's Truth and Reconciliation Commission was that 'torture became increasingly systematic and the death toll in police custody steadily escalated'.[5] In the event, the 90-day provision in the British terror bill was voted down in the House of Commons, thanks to a backbench rebellion by Labour back-benchers and despite the campaigning of the Murdoch press and some senior police officers in favour of the measure.

After the second attempted attacks of 21 July, a shoot-to-kill policy was loudly announced. It soon had tragic consequences, with the shooting dead of a Brazilian electrician.[6] While the government ritualistically acquitted the Muslim community at large of responsibility for the attacks, many of its initiatives contradicted this assurance by the emphasis they placed on extremism within the Muslim community as a major cause of the attacks. An immediate consequence both of the government's response and of the nature of the media's coverage of the attacks was a huge increase across the United Kingdom of racial attacks.[7] But one part of the government's response to the attacks did not strike a chord with public opinion and this was the denial that the attacks had any connection with the war in Iraq. Retrospectively, the British Prime Minister, Tony Blair, has sought to distance himself from this line of argument. A columnist close to Blair, John Rentoul, reported that 'emphatically what he [Blair] really thinks, . . . is that the greater risk of a particular kind of terrorism has to be borne'.[8] The same column contained another piece of Blairite revisionism. It recast Blair's justification for the invasion of Iraq from one of a security threat to Britain to a just war. However, for the most part, the government's response to the attacks resonated with the fears of the majority of the population in the country and the ratings of both the government and Blair rose. One consequence was that Blair's hold on power was strengthened and speculation about his retirement diminished. A disturbing implication of what has happened is that it is by no means far-fetched to conceive of a government that would secretly welcome instances of 'a particular kind of terrorism' in British cities as both strengthening its hold on power and lending legitimacy to an aggressively interventionist foreign policy it wanted to pursue.

The global ambitions of British political leaders need to be seen in the context of Britain as a middle-ranking power, seeking, in the well-worn phrase, to punch above its weight. In practice, the actions of the British government at any one time depend to a considerable degree on the policies prevailing in Washington. However, by no means all American politicians are sympathetic to the British quest to restore its world power status, let alone the hankering to recreate the empire under the guise of the promotion of good governance. America's own penchant for intervention stems from rather different sources. It is based not on a belief that the establishment of American rule over other peoples would be to their benefit, but rather the conviction that America has to put the world to rights in order to be free to get on with its own business. The metaphor of Pearl Harbour for 9/11 was reassuring for Americans because it suggested that the appropriate response to 9/11 would take the form of a war of a limited time-span that would ultimately end in the enemy's complete defeat and the permanent removal of the threat of further attacks.

However, the trend towards greater interventionism cannot be explained in terms of British and American attitudes alone. Many other Western states that, like Britain and the United States, were a party to the UN *Declaration on Inadmissibility of Intervention in Domestic Affairs of States and Protection of their Independence and Sovereignty* of 1965 that condemned intervention by states 'for any reason whatsoever', have shifted their position. The change is a reflection of the structural transformation of the international political system. The norm of non-intervention was perceived as in the West's best interests in the 1960s as a buttress against Soviet ambitions. By the 1990s it had come to be seen as an unwelcome restraint on the West's freedom of action. However, those eager to abandon the constraints of the norm by and large failed to recognize the wider implications of the abandonment of the norm. The norm of non-intervention gave an incentive to those engaged in armed strife to confine their violence to the region or zone in which the conflict was taking place. The removal of that restraint was precisely to create a rationale for terrorism with a global reach. Another highly significant implication of the weakening of the norm of non-intervention is that it has created incentives for fomenting mayhem within states with a view to prompting intervention, as events in both the Balkans and Sudan have underlined.

An argument that is commonly advanced as a criticism of the norm of non-intervention is that it has operated (or might operate) as a bar to military intervention to prevent killings on a mass scale by malevolent regimes. But in fact the basis exists in such cases for intervention to be authorized by the United Nations Security Council under a wide variety of instruments, including the United Nations Convention on the Prevention and Punishment of the Crime of Genocide, which dates back to 1948. But, ask the advocates of unilateral military intervention by states, what if a clash of interests among the powers prevents the Security Council from acting? What this ignores is that in the very limited number of cases in which military intervention might have saved lives, rather than adding to the death toll, what prevented action was not a clash of interests between states, but rather a lack of any interest. Additional Declarations on this subject will not alter that danger in the future, though they may well erode further the norm of non-intervention and the protection it provides against the globalization of conflict. The outstanding examples of where mass killings ran their course for decades while the rest of the world remained virtually totally indifferent were Burundi and Rwanda. Retrospectively, the genocide in Rwanda in 1994 has been used as an argument for expanding the scope of the intervention on humanitarian grounds. Generally, however, intervention is advocated in places, unlike Rwanda, where the strategic interests of major powers are clearly engaged.

The best that advocates of intervention can then offer is that even if the motives of the practitioners of military intervention are impure, it should be welcomed when directed against malevolent regimes because of the beneficial political consequences that are the by-product of the intervention. This was a case often made in relation to the war over Kosovo, where the jockeying for position by the major powers after the war exposed just how mixed the motives for intervention had been. However, this line of argument has become much less persuasive in the light of the humanitarian catastrophe that followed the invasion of Iraq in 2003. The notion of a malevolent regime abusing the human rights of the country's inhabitants out of sheer wickedness is of course in any event a highly simplistic one. In particular, this view commonly fails to recognize that the sources of regime behaviour in a society are often deeply rooted and enduring. That is perhaps most clearly illustrated by how frequently movements for clean government in Africa and elsewhere, when they have come to power themselves, have ended up outdoing their predecessors in terms of their level of corruption.

The weakening of the non-intervention norm is not the only change that has taken place as a result of the end of the cold war and which has had implications for the spread of political violence across state boundaries. For reasons somewhat similar to the

West's change of attitude towards the norm of non-intervention, the absolutist hostility towards secession embodied in the United Nations Declaration of 1970 has also been abandoned. However, just as in the course of the First World War, when Austria-Hungary complained with some justice that the Western allies were highly selective in where they applied the concept of national self-determination so as to suit their war aims, so the post-cold war abandonment of the anathema against secession has also been selective and opportunistic. Thus, the post-colonial anathema against secession has continued to be invoked in defence of the territorial integrity of states such as Spain and Canada, while a much looser interpretation of the norm of self-determination has been applied to less developed regions of the world. For example, the Comprehensive Peace Agreement of January 2005 ending the long-running civil war in Sudan provides for the holding of a referendum in the Southern Sudan on independence in 2011. This provision flatly violates the principle that continues to be insisted on by most established states, including federations, that such separation, if allowable at all, is only permissible with the mutual consent of the centre and the region concerned.

The justification commonly advanced for applying different standards to cases such as Sudan is the existence both of violent conflict and of widespread abuse of human rights. The obvious problem with this approach is that it is an invitation to the fomenting of violent conflict so as to create the conditions for this justification of secession. Its link to the issue of terrorism is that the more indiscriminate the violence that is employed by insurgents the more likely it is to create a situation where human rights are indeed widely abused. Since the existence of violent conflicts also tends to generate support for transnational terrorist networks, the current manner in which the norm of self-determination is being interpreted should be seen as a factor that may be facilitating terrorism in the post-cold war world. By contrast, there is much wider recognition that violent conflicts number among the causes of terrorism and that is reflected in the attention that the resolution of particular conflicts receive, most notably the conflict between Israelis and Palestinians. But what is missing is an appreciation of the role that uncertainty in the interpretation of significant norms of the international political system has played in exacerbating global disorder in the post-cold war world, in internationalizing conflict, and hence, in helping to create the conditions for terrorism with a global reach.

Tariq Ali summarizes the ideological climate at the dawn of the new millennium as follows: 'By the end of the twentieth century, with the defeat of secular, modernist and socialist impulses on a global scale, a wave of religious fundamentalism swept the world'.[9] Ali also includes 'the postmodern defence of relativism' as a significant element in the prevailing ideological climate. Along with such factors as the victory of the clerics in Iran and the defeat of the left in Afghanistan, he blames postmodernism for having 'buried the hopes of women'.[10] However, it is not necessary to endorse every aspect of Ali's account to accept the broad picture he paints. The growth of religious fundamentalism has largely mirrored the discrediting of socialism, a decline in the prestige of science and the erosion of secularism. While Communism only represents one strand of the socialist tradition, the trajectory of Communism from declining vitality to its collapse in Eastern Europe and the Soviet Union was a factor in the discrediting of socialism more generally. Almost all of the governments in newly independent states had adopted some variant of socialism as the basis for the modernization of their societies. The failure of many of these regimes consequently also undermined support for socialism, while in the affluent world the stagnation associated with the oil crises of the 1970s shattered the belief in the viability of the mixed economy that had underpinned social democracy in Europe.

Accounting for the decline in the prestige of science is more difficult in light of its role in continuing and indeed accelerating technological change. Part of the explanation lies in its association in some states with socialism and secularism. But science also suffered because some of the technological innovations with which it was associated, such as the development of nuclear weapons, were seen as threatening rather than benefiting mankind. But also significant was the role that postmodernism played in undermining intellectual confidence in objective truth, an essential foundation of scientific knowledge. A by-product both of the decline in the prestige of science and of the rise of relativism was that it became possible once again to propagate religious cosmologies that science had discredited. This was reflected in the revival in the United States of creationism and in the challenging of evolution by the pseudo-science of intelligent design. Islamism or politicized Islam had long formed a strand of political opinion in Muslim societies. In the new climate, its influence mushroomed. Similar developments also took place in Christianity, Judaism and Hinduism.

These trends should not be overstated. Their significance has varied considerably according to local circumstances. Thus in Europe, secularism has remained strongly entrenched in most countries and the influence of religious fundamentalism on public policies, with the important exception of education, is barely discernible. Further, at least in Europe, arguments about the dangers of particular technologies continue largely to be conducted within a scientific framework. In addition, anti-scientific religious cosmologies generally have had relatively little bearing on political violence even by those who claimed to be religiously motivated. Notwithstanding the central role of religion in Islamist ideology, jihadists have generally advanced instrumental justifications for the use of violence that remain focused on their political objectives. While much tends to be made of the readiness of jihadists to sacrifice their own lives because of the promise of paradise in the next, the use of suicide missions by secular groups underlines that religious belief is not an essential basis for readiness to participate in such attacks.

At the level of the state or region, jihadists may be difficult to distinguish from nationalists and may even attract support as such from other states, including major Western powers, contrary to Huntington's clash of civilizations thesis. In this context, as the case of Afghanistan underlined, one person's jihadists may well be another person's mujahidin. There tends to be much less ambiguity

...s towards global jihadists whose activities constitute a ... to virtually all states. While global jihadists claim to be acting on behalf of the Muslims of the world, the notions of crusader and apostate provide them with a rationale for killing virtually anybody and clearly missing from their ideological perspective is any commitment to the common humanity of all mankind. Thus, there are very good grounds for the hostility that global jihadists evoke. The error that is commonly made, however, is to include in the category of global jihadists, all manner of Islamist groups that operate within the confines of their own conflict zones and have no ambition to wreak havoc at a global level. Their inclusion has the effect of inflating the threat that jihadists represent to global order and it is possible to argue that it helps, in small part, to explain the counter-productive broadening of the war against terrorism.

However, misperception of the nature of the enemy does not explain why the Bush Administration and the Blair government have chosen to magnify the terrorist threat and to stoke up public fears of further attacks. Part of the explanation is to be found in the change in the nature of politics in the two societies during the last two decades of the twentieth century. Focus groups and other means of gauging public opinion have provided politicians with more advanced means for understanding the extent of the public's ignorance and prejudice and their influence is reflected in both the Bush Administration's and the Blair government's relentless exploitation of the issue of terrorism for partisan electoral advantage. The obvious example – at the risk of labouring the point since it has been made repeatedly – is the Bush Administration's promotion of the notion that the regime of Saddam Hussein was connected to the events of 11 September, in defiance of objective reality. In Blair's case, the issue of identity cards was spuriously presented as an anti-terrorist measure to put opposition to the government's proposals from its political adversaries in the most damaging light possible. He also openly appealed to Labour backbenchers for support on the 90-day provision in the terror bill on the grounds of the damage the passage of the measure would do to the opposition parties. No doubt some in the Labour Party considered this behaviour payback for the Conservative Party's somewhat similar political exploitation of Labour's opposition to Conservative anti-terrorist legislation in the 1980s. Crucial to both Bush and Blair in such endeavours, despite the different positions they occupy in the political spectrum, has been the support of Rupert Murdoch's media empire. Murdoch's own neo-conservative convictions are most clearly reflected in a subsidized paper, the *Weekly Standard*. Elsewhere within the Murdoch empire, the neo-conservative message tends to be tempered somewhat by commercial considerations and by tactical political alliances, such as the one Murdoch has established with Blair.

Perhaps even more disturbing than their lack of regard for objective truth have been the indications that the two governments believe that the consensus of opinion of experts in any field does not matter, that they can safely choose any interpretation that suits their interests, that the function of intelligence is to come up with the facts to suit their policy choices and even that falsehoods can be turned into truths through the exercise of power. For example, in 2003 when the Blair government was being pressed on the question of the legality of the Iraq war without authorization from the United Nations, the assurance was airily given in briefings that if need be the lawyers would be found who would endorse the notion that the war was legal without a second Security Council resolution. Admittedly, it might be argued that international law is a matter of interpretation rather than hard fact. But the same logic has been applied by the Bush Administration to the question of climate change, with praise being heaped on maverick scientists who have questioned the scientific consensus on global warming. That some members of the Bush Administration actually believe, like King Canute, that they can order the waves to retreat is suggested by Ron Suskind's interview with a senior White House aide in 2004.

The aide said that guys like me were 'in what we call the reality-based community', which he defined as people who 'believe that solutions emerge from your judicious study of discernible reality'. I nodded and murmured something about enlightenment principles and empiricism. He cut me off. 'That's not the way the world works any more', he continued. 'We're an empire now, and when we act, we create our own reality. And while you are studying that reality – judiciously, as you will – we'll act again, creating other new realities, which you can study too, and that's how things will sort out. We're history's actors . . . and you, all of you will be left just to study what we do.'[11]

Even after the limits of the Bush Administration's power were pointedly underlined by Hurricane Katrina, the radical rightwing columnist, Amity Shlaes robustly defending Bush, claimed that 'the odds of another natural disaster on a Katrina scale are still less than the odds of a terrorist poisoning of a water source or, heaven forfend, a dirty bomb at an airport'.[12] Further, Shlaes argued that the odds on such attacks were actually increasing as 'terrorists see chaos as opportunity' and 'most Americans know all this'.[13] However, while natural scientists can predict the annual frequency of hurricanes with a fair measure of accuracy and even demonstrate the role that global warming has played in raising ocean temperatures and its contribution to increasing the intensity of hurricanes, social scientists have no capacity to predict terrorist atrocities, any more than historians can predict assassinations of political leaders. What Shlaes is counting on is that her readers' fears will lend verisimilitude to an assertion, which is at best a guess that events may well neither negate nor confirm. Of course, Shlaes's purpose is not really to make a prediction about actual events but rather to justify President Bush's priorities so as to acquit him of responsibility for a disaster that was at least in part man-made.

It remains very difficult if not impossible to forecast the future course of terrorism even in the most general terms. A focus on the vulnerabilities of modern societies underlines extremely alarming possibilities of what hypothetically a group bent on wreaking the maximum havoc might be capable of inflicting, assuming the group's preparations for the deed went undetected, which is unlikely in the case of the most elaborate scenarios. By contrast, it is hard to construct an instrumental rationale for attempts to kill large numbers of civilians outside a conflict zone, except perhaps as one-off acts of revenge. Thus, a focus on motivations provides good grounds for the assumption that there will continue to be relatively little spill-over of violence from societies engulfed in conflict to those where much more peaceful conditions prevail. In this context, it is important to bear in mind the distinction between the political violence, including the most appalling atrocities, that takes place within societies engulfed in conflict and terrorism with a global reach. Both the international community and individual governments are more likely to achieve success in eliminating or greatly reducing the latter threat if they both recognize and act on this distinction, notwithstanding the pressures to disregard it on the ground that murder is murder wherever it takes place. The ridicule heaped on the British Prime Minister, Tony Blair, when he sought to draw a distinction between the IRA and al-Qaeda in a press conference in July 2005 nicely illustrates the difficulty of making such distinctions.[14]

The emotive nature of the term terrorism is itself a barrier to the rational analysis of the issue. The justification of this book – to respond to a question posed earlier in this chapter – is that amidst all the millions of words published on the subject, there is still scope for contributions in this spirit. One part of this contribution has been to expose the political exploitation of the issue of terrorism for other purposes, since this constitutes a significant obstacle to the adoption of appropriate and effective policies to counter the threat. In this field, more than perhaps some others, there is much that can be done by both governments and citizens that will shape what happens in the future. In particular, there is little justification for the fatalistic assumption that horrors on a scale many times larger than that of 9/11 are inevitable or to regard the assault on America itself as simply the opening shot in a campaign of global terrorism that will engulf the world for the foreseeable future. At the same time, such a future is not utterly impossible if ideologies that scorn the common humanity of mankind flourish and if leading states seek to monopolize the power, wealth and resources of the world by using their military capacity to that end. While the sources of political violence and terrorism are complex, as this book has shown, it remains a truism that violence tends to breed further violence.

The events of 11 September have cast a long shadow over the first decade of a new millennium and much of this book has focused on the background to these events and their implications for world politics. Hitherto, global jihadists have presented the main threat of similar atrocities in the future. Significantly, none of the atrocities carried out by global jihadists since the attack on the twin towers have been on anything like the same scale as that attack. However, it cannot be ruled out that new sources of terrorism with a global reach will emerge in future years, though reassuringly at present it is hard to identify likely candidates that might follow al-Qaeda's example. Admittedly, religious cults, as they have done in the past, may continue to give rise to acts of explosive and unpredictable violence. Nihilists who wish to cause destruction for its own sake also constitute a threat. But another danger also exists that deserves just as much, if not more attention, than any of these possibilities, but rarely receives it. This is that governments will continue to manipulate the public's fear of terrorism to advance authoritarian agendas at home and aggressive policies abroad. That is why it is so important that the problem of terrorism is viewed objectively and in its proper proportion.

Notes

1 Thus, there were only 23 convictions for terrorist offences under Britain's Terrorism Act 2000 between 11 September 2001 and 30 September 2005, *Independent*, 6 November 2005. The figures for the United States are similar with just 39 convictions for terrorism or national-security related crimes between September 2001 and

September 2004. Dan Eggen and Julie Tate, 'U.S. Campaign Produces Few Convictions on Terrorism Charges', *Washington Post*, 12 June 2005.

2 In this context, Paul Wilkinson's widely quoted aphorism that 'fighting terrorism is like being a goalkeeper – you can make a hundred saves but the only shot that people remember is the one that gets past you' is profoundly misleading. A more apposite analogy would be that counter-terrorism is like hunting for needles in haystacks without being certain whether they are there or not.

3 Kevin Boyle and Tom Hadden, *Ireland: A Positive Proposal*, Penguin, Harmondsworth 1985, p. 16.

4 James Bovard devotes a chapter in his book, *Terrorism and Tyranny: Trampling Freedom, Justice and Peace to Rid the World of Evil*, Palgrave Macmillan, Basingstoke 2003, to American use of the Israeli model for fighting terrorism, see pp. 257–316.

5 *Truth and Reconciliation Commission Report: Volume 3*, Macmillan Reference Limited, Basingstoke and Oxford 1999, p. 529.

6 The disgraceful manner in which this wholly innocent individual lost his life was compounded by false police claims in the immediate aftermath of the shooting. See, for example, Frank Millar, 'Shot man "directly linked" to terrorism, say police', *Irish Times*, 23 July 2005.

7 'Huge increase in race attacks across UK', *Independent*, 4 August 2005.

8 John Rentoul, 'Unlike Clinton, Bush fails as priest in the modern ceremony of death', *Independent on Sunday*, 4 September 2005.

9 Tariq Ali, *The Clash of Fundamentalisms: Crusades, Jihads and Modernity*, Verso, London 2003, p. 67.

10 Ibid.

11 Ron Suskind, 'Without a Doubt', *New York Times*, 17 October 2004.

12 Amity Shlaes, 'Bush was prepared for the hurricane', *Financial Times*, 2 September 2005.

13 Ibid.

14 See, for example, Geoffrey Wheatcroft, 'Blair's dubious logic on Islamism and Ireland', *Financial Times*, 26 August 2005.

Concise bibliography

There is a vast literature on the subject of terrorism and an even vaster literature on the subject of political violence. Even a bibliography restricted to books published since the events of 11 September would be far too lengthy to list here. What follows are items I have found particularly useful in developing the arguments in this book. That has also meant including a few works that have little to do with terrorism as such, but which deal with aspects of the reaction to the events of 11 September or throw light on the nature of the international political system that came into being with the end of the cold war. Most of the items noted here are to be found in the references on individual chapters, though by no means all items referenced are included in this list. It also contains some books that I found of value but had no reason for including in a particular reference. It should be noted that I have included a small number of journal articles, but not magazine or newspaper pieces, any official sources I made use of or material gleaned from the internet.

Ali, Tariq, *The Clash of Fundamentalisms: Crusades, Jihads and Modernity*, Verso, London 2003.

Bar-Siman-Tov, Yaacov, Ephraim Lavie, Kobi Michael and Daniel Bar-Tal, *The Israeli–Palestinian Violent Confrontation 2000–2004: From Conflict Resolution to Conflict Management*, The Jerusalem Institute for Israel Studies, Jerusalem 2005.

Bell, Christine, *Peace Agreements and Human Rights*, Oxford University Press, Oxford 2000.

Bergen, Peter L., *Holy War, Inc.: Inside the Secret World of Osama bin Laden*, Phoenix, London 2002.

Bonney, Richard, *Jihad: From Qur'an to bin Laden*, Palgrave Macmillan, Basingstoke 2004.

Booth, Ken and Tim Dunne (eds), *Worlds in Collision: Terror and the Future of Global Order*, Palgrave Macmillan, Basingstoke 2002.

Bovard, James, *Terrorism and Tyranny: Trampling Freedom, Justice and Peace to Rid the World of Evil*, Palgrave Macmillan, Basingstoke 2003.

Burke, Jason, *Al-Qaeda: The True Story of Radical Islam*, Penguin Books, London 2004.

Campbell, Bruce B. and Arthur D. Brenner (eds), *Death Squads in Global Perspective: Murder with Deniability*, Palgrave Macmillan, Basingstoke 2000.

Chan, Stephen, *Out of Evil: New International Politics and Old Doctrines of War*, I.B. Tauris, London 2005.

Clarke, Richard A., *Against All Enemies: Inside America's War on Terror*, Free Press, New York 2004.

Coll, Steve, *Ghost Wars: The Secret History of the CIA, Afghanistan, and bin Laden from the Soviet Invasion to September 10, 2001*, Penguin Books, New York 2005.

Cooley, John K., *Unholy Wars: Afghanistan, America and International Terrorism* (Second Edition), Pluto Press, London 2000.

Cox, Michael, Adrian Guelke and Fiona Stephen (eds), *A Farewell to Arms?: Beyond the Good Friday Agreement*, Manchester University Press, Manchester 2006.

Crotty, William (ed.), *The Politics of Terror: The U.S. Response to 9/11*, Northeastern University Press, Boston 2004.

Esposito, John L., *Unholy War: Terror in the Name of Islam*, Oxford University Press, New York 2002.

Fisk, Robert, *The Great War for Civilisation: The Conquest of the Middle East*, Fourth Estate, London 2005.

Freedman, Lawrence (ed.), *Superterrorism: Policy Responses*, Blackwell, Oxford 2002.

Frey, Bruno S., *Dealing with Terrorism – Stick or Carrot?*, Edgar Elgar, Northampton, MA 2004.

Gambetta, Diego (ed.), *Making Sense of Suicide Missions*, Oxford University Press, Oxford 2005.

Guelke, Adrian, *The Age of Terrorism and the International Political System*, I.B. Tauris, London 1995.

Guelke, John, 'The Political Morality of the Neo-Conservatives: An Analysis', *International Politics*, Vol. 42, No. 1, March 2005

Halliday, Fred, *Two Hours that Shook the World: September 11, 2001 – Causes and Consequences*, Saqi Books, London 2002.

Hersh, Seymour M., *Chain of Command: The Road from 9/11 to Abu Ghraib*, Allen Lane, London 2004.

Hiro, Dilip, *War without End: The Rise of Islamic Terrorism and Global Response*, Routledge, London 2002.

Huntington, Samuel P., *The Clash of Civilizations and the Remaking of World Order*, Simon & Schuster, New York 1996.

Huntington, Samuel P., 'The Clash of Civilizations?', *Foreign Affairs*, Vol. 72, No. 3, Summer 1993.

Kampfner, John, *Blair's Wars*, The Free Press, London 2004.

Mann, James, *Rise of the Vulcans: The History of Bush's War Cabinet*, Penguin Books, New York 2004.

Misra, Amalendu, *Afghanistan: The Labyrinth of Violence*, Polity, Cambridge 2004.

Sagan, Scott D. and Kenneth N. Waltz, *The Spread of Nuclear Weapons: A Debate Renewed*, W.W. Norton and Company, New York 2003.

Slater, Robert O. and Michael Stohl (eds), *Current Perspectives on International Terrorism*, Macmillan, Basingstoke 1988.

Stedman, Stephen John, 'Spoiler Problems in Peace Processes', *International Security*, Vol. 22, No. 2, Fall 1997.

Tucker, Jonathan B. (ed.), *Toxic Terror: Assessing Terrorist Use of Chemical and Biological Weapons*, MIT Press, Cambridge, MA 2000.

Weinberg, Leonard and Ami Pedahzur (eds), *Religious Fundamentalism and Political Extremism*, Frank Cass, London 2004.

Woodward, Bob, *Plan of Attack*, Simon & Shuster, London 2004.

Index